DISMISSAL

DISMISSAL

There is no easy way —
but there is a better way

WILLIAM J. MORIN
and LYLE YORKS

A Harvest/HBJ Book

Harcourt Brace Jovanovich, Publishers

San Diego   New York   London

To my sons: Mark, Timothy, and Jason Morin
To my parents: Emilie Trindle Yorks and Lyle Yorks Sr.

Introduction

SINCE *OUTPLACEMENT TECHNIQUES* FIRST AP-
peared in 1982 substantial changes have occurred in the
corporate landscape relative to discharge and outplacement
practices. Foremost among these changes is that *downsizing* and
work-force reduction have become part of the terminology of
American business. Outplacement is no longer only a service offered to individuals and the termination of individuals is no
longer a relatively isolated event. The past five years have seen a
wave of large-scale work-force reductions ripple through the
economy. Drake Beam Morin has been repeatedly called upon
not only to provide outplacement support for large groups of employees at all levels of corporate life, but also to assist in devising
guidelines for the process itself. Each downsizing has to be handled within the context of the specific situation. In Chapter
Twelve, we identify what we have come to regard as the basic
steps of the process that need to be addressed by management.

Widespread work-force reductions have led to the
emergence of a number of new concerns in human-resource man-

agement. Voluntary separation packages is one. The need to provide support for those who remain following the work-force reduction is another. Experience indicates that companies must have a strategy—including an explicit goal they are managing toward, of which downsizing is a specific step—if the results are to be positive in terms of organizational performance. Once the downsizing is complete, there must be a focus on corporate revitalization if the envisioned benefits are to be realized. Simply reducing staff is no panacea for accomplishing improved performance.

Those employees caught in the web of company reorganization are not only middle- and lower-level contributors. Senior executives also find themselves considering changes. This group has a unique set of needs, which are discussed in Chapter Ten.

The last five years have seen a change in the legal environment as well. In some states, courts have been aggressively asserting a doctrine of abusive discharge as a counter-balance to the doctrine of employment-at-will. Under the latter, companies have been free to terminate employees for virtually any reason, just or unjust. The only exceptions to this doctrine of employment-at-will were specific instances of legislation, the Civil Rights Act of 1964 being the most visible example. Today, courts are increasingly likely to interpret statements in employee handbooks and other company publications as representing a legal contract with the employee. This provides a course of redress for workers who are abusively discharged. It also makes a review of corporate termination policies and practices critical to safeguarding the company's legal position. Chapter Three reviews many of the issues surrounding this important new dimension to corporate discharge practices.

Outplacement counseling (OPC) has itself developed into an established part of the counseling profession. With the expansion of our practice and with the experience of literally thousands of additional client cases, Drake Beam Morin has made a concentrated effort to refine and extend the formal training counselors receive, incorporating into this training the combined experience of the firm's counselors. In preparing this volume, it seemed appropriate to extend the original chapters on outplacement counseling to reflect this additional experience. Chapters Eight and Nine incorporate this material.

During the past five years, outplacement has been spreading throughout the world as a human-resource management strategy, although both its form and rate of acceptance vary greatly from country to country. Accordingly, Chapter Fourteen provides an overview of emerging OPC practices around the world. Of particular interest is the discussion of Japan, which provides a perspective that is considerably different from popular perceptions of how management in that country deals with its human resource.

In addition to these changes in the context and application of outplacement practice, we have gathered many additional insights into the termination process. In the early part of the decade, the firm undertook a national survey of corporate termination practices. We have included in this volume the key findings from the survey. Our work with clients, not only in outplacement counseling, but also in performance counseling and performance appraisal, has added to our understanding of the range of practical approaches we can draw on in managing the performance problems that often precede a discharge decision. This material has been added to the original text at the appropriate points.

The end result is a substantially revised volume on termination, outplacement, and related performance management issues. Preparing this manuscript has offered the challenge of formalizing and documenting the collective experience of the professional staff of Drake Beam Morin, Inc., and the excitement of contributing to the growing literature in this continually developing area of human resource management. Our intended audience is the human-resource executive and the management community at large, which must concern itself with the establishment and execution of policy in this volatile area of management practice.

Acknowledgments

IN PREPARING THIS BOOK, WE HAVE BENEFITTED from our association with both our colleagues within Drake Beam Morin and our clients. Special thanks, however, are extended to Jim Cabrera, President of Drake Beam Morin, who, as always, has been highly supportive of our efforts. Charles Albrecht, Executive Vice President, has been particularly helpful in sharing his experience in downsizings and work-force reductions. His extensive work in this area with a considerable number of companies was an invaluable resource. So too, has been the expertise of Bob Marshall, another member of the DBM executive team.

Bud Whitney, who manages our Senior Management Program was helpful in preparing the chapter on Senior Executives. We also must acknowledge the efforts of Robert Fischer, who directed the national study on corporate termination practices. Donald Monaco has played a major role in developing the outplacement counselor training process throughout Drake Beam Morin. He has done as much as anyone in the field to document and develop the practice of outplacement counseling. His influence is reflected throughout chapters eight and nine. Don Stevens, who directs DBM's international efforts, made repeated efforts to help us stay current with this fast changing scene. His interest and support are appreciated. Finally, Deborah Jones, a student intern from Eastern Connecticut State University, was particularly helpful in researching the material presented in Chapter Three. To these, and all the members of the Drake Beam Morin professional staff, we extend our sincere thanks.

William J. Morin
Lyle Yorks

All names used in the descriptive case studies are fictitious. Some events have been slightly altered to insure anonymity.

W.J.M
L.Y.

CONTENTS

1

A Look at Corporate
Termination Policies

EXECUTIVE TERMINATION IS AN AWKWARD subject. Although less inevitable, it ranks with death and taxes in popularity. Yet a large number of managers find at some point in their careers that they must face the problem. Companies are increasingly willing to dismiss managerial personnel so as to cut costs or strengthen their management team. Lower-level workers also have to be dismissed either for cause or as a result of relocation or reorganization. Indeed, firing a subordinate is a task that sooner or later confronts most managers.

Termination practices are an ever-present part of corporate life, but until recently the subject has been largely ignored in the literature dealing with personnel problems. Only within the last few years have textbooks begun to devote space to termination. The managers' manual of one Fortune 500 company devotes exactly one paragraph—five sentences—to the handling of terminations. Corporation-sponsored management training programs almost never include skills for dismissing personnel. In more than fifteen years of designing and conducting management training programs for some of the world's largest corporations, we have been asked only once to include the topic.

It is a mistake to believe that severance policies and skills are not important. Many managers report that firing someone is the most difficult part of their job. Few look forward to the task. Most procrastinate until they are forced to confront the issue; then they botch the process. As we will show, the consequences for both of those involved—the person firing and the person being fired—can be formidable.

With the emergence of outplacement counseling (OPC) as a recognized and widely accepted component of human-resource management, the situation is changing. Increasingly, corporations are carefully examining their severance practices and striving to deal with terminations in a professional manner. We have learned much in recent years about how the separation process should be managed to insure that it is appropriate and just and that it minimizes the trauma for all concerned.

Recently, literature on termination has begun to appear, although research on the topic is still sparse.[1] When companies are engaged in work-force reductions, training managers in the do's and don'ts of termination has become part of the support offered by many OPC firms. Despite the current interest, firing people continues to be mismanaged.

BILL AND JOE

It is three o'clock on a Friday afternoon. Bill, the department manager, has decided to fire Joe, his production manager. Joe has been with the company for ten years and has been production manager for two. Bill believes that you have to tell people exactly where they stand. He has never been known to mince words. Today, Bill is going to tell Joe why he's being fired. Bill is going to fire Joe because of the morale problem he has created in his department. Joe's peers consider him a problem, and they frequently complain to Bill that Joe is not performing. Last week, a couple of Joe's supervisors complained that they do not get support from him. In short, Bill realizes that people don't like Joe and he is not part of the team.

When Bill decided he'd had enough of these problems, he talked to management, who agreed that Joe should be dismissed. Bill then went to personnel, had a benefits letter written, and otherwise obtained personnel's support on the termination.

Now Bill calls Joe into his office, tells Joe to sit down, and says, "I have something to tell you that is not pleasant. I hope this doesn't come as a shock, but things aren't working out and we're going to have to let you go."

Joe reacts with shock, asking, "What do you mean, let me go?" Bill tells him that his career with the company is over. "You can't do this to me," Joe protests. Bill replies flatly that Joe's section is clearly not working properly. The morale problems are serious, and there have been a lot of complaints about Joe's performance. He says, "Even your overall attitude is poor."

In response, Joe says Bill has never warned him about his attitude or his performance. A year ago, Bill talked with him about some morale problems in his section, but never about his attitude. Bill responds by stating that Joe's last performance appraisal wasn't good, and he should have seen the writing on the wall. Joe yells that his performance appraisal was average and his technical skills were rated very high.

Bill says, "Look, you knew there were problems in other areas."

Joe: You can't do this to me, Bill. I mean I've worked here for ten years. You can't just wipe me out with the back of your hand.

Bill: Well look, I'm telling you—you're fired. I can't make it any clearer than that. You're not performing well.

Joe: I didn't know I wasn't performing; give me some examples.

Bill: Everybody on your shift says you are not cooperative. You're not leading them; your own people don't even support you.

Joe: Well, that isn't true! I was just talking to some of the people the other night and they thought I was doing a super job . . . a much better job than six months ago.

Bill: Look, I'm telling you to get out of here because you're through as of today. This letter describes your severance arrangements. The company supports this decision, so you better leave. We'll mail your things.

Stunned, Joe leaves the plant.

FRANK AND HARRY

Frank is a department manager. At age 61, he has been with the company for twenty-three years and in his current job for ten. He is popular and well liked by everyone, including management. He generally gets the job done in his department.

Harry, one of his supervisors, has again missed his production schedule. This has been happening on and off for a year and a half, and management has told Frank he must fire Harry. There are to be no more excuses; Harry has to go.

Frank calls Harry into the office and the early conversation goes like this:

Frank: Would you like a cup of coffee? I don't know how to . . . uh . . . how is it going out there on the line?

Harry: It's going well. I'm sorry I missed my production schedule last month, but I'm getting it together.

Frank: Gee, we've talked about that before, haven't we Harry? That you're going to get it together.

Harry: Yes, but I've been working on it. You know I have to put up with Mary out there. She's really been causing a lot of problems, but I talked to her the other night. I think we got our problems solved.

Frank: Well, Harry, didn't we talk about Mary and her problem before? We've been talking about her for some time.

This scene goes on for approximately two and a half hours and through three cups of coffee. Finally, Harry ends up saying, "Well, you know, Frank, I've really enjoyed working with you all these years. Thank God you are going to give me another chance."

Frank answers, "Now look, I'm not really giving you another chance, Harry. I want you to talk to personnel because I'm going to have to take you off the shift in a couple of weeks— maybe a month. We're going to try to find you another job in the company."

Harry leaves, thanking Frank for this opportunity. He wonders where within the company his new job will be.

What Went Wrong?

Which of the two managers handled the firing well? Neither did. In fact, both botched the termination interview in a manner likely to make the dismissal more difficult for the company and the employee.

Bill destroyed Joe. He turned the firing into a widespread condemnation ("Your own people don't even support you"). He wanted Joe out, but he gave only broad, general reasons ("Your overall attitude is poor . . . you're not performing well") instead of citing specific instances (for example, "You haven't met your goals for the last three months"). When Joe challenged Bill's assertions, Bill ignored the challenge and simply told Joe to get out.

Bill's timing (late on a Friday afternoon) compounded the problem. Joe was sent home to a long weekend, not sure why he was fired and suddenly cut loose from his employer of ten years. How can he explain this to his family and fellow workers? Can he say that after ten years his boss finally decided he was a poor worker? That he failed on the job? Joe's dismissal looks both brutal and unfair, which is how some of his colleagues at the plant are likely to view it.

Harry's case is no better, perhaps even worse. Harry doesn't know he is fired. His boss, Frank, beat around the bush and let Harry manipulate the conversation. Frank then confused the issue by suggesting that Harry talk to personnel, with the implication that he was being reassigned, not fired. Harry is in for a shock, of course. Frank hopes personnel will do his job for him.

Both Joe and Harry have been left in the dark as to what went wrong on the job. Neither Bill nor Frank communicated the reasons for their dissatisfaction. Why did they make these and other mistakes?

Several factors contributed to the termination problems. However, the two overriding causes in both these cases and others like them were:

1. *Lack of specific company policies for handling terminations.* In both instances, the companies had almost nonexistent policies beyond a statement to the effect that the supervisor should have job-related reasons for discharging a subordinate and that dismissal should be approved by the boss's immediate superior. No further guidance was offered.

2. *Lack of skill in handling terminations.* Neither Bill nor Frank had any idea of how a manager should approach a dismissal. Both were left to improvise. This was evident later when, during interviews, both managers admitted that they were unhappy with the termination interview. However, they did not know how to improve their performance. They were just aware that during the interview things had gone awry.

Typical Handling of Terminations

Historically, the most common corporate policy on termination has been no policy. Some corporate war stories have become legendary. There are executives who fire people by calling them in, asking for their keys, and having security guards escort them to the street. One large corporation simply transfers executives to dead-end jobs in the field and forgets about them. Gradually, they leave or retire. Hourly employees are easier to dismiss. A notice in the pay envelope—the infamous pink slip—solves the problem.

Such stories aside, what termination practices are typical in corporations? Systematic and reliable studies are almost nonexistent. Our review of 1,200 terminations revealed the following pattern:[2]

- Most often the manager fires the subordinate after obtaining approval from an immediate superior. However, the actual termination interview varies greatly from manager to manager, with little corporate guidance.
- Some people are fired so vaguely and with so many euphemisms that they don't know they are being let go. As in the case of Harry, they may think they have been promised help in finding another job. Some people are told that they would do well to think about other career choices or that they should closely examine how things are going on the job. Still others are told that the boss feels they have been working too hard and need a breather; therefore, some of their key projects and responsibilities are being assigned to others. In these cases, the manager merely hopes they will get the message.
- Still other people are treated with excessive cruelty. Their personalities are attacked, they are charged with being incapable of handling responsibility, or they are yelled at and escorted out of the office. Some are even fired over the phone. In one case a person was fired while ill in the hospital.
- Most terminations happen on a Friday afternoon, with the fired person given little or no guidance about what to do next.
- The support packages offered vary widely. One person

may be given use of the office for several months, while another may be escorted to the street immediately.

Within one company, the variation in personal experience was remarkable. Of twenty-one managers who were let go within a twelve-month period, four were ushered out of the building right after they were fired; several were allowed to clean out their desks but were told to be gone by the end of the day; five were given access to their offices for up to three months; three were given offices in another part of the building; and one had to vacate his office immediately but was permitted to have his former secretary take messages for him for sixty days.

Historically, this casual and at times callous attitude has been reinforced by the courts. As recently as 1980, writing in the *Harvard Business Review*, Clyde Summers noted that common law held that an employer could dismiss an employee with or without good reason.[3] This is known as the employment-at-will doctrine. Summers cited the following cases as illustrative of the past attitude of the courts.

- A salesman for a steel corporation with fourteen years of service was dismissed after informing the vice president in charge of sales that certain steel tubes were dangerous. The company withdrew the tubes but fired the salesman. The Pennsylvania Supreme Court supported the company's position, stating: "The law has taken for granted the power of either party to terminate an employment relationship for any or no reason."
- A secretary, who was fired for reporting her availability for jury duty, on the advice of a senior partner of her firm but against the instructions of her supervisor, heard a California court declare: "Her employer could discharge her with or without cause. It makes no difference if her employer had a bad motive in doing so."
- The Louisiana Court of Appeals declared that a foreman was "an employee at will" and could be discharged at any time without notice.

In the absence of a written employment contract, until recently, court decisions have favored the employer with few exceptions. This has been rapidly changing, however. A flurry of court decisions in recent years has created considerable uncertainty about the circumstances under which employers can rely on the employment-at-will doctrine. Broken promises of job security, discharge contrary to public policy, breach of good faith and fair dealing, and failure to honor a promise of employment have emerged in various court decisions as grounds for challenging employment-at-will. For example, a Michigan court ruled that when an employer hires a person with the understanding that he or she is being retained for an indefinite period and can be terminated only for good cause, that understanding can be enforced. The court held that oral assurances given during the recruitment process by company officials may be binding. So may statements of company policy or other company literature. In addition, some states have enacted whistle-blowing legislation that provides exceptions to the employment-at-will doctrine.

Currently, the situation is fluid, with considerable variation from state to state. For an employer in California, the employee rights movement already poses problems, while for a company in Georgia or Alabama, the issue is not a problem at present. However, all employers in every state should be concerned about this issue. To ignore it is short-sighted indeed. The trend is toward erosion of the employment-at-will doctrine, and employers should take a responsible position to insure that they are dealing fairly with employees.

Civil rights legislation has emphasized correcting discrimination in employment and promotion practices, and it applies to dismissal as well. Under federal law, employees cannot be discharged because of their race, color, religion, sex, national origin, or age. This legislation has placed limitations on the arbitrary nature of termination decisions concerning members of the protected categories.

Because of the risk of being charged with discrimination, companies have exercised increased caution when the person they wish to dismiss is a woman, a member of a racial minority, or over 40 years old. However, even today companies frequently scramble to assemble documentation after a complaint is filed, when the data should have been the basis for the termination decision.

Consequences of Poor Termination Policies

The available evidence suggests that establishing good severance policy has not been a high priority of management. Given the historical attitude of the courts, it is easy to see why. But both organizations and their employees have paid a price for poor termination policies. Let's look a bit more closely at the costs involved in letting people go.

Economic Consequences

Poorly conceived severance policies often add to the cost of discharging a manager. Indeed, most companies end up spending more on severance than is necessary. Generally, a middle- or senior-level manager will leave with a year's severance pay paid in a lump sum at the time of termination. Under such an arrangement, firing a $50,000-a-year executive will cost a company $50,000 plus benefits. However, if the executive receives severance pay at periodic intervals until he or she finds a new job, the economics are different. For example, if that executive finds a job within four to six months, as many do when the termination is properly handled, the cost can be as little as $28,000, including administrative costs associated with the termination—a savings of almost 50 percent.

Other companies permit dismissed managers to remain on the job for up to six months handling many of their usual responsibilities. During this time, they receive full salary and benefits. However, experience indicates that under such arrangements the manager tends to stay on for the full six months and leave without having even identified potential employment contacts. Other managers, who are more effectively let go, find employment in less than six months, again saving the firm thousands of dollars in salary and benefits.

Furthermore, when executives exhaust their severance benefits, the consequences for their personal finances can be devastating. Yet poor severance policies often encourage them to hang around, expecting or hoping the company will have a change of heart and find an available spot.

Beyond the direct costs, poor termination policies typically lead to managerial shelf-sitters, who are a hidden cost to the company. The term *shelf-sitter* is most often used to describe managers who are no longer considered viable candidates for future development and promotion but are kept on the payroll to avoid the problems of termination.[4] Their performance is marginal at best. Most likely, they are not counted on to exercise any real responsibility. For example, one large manufacturing and engineering company was recently advised by its management consultants that close to a 50-percent reduction in managerial staff would be appropriate. The company decided to cut back 25 percent of its managers, a majority of whom were shelf-sitters. The cost of carrying unproductive people for as many as ten years was formidable, so formidable that the company was compelled to clean house in a particularly sudden and sweeping fashion.

Staff cutbacks are made necessary by more than shelf-sitting. Corporate relocations, new product mixes, new technology, and changing economic conditions have produced a wave of corporate work-force reductions. In a period of low productivity and rising administrative costs, corporate sinecures have come to be less and less acceptable to American business.

Psychological Consequences

The psychological consequences of a poorly conducted severance meeting can be devastating. Much has been written about the relationship between self-esteem and work. We are a society that assigns status according to a person's job. As was noted by the special HEW task force on work in America: "In industrial America, the father's occupation has been the major determinant of status, which in turn has determined the family's class standing, where they lived, where the children went to school and with whom the family associated—in short, the lifestyle and life chances of all the family members."[5] With the emergence of women into the mainstream of the work force, family status is increasingly being determined by both the male's and the female's occupation. The report went on to observe that in our society employment provides people with daily evidence of their worth to others. Conversely, being unemployed means not being valued by one's fellow human beings.[6] Psychoanalyst Erich Fromm long ago commented that our society measures people's value as human beings in terms of their success or failure at work.[7]

Research and clinical observation have documented the stress of joblessness. For example, being fired from work ranked eighth out of forty-three events on the Holmes and Rahe Social Readjustment Rating Scale.[8] Harold Kaufman reports that unemployed executives, managers, and highly skilled professionals manifest more stress than their employed counterparts, with approximately two out of five suffering sufficient emotional impairment to need psychological counseling.[9] Donald Monaco, an experienced outplacement counselor, has observed that a high percentage of individuals who have lost their jobs display great difficulty in coping.[10]

As Barrie Greiff and Preston Munter, psychiatrists to the Harvard Business and Law schools respectively, suggest: "It doesn't matter what you call it, fired, axed, socked, canned, kicked upstairs, or allowed to resign. They all feel the same. The only certainty about losing a job is that it hurts. It threatens everybody—the family, peers, even the executive who has to do the firing."[11] This observation is reinforced by the Committee on Psychiatry in Industry, which notes "Our experience in industry and with patients suggests that those who lose their functional role as workers may behave as if their society no longer values them. Because they accept that as true, they suffer a consequent loss in the perception of their value in their families and to themselves."[12]

Recent research shows the relationship between job loss and measurable psychological and physiological changes. Empirical studies reveal statistical correlations with ill health of both a physical and psychiatric nature.[13]

The practical problems that confront a dismissed executive are not trivial. Outplacement counselors report that a significant number of the managers with whom they work encounter accusations of failure rather than support from their immediate family: "What are we going to do about the mortgage?" "We can't take Billy out of school because you screwed up," "You never do anything right." Suddenly, their friends and acquaintances are too busy to see them. The terminated managers themselves feel guilty, so much so that even when family and friends are supportive, they may withdraw. The spouse is unsure of what reaction is appropriate. In a dual career family, the problem can be intensified by the success of the spouse.

The manager without a job is faced with a number of confusing problems:

- How do you prepare a resume?
- How do you get this resume into the right hands instead of into the wastebasket?
- How do you find out about potential jobs?
- What do you tell associates?
- What kinds of references will you get?
- How do you answer when a potential employer asks why you left your last job?

As a result of the wave of corporate mergers and downsizings during the 1980's, being let go no longer automatically carries the stigma it did in years past. Much, of course depends on how the company manages the public perception of the process. Some companies have publicly let it be known that many valuable employees are now available and take steps to facilitate contacts with potential employers, such as job fairs and preparing books of resumes. Unfortunately, some companies do little to discourage the public perception that the organization is "cleaning house". Either way, losing one's job is psychologically traumatic and people face a host of stressful problems. Even with the best support, looking for a job can be one of life's most frustrating experiences. In the beginning, rejections and disappointments outnumber successes.

The termination process can be traumatic for the executive doing the firing as well. In reviewing the experience of occupational psychiatrists and consultants, the Committee on Psychiatry in Industry concludes: "Feelings of guilt are frequent in those who must separate people from their job." These feelings may be related to the sense of aggressiveness inherent in such action, to the failure to maintain one's own ideal and sense of benevolent omnipotence, or the recognition that one's own role and shortcomings may have contributed to the necessity of the layoff or termination.[14] By an overwhelming margin, most managers seek to avoid firing a subordinate. This is a major reason for shelf-sitting; it avoids the need to fire the person. Even managers who fire people with some directness usually experience some guilt over the process. A lack of clear-cut direction on how to handle terminations intensifies such feelings, leading to false starts and poorly handled confrontations. Months after a manager is terminated, the boss may still be trying to rationalize the action. In fact, most outplacement consultants readily admit that the need to relieve the corporate conscience is a major reason for the rapid growth in the practice of providing counseling to discharged managers.

Organizational Consequences

The economic and psychological problems described above can be characterized as organizational costs. But, there are other consequences to the organization as well. A history of awkward terminations and work force reductions becomes known on college campuses and in recruiting circles. This is especially true at the better business schools. Corporate recruiters and campus placement directors are sensitive to the changing reputations of corporations.

One recruiter from a large corporation put the matter succinctly:

We have had a difficult couple of years attracting top graduates. In the past, we have gone through cycles, recruiting heavily for a year or two and then leveling off and letting people go. Sometimes we ended up terminating people we had only recently recruited; other times, we were turning over experienced managers. In either case, it wasn't done with much finesse. Students today are sophisticated. They keep up with what is happening. It's amazing how often an attractive candidate asks about our pattern of letting people go. Who knows about the ones who don't sign up to interview?

The problem is more severe when recruiting experienced executives. The same recruiter commented: "We lost two preferred candidates for a senior-level position once the search firm identified us. Both bowed out graciously. We ended up talking with our third choice. We are going to have to live down our reputation for hatchet jobs on people."

When senior managers are let go, they may begin to talk, and their comments can get into the business press. A manager may say things about his or her former company that are better left unsaid. The comments may not even be true. On the other hand, is the company going to sue for libel? Probably not. The more poorly handled the dismissal, the more likely the grapevine is to pick up on the horror story.

Finally, an important consideration is the reaction of the dismissed manager's peers and associates. If they perceive the manager as a victim who has been treated unfairly, morale can plummet and turnover increase. "What does the future hold for me?" and "Should I be looking elsewhere in self-defense?" are typical reactions among employees who have worked closely with a manager who has been fired.

At the nonexempt level, dismissals that are viewed as arbitrary and unfair contribute to a climate that is favorable to union organizing efforts. The protection afforded by arbitration rights in a collective bargaining agreement is so important to organizing efforts that unions have argued against legislation extending arbitration rights to all workers, fearing an adverse effect on their organizing activities. At a time when many companies feel that enlightened personnel policies can persuade employees that they will be treated fairly without resorting to a union, termination practices are an important aspect of industrial relations.

Earlier, we noted the negative impact poor termination practices can have on recruiting managerial and professional personnel. The same problems exist at the nonexempt level. Local plant and office personnel managers are aware that word-of-mouth communication from employees is an important recruiting device. Poorly handled severance of nonexempts can create a bad reputation in the community, disrupting recruitment efforts.

When members of protected classes under civil rights legislation are involved, lawsuits can mean direct financial consequences as well. Furthermore, lack of a clear policy supported by supervisory training can lead supervisors to believe that protected workers cannot be fired. Thus, they tolerate behavior that undercuts control of the work unit. Of course members of protected classes can be discharged; they just cannot be let go for discriminatory reasons, a distinction many supervisors don't understand. Recent court decisions eroding the employment-at-will doctrine have raised the ante on litigation over the termination of employees.

Growing Awareness of Outplacement

In recent years, a variety of labels have been used to describe the termination process—dehiring, derecruiting, outplacement, executive recycling, and the like. These terms are euphemisms and represent a growing discomfort on the part of many firms with their existing termination practices. With this discomfort has come the realization that termination is a process that can be managed—its negative consequences controlled. Thus, the neglect of termination practices is beginning to be reversed.

This trend has started at the managerial level. Since the late 1960s, a growing number of firms have become aware of the value of providing systematic help to executives who are being dismissed. This awareness is reflected in the growth of the new area of management consulting most commonly referred to as outplacement counseling (OPC).

Descriptive Data on the OPC Process

The results of a national survey of corporate termination practices provide insight into both termination practices and corporate responses to outplacement.[15] In the survey of 244 companies, 49 percent of those responding had established an outplacement counseling policy.

Of the responding companies, 46 percent provided internal outplacement services, while 75 percent reported utilizing the services of external outplacement consultants. Over 65 percent reported that they were currently providing external services for their senior executives. The primary benefits in using external resources were felt to be as follows:

- The ability of external firms to handle sensitive situations, (cited by 68 percent),
- The range of expertise offered by external firms (cited by 53 percent),

• The broad base of services available from external firms
(cited by 39 percent).

In general, the level of involvement in outplacement practices, both those provided internally and those obtained through
external resources, supported the notion that outplacement has
become an established part of the human-resource management
scene in corporations. There had been a 23 percent increase in
the number of firms formalizing outplacement policies and practices since a similar survey was conducted in 1981.[16]

Also of interest was the level of manager training activity in
the area of termination. In 1986, 75 percent of the responding
firms provided training in termination policies and practices, and
68 percent trained managers in effective aproaches to terminating
employees. We believe this demonstrates increasing attention
being given to the discharge process by management.

Companies offered outplacement counseling based on certain eligibility criteria. Length of service was the primary factor
considered by 91 percent of the respondents. The reason for
being terminated was considered by 87 percent; level in the organization of the person being terminated was considered by 76
percent; and salary was considered by 50 percent. Exhibit 1.1
compares the 1986 results with those of the 1981 survey.

Exhibit 1.1 Comparison of 1986 and 1981 Survey Data:
Eligibility Criteria for OPC in Company Policies

	1986	1981
	%	%
Length of Service	91	81
Reason for termination	87	No Data
Organization level	76	69
Salary	50	43
Performance	44	48
Age	39	40

In determining whether or not external services should be offered to terminated employees, the reason for termination ranked as the primary factor for all levels of the hierarchy. At the hourly nonexempt and exempt levels, the second most important factor was length of service. For executive and senior executive positions, salary level was the second most important factor, followed by length of service, age, and performance. The top three corporate situations requiring external outplacement resources were reported to be staff reductions, problem performers, and reorganization. Early retirement seemed to represent a growing trend in the utilization of external services.

The participating companies reported a wide variety of approaches to determining duration and amount of severance pay, with factors such as length of service, salary level, combinations of service and age, pay in lieu of notice, and vacation pay being considered. Few used exactly the same formula. Exhibit 1.2 presents the more generic formulations of the most popular approaches.

Exhibit 1.2. Representative Severance Package Formulas

- One month's salary per year of service; maximum 24 months
- Exempt—2 weeks' pay per year or 4 weeks' pay per year based upon a salary level cut-off amount
  Nonexempt—up to one week's pay per year of service
- Senior executive level—6 to 12 months salary depending on circumstances and level
  Executive level—normally 6 months' salary
- 2 weeks' salary for each completed year of service; maximum 52 weeks
- Years of service multiplied by 1.5 determines number of weeks of severance pay

Each of the formulas in Exhibit 1.2 was applied to the profile of Drake Beam Morin's average client, who is an exempt employee, 46 years old, earning $52,000, with fourteen years of service to the company. The duration of severance ranged from 5.3 months to 14 months, with an average duration of 12.5 months. The amount of severance ranged from $22,966 to $60,666, with average severance of $54,166. This illustrates the considerable range of severance practices evidenced by the survey.

Finally we come to the benefits of external OPC services as reported by responding firms. In terms of benefit to the company, the primary values were seen as, first, helping smooth the transition of the terminated individual into a new work situation; second, maintaining the morale of the work force; third, counseling and training managers in the termination process; fourth, reducing severance costs. This ranking reflects the fact that external outplacement experts are often retained to handle sensitive or potentially difficult cases and employees with long tenure.

In viewing the benefits of outplacement services to the affected individual, participating companies reported that:

- Psychological support was crucial in terms of rebuilding confidence and accepting job loss.
- Training in job search techniques was almost as important as psychological support.
- Ongoing counseling and improved self-awareness led to a smoother and faster transition to the new job.

Over a two-year period (1978–79), discharged executives who were receiving formal outplacement counseling were tracked for purposes of analysis.[17] The results showed that 71 percent of the managers who found employment within a period of four and a half months accepted positions at significantly higher salaries than those they had been receiving. More specifically:

- The average age of the terminated manager was 45.
- The salary range was from $25,000 to $250,000, with a median of $51,000.

- Only 10 people accepted employment at a lower salary; 21 were placed at the same salary; and 116 were placed at a higher salary.
- Of the 15 who made career changes, most left corporate life to start their own businesses.

Equally important, trained counselors identified and dealt with a significant number of people (30 percent of the sample) who presented either behavioral or personality-trait problems.

Would the managers in the above study have found similar positions at the same pay within the same time frame without this formal outplacement counseling? We think not. Unfortunately, a meaningful control group does not exist.

In 1986, a similar analysis was made of executives who had undergone outplacement counseling.[18] The results are shown in Exhibit 1.3. The average outplaced executive was a 46-year-old male earning $55,500 at the time of discharge, which occurred after 12.1 years of service with his former company. His average severance pay was 6.5 months of salary. His average time to find a new job was 5.6 months, with an average total compensation in the new job of $60,100. The new salary represented an increase for 52 percent of those surveyed, a decrease for 35 percent, and no change for 13 percent. Training in job search techniques, self-assessment, and rebuilt self-confidence were considered the most important benefits of outplacement counseling process for the majority of respondents (29, 26, and 24 percent respectively).

Exhibit 1.3. Drake Beam Morin Outplacement Client Profile Based on Data Collected January 1981–June 1986

- Male: 89%   Female: 11%   (Total Entries: 4,800)
- Average age: 46 years
- Average base salary entering program: $51,100
- Average bonus: $4,400
- Average total compensation: $55,500

• Job function entering program:

	%
General Management	19
Operations	14
Administration	15
Personnel	7
Marketing/Sales	7
Finance	18
Engineering/Science	10

• Average service with company: 12.1 years
• Reason for separation from company:

	%
Performance	10
Cutback	31
Reorganization & Merger	29
Chemistry	17
Career Plateau	3
Other	10

• Average severance pay: 6.5 months
• Average base salary in new job: $54,900
• Average estimated bonus in new job: $5,200
• Average total compensation in new job: $60,100
• Job function in new job:

	%
General Management	23
Operations	11
Administration	12
Personnel	5
Marketing/Sales	22
Finance	19
Engineering/Science	8

- Clients benefited most from:

	%
Rebuilt confidence	24
Help accepting loss	6
Self-assessment	26
Search techniques	29
Faster relocation	8
Other	7

- Source of new job:

	%
Advertisement	9
Company letter	8
Search firm	15
Personal contact	68

- Average time to new job (mean): 5.6 months

  40% placed in 3 months or less
  50% placed in 4.5 months or less (median)
  68% placed in 6 months or less
  (percents are cumulative)

- Salary change, old to new job:

	%
Increase	52
No change	13
Decrease	35

These results are more favorable than those generally observed by personnel specialists. The average time out of work for an executive in this salary range is usually over six months, and the odds of locating a job at a higher salary are thought to be no better than fifty-fifty. Our data reinforce the belief expressed by the companies responding to our corporate survey that outplacement counseling provides clients with significant psychological benefits.

During 1988, DBM outplacement clients who had accepted a job offer were in the program for an average of 5.3 months until their job offer was received. This number varies, of course, by region and industry. For example, during this particular period, those in energy related jobs in the southwestern United States had a more difficult job search than in some other regions and industries. During the first six months of 1969 the national average was 5.7 months.

Initial corporate outplacement efforts were targeted toward managerial jobs. However, restricting concern solely to the executive levels is a mistake. As noted above, a poorly handled dismissal creates stress for the individual—exempt and nonexempt alike—and the individual's family. It can also have disruptive organizational consequences, including lower morale of other workers, a poor reputation in the community (the employment grapevine), and pressure for unionization. Many companies have come to recognize the disruptive effects of poor termination practices and are extending some type of outplacement support to all employees, especially those caught in work-force reductions.

This book provides both an understanding of the termination process and a framework for managing that process effectively.

Endnotes

[1]Robert Coulson, *The Termination Handbook* (New York: The Free Press, 1981); David Ewing, *Do It My Way or You're Fired!* (New York: John Wiley & Sons, 1983); Paula Michal-Johnson, *Saying Good-bye* (Glenview, Ill.: Scott, Foresman and Company, 1985); William Morin and Lyle Yorks, *Outplacement Techniques* (AMACOM, 1982); and *Employee Termination Handbook* (Englewood Cliffs, N.J, Executive Enterprise Publications, 1981).

[2]These were people whose use of Drake Beam Morin's outplacement services was sponsored by their former employers.

[3]Clyde W. Summers, "Protecting All Employees Against Unjust Dismissal," *Harvard Business Review* (January–February 1980), 132–39.

[4]Samuel R. Connor and John S. Fielden, "Rx for Managerial Shelf-Sitters," *Harvard Business Review* (November–December 1973), 113–20.

[5]*Work in America: Report of a Special Task Force to the Secretary of Health, Education and Welfare* (Cambridge, Mass: The M.I.T. Press), 4.

[6]Ibid.

[7]Erich Fromm, *The Revolution of Hope* (New York: Harper & Row, 1964).

[8]Thomas Holmes and Richard H. Rahe, "The Social Readjustment Rating Scale," *Journal of Psychosomatic Research* (August 1967), 213–18.

[9]Harold Kaufman, *Professionals in Search of Work: Coping with the Stress of Job Loss and Underemployment* (New York: Wiley Interscience, 1981).

[10]Donald Monaco, "Outplacement Counseling: Business and Profession" in James S. J. Manuso, *Occupational Clinical Psychology* (New York: Praeger, 1983), 189–201.

[11]Barrie S. Greiff and Preston K. Munter, *Tradeoffs: Executive, Family and Organizational Life* (New York: New American Library, 1980), 117.

[12]Committee on Psychiatry in Industry of the Group for the Advancement of Psychiatry, *Job Loss—A Psychiatric Perspective* (New York: Mental Health Materials Center, 1982), 5.

[13]Harold Kaufman's *Professionals in Search of Work* contains an extensive review of the literature. Mental health professionals and counselors will have a particular interest in the evidence reviewed and presented in *Job Loss—A Psychiatric Perspective*.

[14]Committee on Psychiatry, *Job Loss*, 54.

[15]Drake Beam Morin survey of 244 companies, 1986. The number of employees in the participating firms ranged from 60 to over 10,000, with the median at 6,000; 23 percent of the firms employed 20,000 or more, and 31 percent employed 3,000 or less. In terms of sales or assets, the range was from $1.2 million to over $90 billion, with the median at $1.4 billion. 32 percent of the firms reported sales or assets under $500 million and 26 percent over $2.5 billion. Responding companies represented the full range of industry classification (SIC) framework. 61 percent identified themselves as manufacturing companies, and the following industries accounted for over 50 percent of the respondents: finance, insurance, real estate, food, fabricated metals, chemicals and pharmaceuticals, electric and electronic, transportation, communications and public utilities.

[16]Drake Beam Morin, *Survey of Outplacement and Termination Practices*, 1981. Responses were obtained from 449 companies, just under half of which were from the Fortune 1000.

[17]Donald Monaco, "Outplacement Counseling."

[18]Drake Beam Morin survey of 4,800 clients counseled in field offices throughout the United States between January 1981 and June 1986.

2

Organizational Development and Change

S URPRISING AS IT MAY SEEM, MANY EXECUTIVES can look back on their careers and say that getting fired was the best thing that ever happened to them. Depending on the person and the situation, being dismissed can force people to examine their career progress. Often they are blasted from complacency and come to realize that their career has been stagnant for some time. This realization can be blunted or vitiated by poor termination practices, however.

All too typical is the case of Harry Morgan. Harry was effectively placed on the shelf eleven years ago at the age of 42. "After all," went the reasoning, "Harry joined us right out of school; he has given us the best years of his life. It has been almost twenty years. Keeping Harry on is the responsible thing to do." Since that time, Harry had been given makeshift work, special projects, and, much of the time, nothing to do.

Then the economy went into a deep recession. The company's ability to respond was hampered by, among other things, too much deadwood. Senior management found complacency among many people in key customer service spots. As part of the corporate redevelopment plan, Harry and others like him would have to go. Budgets were being cut. Harry was a luxury the company could no longer afford.

Now Harry was 53 and out of work. Furthermore, he had not received a promotion in more than thirteen years. Nor was he in a position to talk to a potential employer about any recent accomplishments. Not having been challenged in more than a decade, his approach to the job search process was timid and uncertain. In short, Harry was not an attractive job candidate. Corporate responsibility had backfired.

Replacing Managers for Organizational Development

Replacing a manager is often a necessary means of organizational change, one that has been given short shrift in the voluminous literature on organizational development. Porter, Lawler, and Hackman have noted that:

> Just as organizations can be changed by recruitment and selection practices, so also can they be changed by practices regarding who is encouraged or required to leave the organization . . . It is true that by systematically eliminating from an organization those individuals who cannot or consistantly will not work effectively toward organizational goals, the overall level of organizational effectiveness often can be improved.[1]

They suggest that, in the long run, "the best interests of the organization and the employee are served by the individual not staying in a position to which he is not suited."[2]

Similarly, Beer has noted that "there are few major organizational transitions where managers are not faced with decisions about replacement or termination."[3] Executives of developing companies in particular often find themselves in the difficult position of having to discharge those who can no longer meet the requirements of managing in a more complex organization. Such terminations are painful because of the close identification between these individuals and the early years of the business, yet their inability to grow with the organization's needs can restrict the company's progress.

Several scholars have developed theories to describe the identifiable stages of organizational growth. One of the more prominent models is the one formulated by Larry Greiner.[4]

Greiner's analysis makes three points:

- As organizations grow, they are forced to adopt structures and management systems that are appropriate to their stage of development. Such adaptation is a prerequisite of continued growth.
- With continued growth, management structures that permitted past growth to occur will become obsolete.
- As the organization moves from one stage to another, an atmosphere of considerable turmoil is often generated as the management styles, techniques, and structures that led to success in the previous stage prove problematical for the growing organization.

In other words, successful managerial methods often generate their own demise. The very growth that the methods helped generate creates new conditions, for which new methods and structures must be employed.

Consider the practical effects of Greiner's arguments for individual managers. Although many managers can adapt from the informal structure of a small company to a more centralized bureaucratic environment, company histories are replete with examples of senior managers, even founders, who have had to be replaced in order for proper management systems to be installed. An autocratic manager may be highly effective at a certain point in a company's history; at another point, that style will begin creating problems rather than solving them. Similarly, a manager whose delegation skills have been critical to the success of the company to date might find these same skills counterproductive as the organization evolves.

Managers caught in the middle of such organizational crises are often confused when faced with the reality that they are not as effective as in the past. The executive may resist the new managerial approaches being implemented, seeing them as a personal repudiation. Yet it is not that these managers are less skillful than before, just that their managerial strengths are no longer appropriate to the new set of organizational challenges their past successes have helped generate. Other organizations may be floundering for lack of managers with their particular skills and abilities.

Appropriately, most organizations turn to training and development in an effort to help managers adapt. Some managers respond to this training and once more become contributors to the organization. For others, however, the occupational habits of a lifetime prove hard to break. Some cannot or do not want to make the adjustment. These come under increasing fire for their methods and eventually find themselves outside the mainstream of the company in which they were once important performers. Either they are bypassed, or worse, they may remain in key positions, hindering rather than helping the organization's progress.

Fiedler has presented data on the difficulty of changing a manager's style.[5] He suggests that at times it might be simpler to redesign the job around the manager than to try to adapt the manager's style to fit a particular situation. Unfortunately, there are few circumstances in which this solution would work.

An example of the dilemmas that can confront a growing organization was observed by one of the authors in a small manufacturing organization ($15 million in sales), located in western New York State. The president of the organization inherited the C.E.O. job following the sudden and unexpected death of his father, who was the founder of the company. The father, a brilliant engineer, ran the organization as a paternalistic autocrat.

His key associates would describe problems to him; he then made the decisions and told them what to do. Over a twenty-year period he built a team that had good technical skills but no experience with managerial problem-solving.

Prior to the father's death there were signs that the growing complexity of the company was beginning to create problems for his style of managing. All indications are that he had been postponing certain organizational decisions while he groomed his son to take over the business. Then he fell ill. Any plans for a smooth transition evaporated as the son was thrust into the leadership role. No interim successor was on the scene.

The son was confronted with a number of difficult management decisions. Recent technological advances were threatening to render the company's production processes obsolete. The cost of the new equipment was such that it had to be run continuously, thus requiring a search for new markets and an internal reorganization. Used to the father's style, key subordinates continued to wait for the son's answers on rather minute problems rather than taking initiative. This continued despite the son's efforts to put new management systems in place. Worse, several of his father's long-time subordinates resisted change, arguing over proposed solutions rather than helping to find new ones. Frustration set in as the organization was locked in recurring debates with little action taking place.

Finally, the son fired two managers because they failed to implement the policies and practices he wanted. He replaced them with two more sophisticated managers to serve as role models for his future management team. The change came as a shock to the organization, but as the earlier negativism subsided, new voices began to be heard. He encouraged the managers who remained to attend a number of training programs to develop better understanding of the managerial issues confronting them. At present, some momentum has been generated as the organization moves toward implementing its new business plan.

Impact of Humanistic Psychology

The impact of humanistic psychology on management development programs can be seen in the emphasis placed on personal growth in managers. Throughout the 1960s and 1970s, most training and development specialists were influenced by the theories of writers such as Douglas McGregor, Chris Argyris, Warren Bennis, Robert Blake, and Jane Mouton. Although these writers are associated with different organizational development methods, they share a common belief in the responsiveness of most managers to organizational structures that encourage a fuller utilization of their abilities. The cumulative effect of their collective influence has been an industrial human potential movement. This humanistic approach asserts that organizations that evolve into open, organic structures tend to be more effective than those that are autocratic and mechanistic. However, the weight of existing research evidence supports a more complex theory of organizational management.

Organizational research suggests that although open, organic, and participative organizations are highly effective in turbulent and rapidly changing market conditions, they are less effective in stable environments than more centralized and bureaucratic organizations.[6] This research has provided the foundation for the so-called contingency approach to organizational management and the "fit" models currently being developed by organizational experts.[7]

Distilling managerial principles from such data requires care, since the relationships involved are complex, but the studies seem to support the view that, under differing conditions, certain managerial styles are more effective than others.

Couple this research to the possibility that many managers will find adapting their style to changing organizational conditions to be an unrewarding task, and termination emerges as a periodically necessary method for furthering the development of both the organization and the careers of individual managers.

When a manager is no longer performing, and this failure threatens the vitality of the organization and is coupled with passivity or resistance to change, then a compelling reason for termination exists. Often only the shock of being let go will initiate the kind of self-assessment that is likely to generate more realistic career aspirations. Of course, the discharged manager needs support far beyond that provided by our traditional approaches to termination.

The Human-Resources Perspective

In the mid-1960s, as part of the maturing of the humanistic movement, behavioral scientists began to differentiate between traditional human relations in management and a new alternative: the human-resource model.[8] Human-relations practices, went the argument, emphasized treating people better but overlooked the issue of utilizing them well.

This new perspective argued that people are an economic resource requiring full utilization of their talents if they are to maximize their performance potential. Some writers suggested that human resources should be audited, much like the financial and capital resources of the corporation, since they are a significant factor in an organization's ability to perform.[9] Such human-resource accounting practices would require management to pay more attention to the state of the firm's human assets.

The emergence of the human-resource perspective has been a watershed in the history of personnel management, clearly separating paternalism from the genuine development of people. This new perspective has some interesting implications for termination policy.

Although historically the human-resource model has focused on the training, development, and utilization of people, it also provides a rationale for management's assessing people carefully and terminating those who cannot or will not meet the organization's needs. When organizational conditions change, preserving or redeploying people is often a problem. And as the human-resource model makes clear, paternalism is often destructive to the individual in the long run.

However, human resources are different from other resources in a most important sense: people have both a need for and a right to individual dignity. People are neither extensions of nor analogous to machines. Other resources can simply be scrapped; employees expect and deserve more. Discharge should be resorted to only when other options are not viable. Further, terminations must be handled according to policies that strive to avoid degrading the value of the human resource.

We are not suggesting that terminating an employee is something managers should look forward to doing with great frequency. Termination is not the primary method of changing organizations. Although it is often a necessary tool for change, it is not a particularly desirable one. Indeed, a high termination rate is generally an indicator that other personnel management systems are not operating effectively. However, given our form of industrial organization, periodic dismissals are a fact of corporate life. Our argument is for recognizing the possible need for occasional dismissals and developing policies that will manage the process effectively.

The Causes of Termination

In analyzing the reasons for termination in cases handled by our organization over the last eight years, a definite pattern emerges. At the lower levels of the organization (nonexempt administrative personnel, first-line supervisors), competency is the main reason for dismissal. At the upper managerial level, however, the reason for firing is likely to be related to personality and the degree of fit between the person and the organization.

Although the files seldom stated the matter explicitly, managerial terminations were traceable to personality-related conflicts between boss and subordinate more often than any other factor except that of work-force reductions. The corporate personnel managers we interviewed supported this conclusion, stating that in the majority of instances managers are fired because they can't integrate themselves into the boss's "way of doing things."

In other words, it is the inability of managers to fit into a given organizational setting that generates problems in personal effectiveness. Most often, the disagreement is over how the job should be done. At the root of these differences are the attitudes, traits, and personal styles of the people involved.

Occasionally we encounter a person with a style so extreme that he or she runs through a number of jobs in different companies. Such cases require professional counseling. More typically, a clash with a specific boss results in the individual being let go, although he or she may have functioned very well in the past. As one manager expressed it: "You work for one guy, you're a hero; another tells you you're a bum; on the next job, you're a hero again."

Job incompetence is the basis for only a small percentage of terminations at the managerial level. Included among these are the shelf-sitters, who are considered ineffective and are continually passed over for promotion. When subordinates are easy to get along with, or have "been on the team," the first response of the boss is to protect them. They are given noncritical jobs and placed on the shelf. It is when subordinates clash with their superiors that incompetence leads to termination.

Incompetence is, of course, relative. To be incompetent at one job does not mean a person is unemployable. In another job, with other responsibilities, the same person might prove quite capable.

What does our discussion imply for a company's human-resource planning systems? Termination is one of the ways in which an organization can control its employment mix. Let's examine some of the others.

Recruitment and Termination

A systematic analysis of a company's termination patterns often suggests the need for improved recruiting practices. If a firm takes a hard, realistic look at why it ends up dismissing people, it often finds that many problems can be headed off during the employment selection process.

Analysis of our client organizations has revealed that attention is too seldom given to the personal style of potential applicants and how they and their future bosses might work together. Is the manager detail-oriented and the immediate supervisor impatient and decisive? What if one is creative and innovative and the other is cautious? Although such differences do not always forecast interpersonal conflicts, it is reasonable to make them explicit before offering employment to an applicant. It requires maturity to tolerate significant personality differences and to view these differences as compensating for one's own blind spots.

Cabrera and Galiskis recommend that the recruitment manager give careful consideration to the personal characteristics that the boss thinks are important to success in the job before the search is initiated.[10] What kind of environment does the boss create for subordinates? Is it highly structured, with close supervision, or do subordinates have considerable autonomy? How much emphasis does the boss place on personal organization and adherence to formal procedures in carrying out work assignments? How does the boss make decisions? Does the boss prefer to be presented with a subordinate's best recommendation or to examine all the options personally?

Such data, collected through interviews with the boss and subordinates, can be translated into specific characteristics that the successful applicant should have. It is important that the characteristics be limited to those that experience indicates are important to interpersonal effectiveness between this particular executive and subordinates. These should be discussed frankly before the search process begins.

Unfortunately, such an analysis doesn't always precede a job search, so that an applicant might be selected who does not have the temperament needed to perform well in the new environment. Instead, two or three years later, the recruit is a candidate for dismissal.

Simply stated, when hiring subordinates most managers are basically interested in whether the person has the technical ability to do the job and whether they can work with this person. Failure on one or both of these points should lead to rejection.

Future-oriented Job Specifications

Job specifications should be oriented to the future, not the past. Industrial psychologist John Drake notes that recruiters frequently rely heavily on past managers as models in developing job specifications.[11] But people who were successful in the job over the past five or ten years are not necessarily good models for future success. This is especially true when the organization is undergoing rapid change.

Peter Drucker relates a story about the selection of a relatively low-level manager by Alfred Sloan. Mr. Sloan, the legendary C.E.O. of General Motors, appeared to be spending an inordinate amount of time pondering his selection. His rationale was that each time the job had to be filled, the terms of the assignment were quite different.[12]

When developing job specifications, a corporate recruiter should focus on (1) the current demands of the job in question and (2) anticipated future demands. How does the boss see the job evolving? Where will the new manager be expected to move in terms of long-range development? What new skills will be required of the person holding down the position? Conscious consideration of questions such as these can help avoid unnecessary terminations. Attention should be focused during the recruitment process on the characteristics required if the person is to grow with the company.

A considerable body of literature exists on recruitment and selection. Our intent in this book is neither to duplicate nor to supplement it. Suffice it to say that analysis of termination patterns often reveals weaknesses in a company's recruitment practices.

Human-Resource Planning

Beyond selecting the proper people tor the organization, there is the matter of effectively planning their utilization. Analysis of an organization's termination patterns often reveals that people are terminated because the company failed to identify certain developmental needs early in their careers or, in other cases, simply misassigned them.

Performance appraisal emerges as an important part of any human-resource planning system. Properly managed, the appraisal process can help provide reasonably accurate assessments of a person's capabilities and developmental needs. Even more important, a well-conceived approach to appraisal helps avert problems before they become severe.

Unfortunately, most organizations fail to maintain effective appraisal systems. All too often the appraisal becomes a tool for justifying salary decisions. Under such conditions, appraisals reflect more about what the company is willing to pay than about the employee's actual performance, strengths, and weaknesses. Furthermore, the appraisal information is often not transferred to a centralized human-resource information bank where it would be readily available when staffing and training decisions were made.

A much-underestimated device for managing an organization's human-resource flow is the management inventory. Essentially, a management inventory is to a business what a depth chart is to an athletic team. Every year, key managers (division, plant, and department heads) complete the inventory on crucial managerial and administrative slots that report to them.

The incumbent of each slot is usually evaluated on several levels:

- Current performance
- Qualifications for current positions
- Anticipated future performance
- Promotability

Successors to these positions are typically evaluated as well, with the manager often required to identify two or three possible backups for each slot, along with their degree of preparedness for assuming the job. Development plans for improving the preparedness of these successors are also required. This information is then integrated with a statement on how the managers expect their human-resource requirements to change given present and future business plans. This information is reviewed with the managers' superiors and then fed into the centralized human-resource information system.

A management inventory does not provide automatic answers. When completed annually, however, the inventory imposes the rigorous discipline on human-resource planning that comes with repeatedly asking the right questions. Individuals who have not made any progress or whose performance is slipping are likely to be identified at an early stage and targeted for corrective action. Alternative career paths resulting from changed business objectives are likely to be illustrated by the inventory. In short, management inventories can help an organization stay on top of many career-path-related issues.

Of course, both appraisals and management inventories must be supplemented by an investment in management development training if the organization is to maximize its efforts to avoid unnecessary terminations.

Establishing and maintaining an effective human-resource system is a topic beyond the scope of this book except to say that a frequent need to resort to termination should lead a company to audit its practices in this area.

Mid-career Guidance

Although large organizations are increasingly examining their outplacement policies, few have seriously looked at mid-career guidance. In essence, mid-career guidance is evolving today as an effort to stave off termination. As noted previously, a majority of people at managerial levels are fired because of the chemistry between them and their bosses or other managers above them. Mid-career guidance can help them modify the behavior that is creating difficulties.

Often, if people know that they are doing certain things that are not acceptable to their superiors or peers, they will strive to change that aspect of their behavior. All the boss wants many times is a change in behavior, not a personality change.

For example, we were asked to work with one manager whose job was in jeopardy because his superiors were uncertain whether they could trust his judgment. In pressing this issue with his superiors, we found that the individual involved tended to hesitate when expressing his opinion, a trait others interpreted as indicating a lack of confidence in his opinion. Conversations with the manager revealed that he felt he was not really being asked for his opinion. He was unaware of how his behavior was being read by others.

Once he understood the problem, he worked to eliminate the hesitant behavior that communicated uncertainty on his part. He also worked on skills that helped him to clarify his boss's expectations. Subsequently, his superiors came to view him as having "grown and developed more confidence." Less than a year after having received what we now call mid-career guidance counseling, the manager was promoted to a more responsible position in his division.

This kind of counseling often comes from a boss or other mentor within the company. Sometimes, however, performance problems create a tension that the boss finds difficult to overcome. Either the boss lacks the skills to counsel the subordinate effectively, or the subordinate is too defensive. In such situations, a third-party counselor can often provide the assistance that is needed to salvage the person's career for the company.

Simply helping to clarify expectations is a useful role when one considers that today a company may have $500,000 to $1 million invested in an employee after twenty to thirty years of service. To fire such people or say that they have "Peter principled" or "plateaued" out without first making an effort to turn their careers around is to write off a significant investment. Replacement costs add to the expense.

It is our opinion that the poor quality of communication that characterizes many performance appraisal systems, coupled with a tendency for subordinates to claim they understand the feedback they are getting from a boss when in fact they do not, generates considerable waste in our utilization of people. There are a great many needless terminations. Mid-career guidance can help avoid them. This guidance can be oriented toward eliminating a specific problem, as in the illustration above, or it can be directed toward overcoming more general problems, such as a leveling off in performance.

When Not Terminating Is a Mistake

Few things in life are as traumatic as being fired. It is our hope that the above discussion makes clear our belief that dismissing someone should be considered only when other human-resource management approaches have not produced results. Managers should not expect termination to be a regular part of their job. In fact, an excessive termination rate is usually indicative of a deep-rooted managerial problem.

Nevertheless, as we have indicated above, there are times when termination is an appropriate managerial strategy. More specifically, such situations include:

- *Poor job performance.* When an employee's work performance continues to be unsatisfactory, although specific performance criteria have been repeatedly explained to the employee, failure to discharge the employee is a mistake. The firm is not realizing a return on its investment in the person. Furthermore, someone else usually has to pick up the slack. In addition to imposing extra costs, this can generate a morale problem, leading to other problems. The longer the poor performer is carried, the less management can expect other workers to be responsive to performance standards.

- *Failure to comply with company regulations and rules.* Included here is failure to comply with personnel regulations as well as any other set of established organizational policies. For example, excessive absenteeism or tardiness that violates existing standards for a job classification must be corrected to maintain management credibility. When an employee has been warned repeatedly that his or her behavior violates published standards and the employee still refuses to comply, termination is a reasonable solution.

- *Insubordination.* When a subordinate refuses to carry out the boss's directives, termination looms as the only solution. Insubordination threatens the authority structure of the organization as well as the manager's ability to meet organizational goals.

In every instance, termination should be preceded by either corrective or career-oriented counseling. However, once it becomes clear that these strategies are not providing a solution, termination becomes a viable, indeed necessary, vehicle for organizational change.

Endnotes

[1] Lyman W. Porter, Edward E. Lawler III, and Richard Hackman, *Behavior in Organizations* (New York: McGraw-Hill, 1975), 442.

[2] Ibid.

[3] Michael Beer, *Organization Change and Development* (Santa Monica: Goodyear, 1980), 196–97.

[4] Larry E. Greiner, "Evolution and Revolution as Organizations Grow," *Harvard Business Review* (July–August 1972), 37–46.

[5] Fred E. Fiedler, *A Theory of Leadership Effectiveness* (New York: McGraw-Hill, 1967).

[6] Tom Burns and G.S. Stalker, *The Management of Innovation* (London: Tavistock Publications, 1961); Richard H. Hall, "Intraorganizational Structure Variation," *Administrative Science Quarterly* (December 1961); Paul F. Lawrence and Jay W. Lorsch, *Organization and Environment: Managing Differentiation and Integration* (Homewood, Ill.: Richard D. Irwin, Inc., 1967); J. W. Lorsch and J. J. Morse, *Organizations and Their Members: A Contingency Approach* (New York: Harper & Row, 1974).

[7] Jay R. Galbraith, *Organization Design* (Reading, Mass.: Addison-Wesley, 1977); John Kotter, *Organizational Dynamics: Diagnosis and Intervention* (Reading, Mass.: Addison-Wesley, 1978); Robert Duncan, "What Is the Right Organization Structure?" *Organizational Dynamics* (Winter 1979); and Henry Mintzberg, "Structure in 5's: A Synthesis of the Research on Organizational Design, *Management Science* (March 1980).

[8] Raymond Miles, "Human Relations or Human Resources," *Harvard Business Review* (July–August 1965), 148–63.

[9] Rensis Likert and D. G. Bowers, "Organization Theory and Human Resources Accounting," *American Psychologist* (June 1969), 585–92.

[10] James C. Cabrera and Edward A. Galiskis, "A Participative Executive Search," *Personnel* (January–February 1974), 69–72.

[11] John D. Drake, *Interviewing for Managers* (New York: AMACOM, 1982).

[12] Peter F. Drucker, "How to Make People Decisions," *Harvard Business Review* (July–August 1985).

3

The Employment-at-Will
Controversy

IN RECENT YEARS THERE HAS BEEN AN UNMIS-
takable trend in many state courts of permitting redress to
employees when a discharge is grossly unjust. This trend has
had the practical result of limiting management's ability to fire at
will.

The traditional prerogative of management to fire at will
has, since the nineteenth century, been institutionalized in
United States common law as the right to "discharge an employee at any time, or even for cause morally wrong."[1] Based in
English common law, this right emerged in the United States as a
means of balancing the relationship between employees and employers.[2] Essentially, the employment-at-will doctrine holds that
an employer has the right to dismiss an employee for good cause,
no cause, or even a bad cause (one that is morally wrong), just as
an employee has the right to leave the service of an employer for
any reason.

Throughout the twentieth century, however, a series of specific restrictions have been placed on an employer's rights under
the employment-at-will doctrine. Shortly after the turn of the

century, a number of state legislatures enacted worker's compensation statutes that prohibited retaliatory discharge against employees who filed for benefits. At the federal level, the Fair Labor Standards Act, the National Labor Relations Act, and the Occupational Safety and Health Act provide protection from retaliatory discharge for employees asserting their rights by filing charges under the act in question or testifying during proceedings.

In writing such provisions into these acts, legislators recognized the extent to which employment-at-will was more than just a counterpart to an employee's right to leave an employer. It was a lever of power that could be used by employers to frustrate the intent of such legislation.

Indeed, management has often invoked the employment-at-will doctrine in an arbitrary fashion. And until recently the courts have supported such action as among the rightful prerogatives of management. The restrictions cited above apply only to the specific statutes in question. In the absence of statutory or contractual provisions, judges have been reluctant to intervene in the private employment relationship and have traditionally ruled for employment-at-will, no matter how abusive the discharge. Only the antidiscrimination legislation and executive orders of the 1960s and early 1970s afforded any additional limitation on an employer's right to discharge. Until the late 1970s, *good cause* was a concept recognized in collective bargaining agreements, but without legal standing beyond the framework of negotiated contracts.

Rationale for Modifying Employment-at-Will

About twenty years ago, however, Professor Lawrence Blades wrote a classic article on abusive discharge, published in the *Columbia Law Review*, challenging the idea that, in contemporary American society, the employment-at-will doctrine was an equitable counterpart to the Thirteenth Amendment.[3] When formulating and enforcing corporate termination policies, it is well worth a manager's time to give thoughtful consideration to Blades's concerns about the employer-employee relationship.

"Obviously," Blades noted, "if every employee could go from job to job with complete ease, there would be little need to provide other means of escape from the improper exertion of employer pressure. In reality, however, because of his comparative immobility, the individual worker has long been highly vulnerable to private economic power."[4]

The focus of Blades's argument was those situations in which a company might force an employee to go beyond the employer's legitimate business interests: to commit illegal acts, subvert public policy, or—in the case of licensed professionals such as lawyers, accountants, or medical personnel—engage in unethical activities. The issue for Blades was not how widespread such abuses were but that "some less scrupulous employers are unable to resist exercising a power" that common law placed in their grasp.[5]

While arguing against the right of discharge as absolute and inviolable, Blades recognized that "the employer's prerogative to make independent, good faith judgments about employees is important in our free-enterprise system" and went on to suggest that in such cases the employee "be held to a higher burden of proof than normally required of civil actions."[6] Since such cases would often center on the word of each of the parties, Blades's opinion was that to prevail the employee should be required to provide proof by "clear and convincing" evidence.[7]

Blades raised these issues in terms of legal theory. Contemporary employers are confronted with recent court decisions that reflect his arguments but are not unanimous in their interpretations. For example, the issue of which side carries the burden of proof is crucial and one on which various courts have differed. For purposes of framing policy implications, it is instructive to examine the particular concerns that have characterized legal rulings to date.

Wrongful Discharge vs. Employment-at-Will

Recently, a doctrine of wrongful discharge has emerged in certain state courts, which establishes exceptions to the doctrine of employment-at-will. Evidence of this trend was already apparent by the late 1970s. Early exceptions to the employment-at-will doctrine have led state courts to an increasing number of wrongful-discharge decisions that have gone to the appellate level, where the doctrine of wrongful discharge is currently being shaped.[8] Despite near hysteria over erosion of the employment-at-will doctrine, the emerging standards are not all negative toward management's prerogatives.

Essentially, certain courts have ruled against the employment-at-will doctrine in specific instances when:

- The discharge appears contrary to public policy.
- The discharge implies breach of an implied contract between the employer and employee.
- The discharge involves breach of an implied covenant of good faith and fair dealing.[9]

A number of courts have ruled that an employee can sue if his or her discharge was in retaliation for refusing to commit an unlawful act, exercising a legal right, satisfying a legal obligation, or opposing an employer's unlawful conduct.[10] In *Tameny* vs. *Atlantic Richfield Company* a case involving an employee who alleged he was fired for refusing to participate in an illegal price-fixing scheme, the California Supreme Court asserted as part of its opinion:

We hold that an employer's authority over its employee does not include the right to demand that the employee commit a criminal act to further its interests . . . And an employer may not coerce compliance with such unlawful directions by discharging an employee who refuses to follow such an order. An employer engaging in such conduct violates a basic duty imposed by law upon all employers, and thus an employee who has suffered damage as a result of such discharge may maintain a tort action for wrongful discharge against the employer.[11]

Similarly, in *Nees* vs. *Hocks*, an Oregon court awarded an employee compensatory damages for emotional distress suffered when she was discharged for serving on a jury.[12]

However, the fact that a plaintiff's behavior is laudable does not necessarily give rise to a public policy case.[13] In *Adams* vs. *Budd Company*, the plaintiff alleged that his discharge was for reporting defects in Budd's railway cars to his superiors. As Baxter and Wohl report, "The court stated that it empathized with Adams's strict compliance with the Budd quality control manual . . . Yet the court held that under Pennsylvania law it had to dismiss the suit because Adams had not shown that the defects had posed a safety hazard to the public or that Budd was hiding the defects or refusing to take responsibility for them."[14]

Perhaps no aspect of the current changes in employment-at-will has been more shocking to executives than the extent to which courts have found certain language in company documents and employee handbooks and certain oral statements to constitute an implied contract to terminate only for cause.

In *Pugh* vs. *See's Candies, Inc.*, a California appeals court concluded that an employee who had been thirty-two years with the company and had advanced from dishwasher to vice president of production and member of the board of directors, but had no written employment contract, nevertheless did possess an implied contract. Because this case is often cited in the literature, the specifics of the judge's opinion are worth examining.

In his opinion, Judge Grodin observed:

When Pugh first went to work for See's, Ed Peck, then president and general manager, frequently told him: "If you are loyal to [See's] and do a good job, your future is secure" . . .

Laurence See, who became president of the company in 1951 and served in that capacity until his death in 1969, had a practice of not terminating administrative personnel except for good cause, and this practice was carried on by his brother, Charles B. See, who succeeded Laurence as president. During the entire period of his employment, there had been no formal or written criticisms of Pugh's work. No complaints were ever raised at the annual meetings which preceded each holiday season, and he was never denied a raise or bonus. He received no notice that there was a problem which needed correction, nor any warning that any disciplinary action was being contemplated. Here, similarly, there were facts of evidence from which the jury could determine the existence of such an implied promise: the duration of the appellant's employment, the commendations and promotions he received, the apparent lack of any direct criticism of his work, the assurance he was given, and the employer's acknowledged policies. While oblique language, standing alone, will not be sufficient to establish agreement [*Drzewiecki* vs. *H&R Block, Inc.,* supra, 24 Cal. App.3rd 695, 703, 101 Cal.Rptr. 169], it is appropriate to consider the totality of the parties' relationship: Agreement may be shown by the acts and conduct of the parties, interpreted in the light of the subject matter and the surrounding circumstances. [*Marvin* vs. *Marvin* (1976) 18 Cal.3rd 660, 678, fn.16, 134 Cal. Rptr.815, 557 P.2nd 106 see Note, Implied Contract Rights to Job Security (1974) 26 Stan.L.Rev. 335] We therefore conclude that it was error to grant respondents' motions for non-suit as to See's.[15]

The court let the case be tried, an event considered important by experts in employment law, although Pugh subsequently lost the case. In letting the case go to trial, Justice Grodin's opinion recognized the need for caution in overruling the employment-at-will doctrine, stating: "And where, as here, the employee occupies a sensitive managerial or confidential position, the employer must of necessity be allowed substantial scope for the exercise of subjective judgment." In providing guidance to the trial court, Justice Grodin wrote that Pugh "bears, however, the ultimate burden of proving he was terminated wrongfully,"[16] a burden which Pugh failed to carry.

California courts have been particularly aggressive in applying contract law to employment-at-will situations, and Baxter and Wohl's review of appellate decisions in that state is especially enlightening. For example, in *Crosier* vs. *United Parcel Service*, a California case subsequent to *Pugh* vs. *See's Candies, Inc.*, the court also imposed the burden of proof on the employee, leading Baxter and Wohl to observe that "this evidentiary presumption in favor of the employer further protects its discretion to terminate."[17]

Baxter and Wohl also cite *Hillsman* vs. *Sutter Community Hospitals of Sacramento*, a recent case before the California State Court of Appeals, which suggests further limitations on the circumstances in which an implied contract to terminate employment only for cause may be said to exist. Dr. Hillsman alleged he was fired as a hospital physician in breach of contract, based in part on a letter Sutter had sent him at the time of hiring, which stated that, "it looked forward to a long, pleasant, and mutually satisfactory relationship." He also claimed he was fired in violation of the hospital's disciplinary bylaws. The court found no evidence of a promise that Dr. Hillsman's employment could be terminated only for cause. It noted that the hospital's statement that "it looked forward to a long, pleasant, and mutually satisfactory relationship" was no more than a "polite closing salutation [intended] simply to add a touch of personal warmth to an otherwise businesslike letter."[18]

However, because the hospital had adopted discharge procedures in its bylaws, the court agreed with Hillsman that he had an implied contract and that he could not be terminated in violation of those procedures, noting a mutual understanding that rules and procedures applying to an employee may indeed be part of an implied contract of employment. The court held that Hillsman had a cause for legal action despite language in the letter of understanding that either side could terminate its provisions upon thirty days' notice, since the letter was silent on the cause for termination, leaving open the possibility that the procedures were part of the agreement. Hence, Sutter would have to rebut Hillsman's allegations at trial.

Baxter and Wohl find three points of significance in the Hillsman ruling, points that have some support in other cases as well: (1) employers may reserve their prerogative to discharge at will through explicit language in a formal agreement; (2) *vague* salutations of long-term employment were not considered by the courts to constitute a binding contract; and (3) if employer and employee have a mutual understanding that a given set of rules or procedures apply to the employee in question, then they may give rise to an implied, binding contract.[19]

In Hunt v. IBM Mid America Employees Credit Union, the Supreme Court ruled that the disciplinary and termination procedures in the handbook in question were too vague to constitute a contractual offer. The absence of detailed procedures would require the jury to determine the terms and conditions of employment, which the court ruled would be inappropriate.[20]

That the language in an employment handbook may modify an original employment contract was noted in a 1983 opinion of the Minnesota Supreme Court in *Pine River State Bank* vs. *Richard E. Mettille*:

> An employer's offer of a unilateral contract may very well appear in a personnel handbook as the employer's response to the practical problem of transactional costs . . . An employer, such as the bank here, may prefer not to write a separate contract with each individual employee. By preparing and distributing its handbook, the employer chooses, in essence, either to implement or modify its existing contracts with all employees covered by the handbook. Further, we do not think

that applying the unilateral contract doctrine to personnel handbooks unduly circumscribes the employer's discretion. Unilateral contract modification of the employment contract may be a repetitive process. Language in the handbook itself may reserve discretion to the employer in certain matters or reserve the right to amend or modify the provisions.[21]

Implied covenant of good faith and fair dealing is well established in contract law, and courts will find it applicable when a discharge appears abusive. A recent California appellate court decision (*Rulon-Miller* vs. *IBM Corp.*) confirmed "the right of an employee to the benefit of rules and regulations adopted for his or her protection."[22] In addition, the court found the supervisor acted in "bad faith" in making charges against the employee without any basis of substantiation. Further, the court found that, in claiming that the firing was in the employee's best interest, thus leaving her powerless to assert her rights as an IBM employee, the supervisor's behavior was sufficiently outrageous to merit recovery against IBM for intentional infliction of emotional distress.

Implications for Management

What does the above sampling of wrongful discharge vs. employment-at-will cases imply for management? As Robert Coulson, president of the American Arbitration Association, stated to us in a recent interview, the issue is a "serious legal problem and should be treated as such. But in most instances an unjust dismissal case remains a very hard case for an employee to win."

During the initial period of rising concern about the erosion of the employment-at-will doctrine, D. W. Ewing wrote, "Contrary to a widespread impression in the management community, no court that I know of questions a manager's prerogative to fire a subordinate who is demonstrably incompetent, lazy, uncooperative, or abusive toward associates."[23] Ewing further observed that, while restrictions on management's right to fire are spreading, there is no reason to believe that American companies will be shackled. Rather, he suggested, "American courts and legislatures will continue to protect and preserve corporate rights, except when they come into conflict with individual civil liberties, the general public welfare, or contractual obligations to employees. Even then, corporations will win their share—or more—of the cases."[24]

According to Pingpank and Mooney, "We must recognize that in this area, wrongful discharge, the facts make the law. . . In most instances where recovery was granted, or the case was allowed to proceed, the fact situation cried out for recovery."[25] Colosi makes a similar argument when he notes that the "new judge-made" law has arisen from bad cases making bad law: In other words, courts faced with employees who received intolerable and onerous treatment from their employers elected to give relief to the employee, despite the apparent roadblock of the at-will doctrine.[26]

Hames has concluded that as of 1988 definitive conclusions regarding employment-at-will cannot be made, even for each state. However, the majority of states have imposed some restrictions on an employer's right to fire, especially in cases involving public policy or termination procedures or requirements contained in employee handbooks or made orally.[27]

These observations place the problem in perspective. They indicate that managers no longer have an unqualified right to fire an employee but must use judgment, show a sense of fair play, and recognize an obligation to the employee in question. Restrictions on the employment-at-will doctrine are emerging, but the doctrine has not and probably will not be replaced by a total disregard for employer interests. Good employee relations can help a corporation effectively exercise its rights. Moveover, such relations can help shape the legislative environment in which the issue is likely to be resolved in the future.

Following an extensive study of the legal cases and the interpretive judgments of experts in employee-relations law, we have found four conclusions reasonably evident.

First, the trend toward restricting employer's right to discharge is clear, although considerable variation continues to exist between courts in different states. However, it is our opinion that, even in states in which the employment-at-will doctrine remains well established and without significant modification, retaliatory or abusive discharge makes little sense from an employee-relations standpoint, raises serious questions of ethics, and from a policy standpoint is very short-sighted. Given the tendency of bad cases to make bad law, the business community has a vested interest in minimizing the number of questionable discharges that occur. Even firms seeking to preserve their at-will status, which is one of several policy options, should do so in a constructive fashion.

Second, the courts do not appear to be disregarding corporate interests. The challenge to the employment-at-will doctrine is rooted in the courts' desire to rectify the injustice of specific retaliatory or abusive discharges, which have placed in sharp relief the power imbalance between employer and employee. The consequences, however, are troublesome for *all* discharges.

Third, companies should expect terminations with public policy implications to be especially sensitive. Given the potential for significant financial exposure under tort claims, corporate termination policy should be explicitly communicated to all managerial employees and compliance carefully maintained. It should be clear, for example, that all terminations will be reviewed and that no employee will be discharged for refusing to comply with laws or regulatory guidelines.

Fourth, the courts are taking corporate handbooks and similar publications seriously, assuming that employees take management at its word and even make career decisions based on such assurances. Given the reaction of most companies caught in such legal actions, the courts are taking such communications much more seriously than the people who write and publish them do. This is a situation in which it is incumbent upon senior human-resource executives to take corrective action. Here again there is a potential for tort claims resulting in substantial recoveries.

Despite the unpredictability of the judicial process, the emerging trends in court proceedings seem to be gravitating toward a balance of employer and employee rights similar to that envisioned by Professor Blades. Such a balance will no doubt be an imperfect one, occasionally marked by unanticipated rulings resolving cases characterized by inconsistent behavior on both sides of the employer-employee relationship.

Formulating Corporate Policy

The current uncertainty surrounding employment-at-will provides corporate management with an opportunity to explicitly define company policy toward its employees. It is essential that this policy be defined within the framework of the organization's strategic and tactical needs and not with the myopic goal of trying to preserve some eroding corporate right. Organizations tend toward congruency in their various strategies, policies, and cultural settings.[28] Management's response to the issue of employment-at-will may create more problems than it solves if it runs counter to strategic initiatives that are being undertaken to build and sustain organizational performance.

Much of the recent literature in the personnel journals has focused on what management should do to avoid compromising its legal position on employment-at-will. This is a serious concern, lest management unintentionally reduce its area of legitimate discretion and complicate its dealings with employees. Properly implemented, many of the recommended precautions can facilitate communication between employees and management, lessening the potential for misinterpretation. Carried to an extreme, however, some of these actions, although prudent from legal counsel's view, could significantly inhibit the existing sense of corporate community and commitment to organizational goals.

There is a need for human-resource policies that protect the organization both legally and culturally. The challenge confronting management is to develop and enforce a strategic stance on employee discharge that encompasses and goes beyond protective and reactive legalistic positioning. A constructive phrasing of the policy issue might be: To what extent can management protect employees from retaliatory and abusive discharge while also protecting the interests of the corporation within the framework of explicit policy decisions?

The managerial challenge inherent in the employment-at-will controversy goes to the heart of the issue of corporate decency and the ethical use of power. D. W. Ewing asserts that, in today's business environment of complex technologies, rapidly changing markets, and large corporations, employees must have a basis for faith in the professional decency of management if a company is to function effectively.[29] Ewing's work takes an important step toward integrating Blades's concept of abusive discharge and the shifting framework of employment-at-will being imposed by the courts into a coherent and practical management philosophy. Many organizations are explicitly seeking more effective ways of forging a partnership between employees and organization in order to enhance the quality of products, raise productivity, lower costs, and improve corporate image. Managers in such companies need to perceive not only what they *can* do but, as Ewing suggests, what they *should* do relative to economic and social needs.

Recently, Richard Walton has drawn a sharp contrast between what he refers to as the "control" and the "commitment" strategies of managing the work force.[30] A control strategy is embodied by policies and procedures that closely direct and regulate employee behavior, generally emphasizing management's rights to make arbitrary decisions that affect employees. Under a commitment strategy, a company seeks to de-emphasize distinctions between levels of the organization, encourage participative decision-making, and obtain commitment of all employees to company goals. Whichever strategy is chosen, companies are best served by pursuing an internally consistent strategy toward their

work force and that corporate policies concerning discharge are
an integral component of any such strategy.

In a very real sense, the employment-at-will controversy forces
companies to confront the issue of work-force strategy. Organizations striving to preserve employment-at-will prerogatives are confronted with the need to state explicitly on employment forms, in
employee handbooks, and in similar documents that the company
reserves the right to fire for any reason whatever, and to purge such
communications of any promises of job security, just cause, and the
like. To expect employees to demonstrate commitment to the organization in the absence of any reciprocal commitment to its employees is in most instances unrealistic. At minimum, the threat of
arbitrary discharge, even if seldom exercised, makes the commit-
ment-building enterprise more difficult.

Assessing the Trade-offs

Effective policy in this area requires a clear understanding at
the board of directors and executive committee levels of the possible strategic implications of the company's position. Policy options cover a broad range from a totally at-will employer to an
employer that never discharges an employee unless the organization itself goes out of business.[31]

In practice, few, if any, American business organizations are
willing to commit themselves to lifetime tenure for employees
with no restrictions whatsoever. Even university tenure systems
attach certain qualifications to the promise of lifetime employment. Thus, as a practical matter, total commitment simply represents the logical end of the continuum. Options very close to
that end of the continuum might prove appealing to some organizations willing to risk the associated trade-offs, however. For example, lifetime employment could be offered to employees
selected after a specific period of time subject to continued compliance with certain ethical, job abandonment, (time constraints
in which an employee is required to communicate with manage-

ment when absent, before management assumes the employee has voluntarily forfeited employment), and performance standards. Both the American university system and certain large Japanese corporations provide examples of variations on this choice. Exhibit 3.1 illustrates some of the basic choices along the continuum, although other options are conceivable and some could be used in combination.

The totally at-will choice is on the surface least problematic. It strives to protect the full range of employer options, but it has potential drawbacks, including possible negative implications for recruitment, turnover, and labor relations. Organizations in which arbitrary discharge is official policy may find it difficult to attract and retain qualified workers who have more secure options. Additionally, job security is a very effective issue for union organizing committees, which could be a concern for non-organized companies.

Note, however, that these are *possible* disadvantages. While such problems are reasonable to presume, no empirical evidence establishes a direct link between explicitly implementing an at-will policy and these negative consequences. Further, they may be countermanded by other influences such as a weak local job market or generous compensation practices. Companies that seldom discharge people anyway, except for obvious disciplinary reasons, or that normally operate at the lower end of the labor market at most levels of the organization, using specific contracts to attract key professional and management personnel, might well find such risks tolerable, in striving to protect their right to fire in any fashion.

Note also that, while companies can take many precautions to preserve their at-will prerogatives, they are in the end only precautions. While a company may attempt to preserve its at-will status, there is no guarantee that it will be able to do so, especially in cases involving public policy in progressive states.

Recent rulings do suggest employers can avoid contractual liability by placing disclaimers on employee handbooks, employ-

Exhibit 3.1 Some Possible Policy Choices Regarding Termination. Combinations Are Possible.

Total At-Will Employer	Discharge at Any Time, with or without Just Cause and without Warning, with a Specified Severance Package	No Discharge for a Specified Period of Time other than for Just Cause	No Discharge for a Specified Time	Discharge Only In Accordance with Specific Procedures	Discharge Only for Just Cause	Discharge Only for Economic Necessity at the Discretion of Management	Discharge Only Before a Certain Period of Time	No Discharge for Any Reason During the Life of the Firm
Possible Advantages	*Possible Advantages*	*Possible Advantages*		*Possible Advantages*		*Possible Advantages*	*Possible Advantages*	*Possible Advantages*
Protects the employer's interest to the maximum extent possible under the law . . . protects freedom of action to the maximum extent possible.	Largely the same as Total At-Will Employer, although the cost of insuring severance properly is increased. At the margin may be better for recruiting and retention than Total At-Will.	Can assist in the recruitment and retention of employees without permanently compromising freedom of action. Renewal option can provide control on performance.		Management has established a definite commitment to its employees. With proper managerial style this can be used as the foundation for a strong reciprocal relationship. Employees are likely to view the organization as just. Can be used as part of retention strategy.		Largely the same as Just Cause option.	Retain flexibility with non-tenured employees. Properly used, can provide a performance incentive.	Recruiting tool.

Possible Disadvantages

May make recruitment more difficult . . . may expose the company to higher turnover, incurring higher recruiting and training costs . . . may expose the company to unionization attempts

May cause employees to be insecure, interfering with open communication.

Possible Disadvantages

Largely the same although possibly somewhat lessened.

Possible Disadvantages

Management loses flexibility in dealing with employee during specified period.

Possible Disadvantages

Management loses flexibility of immediate termination.

Must defend decision in terms of the procedures.

Managerial time is required to process a discharge case through the steps.

Decisions are possibly subject to external legal review.

Difficult exceptions may arise.

Possible Disadvantages

Loss of flexibility.

Performance inequities cannot be addressed.

Must defend actions as necessary.

Possible Disadvantages

Employees discharged prior to tenure may claim bad faith.

Management has lowered leverage on tenured employees.

Possible Disadvantages

Cannot dismiss for any reason, sacrifices all flexibility; can make certain survival choices impossible.

Turnover is likely only among stronger and more marketable employees.

ment applications and similar documents. Handbook disclaimers should be conspicuous (on the front cover, introductory page or contents page), in bold type and in straightforward language which clearly states that the handbook is for employee guidance only, expresses general corporate philosophy and does not form a contract between the company and its employees.[32] Placing disclaimers on the pages of documents which list disciplinary reasons, related procedures and benefits further strengthens this protection.[33]

Management must carefully consider its options in choosing the specific strategic relationship it wishes to establish with its employees. It must then make certain that the structures and systems that embody this relationship are functioning effectively. Thus, an organization can strive to protect its position with regard to employment, possibly avoid nuisance suits, and defend its stated philosophy.

Walton's dichotomy between control and commitment strategies is instructive in considering this choice. Organizations that are more closely aligned with a control strategy, in which employees are regarded as variable costs, pay is geared to job evaluation, a strong emphasis is placed on top-down controls, and a tendency exists toward an adversarial posture in employee relations, should give careful consideration to implementing an employment-at-will policy, or some option close to it. Organizations characterized by a commitment strategy, in which retraining is used to avoid unemployment, pay is linked to skills, active use is made of participation to solve problems, and a collaborative posture exists toward workers, will probably be better served by an option that contains some form of internal due process for employees.

These decisions require careful consideration. Given the tendency of some executives to talk in terms of commitment yet manage through control, and the difficulties associated with maintaining a true commitment strategy over long periods of time, the human-resource executive needs to press for an accurate determination of management's desired posture. Otherwise, the necessary support for required systems and processes, such as accurate performance appraisals, may not be forthcoming, thereby placing the organization at risk.

Adopting any posture other than employment-at-will concedes the fact that social relationships are highly complex, the number of possible situations virtually infinite, and the outcome of any particular legal encounter uncertain. Companies that modify their at-will posture are in effect stating that such risks are worth tolerating in light of the larger employee-relations strategy through which they choose to manage their business.

Communicating the Policy

For some years now, human-resource executives have spoken of the value of establishing psychological contracts through which manager and employee share a set of expectations about their rights and obligations.[34] Handbooks, written policies, and slogans repeated in a way that communicates seriousness of intent are elements of such a psychological contract. Employees believe such statements and even make lifestyle decisions based on them. The courts are now deciding cases in a manner that suggests they are taking them seriously as well.

Companies wishing to protect their at-will prerogatives should state plainly on job applications, in other printed material such as employee handbooks, and orally at the time of employment that all employees are employees-at-will who can be discharged at any time for any reason. Companies seeking maximum protection should have employees sign a written statement which states the at-will arrangement and disclaims that statements made in other documents such as the employee handbook can be construed as a contract. Companies choosing to establish a different psychological contract with their employees must give careful consideration to the exact nature of the policy statement, review company literature to insure that potentially contradictory statements and language are reworded, and train management and supervisory personnel in the intent and content of the company's position.

Managers and supervisors must be trained not to make oral representations that are contrary to corporate policy. Employee handbooks and similar materials should clearly state that managers and supervisors do not have the authority to modify corporate policy through their oral representations. While there is evidence that courts will recognize the difference between pleasant salutations and intended policy, assuming the latter is clearly stated, it is obviously safer for managers to learn to say exactly what they mean: for example, "We look forward to your joining us" or "We hope to have a productive relationship" instead of "We look forward to a long relationship."

It is within this context of policy that references to *permanent employment* should be changed to *regular employment*, *probationary* to *introductory*, and *when* (as in *when you retire*) to *if*. Statements that dismissal will take place only for *just cause* should be made specifically contingent on certain critera or else replaced with less certain language. When discussing benefits, management's future discretion should be protected with statements such as *under the present plan*. Management may also state that employment may be a function of economic conditions and that management has the right to reduce staffing as a response to business conditions. Also, procedures established solely to structure decision-making processes should be clearly designated so that there is no confusion over their meaning. For example, a policy of supervisory review of terminations should be clearly labeled as a required process for managers and not a contractual agreement with employees.

Establishing Review Policies

Responsibility for the enforcement of company policy should be established at three points in the termination process: with (1) the manager conducting the termination, (2) the superior who reviews the decision, and (3) a professional in the personnel department who is responsible for monitoring policy in this area. A policy of managerial review tends to discourage emotional firings and gives the next level of management an opportunity to determine whether the termination is appropriate—indeed, whether the problem really lies with the person designated for discharge.

In a large, highly diverse organization, policies in sensitive areas, especially new policies that have not yet become embedded in the character of the firm, are best reinforced through the creation of a specific review function. Many firms have established a specific function in the personnel department to oversee the termination process and the administration of outplacement services. This should include the review of terminations to insure that policy and procedures are followed in a consistent fashion and that each termination conforms to the company position. In this way, potentially troublesome situations can be identified and managed so as to avoid placing the company in a difficult legal position. Without such a centralized review procedure, it is doubtful that termination policies will be effectively carried out in practice.

This function should also have a working relationship with those human-resource professionals who monitor systems such as performance appraisal that impact significantly on the execution of discharge policy.

The flowchart in Exhibit 3.2 depicts a series of checkpoints for reviewing a specific termination to help avoid problems. If managers who might discharge employees are familiar with such a chart along with the specific procedures that embody the organization's policies, the risks of wrongful discharge should be given appropriate consideration. The termination should be carefully reviewed in consultation with senior human-resources executives, with concern for protecting the integrity of both the letter and spirit of procedures. What is the explanation for variance from procedures? Should policies be revised? Are there al-

Exhibit 3.2 Reviewing Termination Circumstances to Avoid Wrongful Discharge*

	Questions to Be Asked		Action to Be Taken
Contractual Concerns	Do the circumstances stand as an exception to any written organizational policies or procedures? IF NO →	IF YES →	Assign appropriate staff to investigate the issue, make the decision within the context of corporate policy, and communicate the same to the person involved.
	If performance-based, do the person's past performance appraisals reflect the problem? IF YES →	IF NO →	Put the individual on a formal performance improvement program.
	If disciplinary, have the published progressive disciplinary procedures been followed and exhausted? IF YES →	IF NO →	Reinstate until all elements of progressive discipline procedures have been complied with.
Public Policy Concerns	Is the discharge especially abrupt? IF NO →	IF YES →	Investigate the issues surrounding the dismissal, including employee complaints or allegations. Have steps 1 and 2 or 3 above been complied with? Abrupt discharge decisions usually involve issues other than legitimate performance failures and may be symptomatic of a problem that is not caused by the employee.
	Does the discharge center around some external obligation on the part of the employee, such as jury duty or military service? IF NO →	IF YES →	Seek advice of counsel, with bias toward allowing the employee to fulfill obligations regardless of state climate. Do what is right, not what is legally possible.

Is there a claim of retaliation for some behavior that displeased a supervisor, possibly raising questions about the performance of the supervisor's work unit?
IF NO →

IF YES → Take no action until a management review is completed.

Has the employee recently filed any claim that may be associated with the discharge?
IF NO →

IF YES → Take no action until a management review establishes that there is no link between the termination and the claim. Act with the advice of counsel.

Are any state laws applicable?
IF NO →

IF YES → Act with the advice of counsel.

Does the dismissal center around an issue of potential concern to the external community at large?
IF NO →

IF YES → Act on advice of counsel in a manner that does not jeopardize the company's position in the community.

Implied Covenant of Good Faith and Fair Dealing

Does the organization owe the discharged person any bonus, back pay, compensatory time, or similar reward that has been earned but will not be received as a result of this action?
IF NO →

IF YES → Make good on all such rewards in addition to the standard severance package. Be sure the discharge is not related to any such claims on the organization's resources.

Implement termination decision within the guidelines of corporate outplacement policies.

*These steps assume that precautionary measures regarding contractual obligations have already been taken by the organization, such as the establishment of a specific policy and the adoption of specific language in company literature, forms, and processes.

ternatives to termination (reassignment, disciplinary action)?
What would be procedurally correct? All decisions should be reviewed by counsel.

Linking Policy to Management Systems

Depending on the specific policy stance adopted, support
systems such as performance appraisal, performance standards,
and progressive disciplinary procedures must be provided to support the policy. Two issues are involved here: (1) the design and
implementation of such tools and (2) ongoing monitoring to insure that they are being properly utilized. For example, an annual audit of the effectiveness of the appraisal system is virtually
mandatory if meaningful application is to be achieved.[31]

Such monitoring maintains the link between the discharge
policy, the larger employee-relations strategy, and the actual
managerial processes of the organization. Full discussion of the
issues involved in maintaining this link is beyond the scope of the
present chapter. Suffice it to say that such linkage can be difficult
to maintain.

Employment-at-will will continue to be a volatile area of employment law for the foreseeable future. The challenge to management is to install policies to help insure that termination
decisions are not made impulsively. Over time, management can
create a value system in a company's culture that regards such
behavior as unprofessional, and does not tolerate it. This should
be true regardless of the policy posture adopted.

When management is confronted with evidence that specific
supervisors have acted to subvert public policy, laws, or regulations or have been dealing vindictively with employees, it must
move to assert the rights of the employee (and ultimately the
rights of society at large). To do otherwise risks incurring legal
liability and compromising the credibility of the company. All too
often management has failed to recognize these obligations. In
the process, it has helped to hasten the erosion of the employ-

ment-at-will doctrine by producing the kinds of bad cases that now mark the common law landscape. The claim "We thought we had the right to do it" is weak justification for abusive behavior in a society that, however imperfectly, seeks in the long run to be decent.

Action on this issue is of immediate concern if companies are not to be taken by surprise should the legal climate in their state change. Delay simply increases the potential for difficulty in this critical area of employee relations.

Endnotes

[1]C. W. Summers, "Protecting All Employees against Unjust Dismissal," *Harvard Business Review* (January–February 1980), 134.

[2]J. L. Liddle, "Malicious Terminations and Abusive Discharges: The Beginning of the End of Employment at Will," *Employee Termination Handbook* (Englewood Cliffs, N.J.: Executive Enterprise Publications, 1980), 1–19.

[3]L. E. Blades, "Employment at Will vs. Individual Freedom: On Limiting the Abusive Exercise of Employer Power," *Columbia Law Review* (December 1967), 1404–35.

[4]Ibid., 1405.

[5]Ibid., 1410.

[6]Ibid., 1428–1429.

[7]Ibid., 1429.

[8]R. H. Baxter, Jr., and J. D. Wohl, "Wrongful Termination Lawsuits: The Employers Finally Win a Few," *Employee Relations Law Journal* (Autumn 1984), 258–75.

[9]S. C. Kahn, B. A. Brown, and B. E. Zepke, *Personnel Directors Legal Guide* (Boston, Mass: Warren, Gorman and Lamont, 1984).

[10]Ibid., 54.

[11]*Tameny* vs. *Atlantic Richfield Company*, 610 P.2d 1330 (1980).

[12]*Nees* vs. *Hocks*, 536 p.2d 512 (1975).

[13]Baxter and Wohl, "Wrongful Termination Lawsuits," 261.

[14]Ibid., 262.

[15]*Pugh* vs. *See's Candies, Inc.*, 171 Cal. Rptr. 917 (1981).

[16]Ibid.

[17]Baxter and Wohl, "Wrongful Termination Lawsuits," 269.

[18]Ibid., 263.

[19]Ibid., 265–66.

[20]Hunt v. IBM Mid America Employees Credit Union, 384 NW 2d 853 (1986).

[21]*Pine River State Bank* vs. *Richard E. Mettille*, 333 NW 2d 622 (1983).

[22]R. H. Baxter, Jr., and J. D. Wohl, "A Special Update: Wrongful Termination Tort Claims," *Employee Relations Law Journal* (Summer 1985), 125.

[23]D. W. Ewing, "Your Right to Fire," *Harvard Business Review* (March–April 1983), 33.

[24]Ibid., 42.

[25]J. C. Pingpank and T. B. Mooney, "Wrongful Discharge: A New Danger For Employers," *Personnel Administrator* (March 1981), 31–35.

[26]M. L. Colosi, "Who's Pulling the Strings on Employment-at-Will?" *Personnel Journal* (May 1984), 60.

[27]D. S. Hames, "The Current Status of the Doctrine of Employment-At-Will," *Labor Law Journal* (January, 1988), 19–32.

[28]R. E. Miles and C. C. Snow, "Designing Strategic Human Resources Systems," *Organizational Dynamics* (Summer 1984), 36–52.

[29]D. W. Ewing, *Do It My Way or You're Fired!* (New York: John Wiley & Sons, 1983).

[30]R. E. Walton, "From Control to Commitment in the Workplace," *Harvard Business Review* (March–April 1985), 76–84.

[31]T. H. Williams, "Fire at Will," *Personnel Journal* (June 1985), 72–77.

[32]H. G. Baher, "The Unwritten Contract: Job Perceptions," *Personnel Journal* (July 1985), 36–41.

[33]M. R. Witt and S. R. Goldman, "Avoiding Liability in Employee Handbooks," *Employee Relations Law Journal* (Summer, 1988) 5–18.

[34]Ibid.

[35]R. J. Butler and L. Yorks, "A New Appraisal System as Organizational Change: GE's Task Force Approach," *Personnel* (January–February 1984), 31–42.

4

Effective Corporate Termination Practices

HAVING SURVEYED HOW ORGANIZATIONS TYPically deal with terminations, the problems caused when they are handled poorly, the reasons discharge is often appropriate, and the emerging legal complications, we are left with a practical question: How can a company manage terminations effectively? As with all organizational activities, consistency in the handling of firings requires a well-defined policy. In the absence of clearly articulated policy, termination practices will vary not only from division to division but from department to department and even within departments. As suggested in the previous chapter, the first step in establishing effective termination practices is for the senior corporate personnel officer to obtain top management agreement on several policy issues. Foremost among these issues is what constitutes grounds for termination.

Grounds For Termination

It is our belief that corporate termination policy should make it clear that the company will not tolerate dismissals supported by vague reasons; that managers have to document their cases for termination with concrete business reasons consistent with corporate human-resources strategy. Surprisingly, this is not often the case. Outplacement consultants find that in most cases the boss is unclear in describing why a person is being fired. Such reasons are given as: "He's not on my team," "I can't communicate with him anymore," "She didn't understand the new direction," "He always seemed to be confused." Consultants hardly ever hear that a person failed to accomplish specific goals or do specific tasks.

In actuality, however, the discharged employee's performance has usually been marked by problems. Over a period of time, he or she has hurt the organization, but it has tolerated the poor performance. At some point there has been a change: perhaps new management has taken over, or the employee has made some particularly bad decision. Many things can change to produce a sense of urgency and lead to swift action. The problem, however, has frequently been obscured by personality conflicts, and real performance indicators have not been addressed. Management has failed to articulate the lack of performance and instead gives its rationale for dismissal in vague, superficial terms.

Poor Performance

- Harry's department has repeatedly had low efficiency ratings. For some time now, Harry has been unable to improve the situation, despite the urgings of his boss.
- Mary submits marketing plans that consistently fail to demonstrate either increased sales or consumer awareness of the product.
- Fred has not yet evaluated the impact of the message con-

sumers will get in the advertising campaign to introduce a new product. The campaign is scheduled to begin in five weeks. Fred is late on other deadlines as well.

- John's people frequently violate personnel policies, creating a great deal of discontent in other departments. It appears that John either cannot or will not maintain discipline over his people.
- Diane has been rated poorly on several of her major projects. It is unlikely she will be promoted. Her firm operates on an "up-or-out" policy.

All five of these people represent the most justifiable of reasons for termination: repeated poor work performance. Unfortunately, in each of the cases, the company botched the termination badly. Documentation was shaky (although thorough investigation substantiated the performance problem); previously held performance counseling sessions were not well recorded; and there was reason for each to believe management would be tolerant of their current level of performance for at least the near future. Making matters worse, the companies planned to obscure the reasons for discharge, in two instances trying to soften the blow with comments like "Things just didn't work out."

It is remarkable how often companies muddle a termination even when strong evidence of poor performance exists. Company policy should be directed toward avoiding this mistake.

When considering a performance-based discharge, management should identify specific reasons why the individual should be terminated—for example, failure to reach certain agreed-upon objectives or repeated failure to meet specific job performance standards. The following performance-oriented guidelines may be part of corporate termination policy.

Three Consecutive Below-Average Performance Appraisals

In many instances companies have no poor appraisals on record at time of termination. This indicates that:

- Performance appraisals are not conducted properly.
- Managers tend to terminate on an emotional basis.

Most probably, the fired person has gotten by with average performance appraisals. To the boss, however, *average* means "below average"; better people are all rated "above average" or "outstanding." These ratings support the boss's compensation and promotion decisions without causing unnecessary confrontations with the poor performer. Confrontations, in this boss's experience, only lead to increased tension on the job.

One consequence of this philosophy is that documentation for the termination decision is nonexistent. This seriously hurts the firm if litigation is initiated, since courts base their decisions on the contents of the appraisal file. Beyond the matter of legal defense, however, when reviews fail to document performance problems they also fail to provide employees with an accurate picture of where they stand with the boss. Even when specific problems and conflicts have arisen on the job, the employee is able to conclude that, overall, things are going all right. A false sense of security is generated, setting up the individual for a real shock. Failure to provide comprehensive and thorough appraisals of poor performance shows a lack of managerial integrity. Managers who avoid giving such feedback are sidestepping their responsibility.

Often in a termination the boss is reacting to a specific incident, the straw that broke the camel's back: "I don't like him. That's it. I've had it with him. He is going today." The boss has not thought out the specifics, nor are they documented anywhere. A policy of three consecutive below-average performance appraisals reduces this reactive, impulsive element and insures proper documentation. Note that such a policy does not require a three-year time frame for performance-based dismissals. An "unsatisfactory" or "needs improvement" rating can trigger a performance review on a much shorter than annual basis.

Missed Performance Objectives

A discharged person should be given specific reasons for being fired in addition to the required documentation on the performance appraisals. This helps the person digest what went wrong. These reasons are best spelled out in terms of specific job objectives that were not met.

Obviously, this policy is easier to implement when managerial and professional staff responsibilities are expressed in results-oriented objectives on an annual basis. Even in the absence of a management-by-objectives program, however, corporate policy can specify that a terminated employee be given specific reasons for the termination and that these reasons be expressed in terms of objectives shared previously with the person involved. Such a policy places pressure on those thinking of terminating a subordinate to communicate specific, job-related performance objectives before making the final termination decision.

Outplacement consultants find that when specific objectives have been clearly articulated, there is less conflict during the termination process. It is when the reasons given are vague ("I don't think you are doing too well in your job") that the person being terminated will argue. When there are specific failures that management can delineate, the dismissed person might say, "I'm sorry, I don't see it that way; I disagree with you. I think there were a lot of extenuating circumstances." But there is usually not a heated argument.

It is when the reasons are not specific that people feel wronged and want their day in court. Psychologically, a person needs to have specific reasons, ideally more than one, for termination in order to be able to assess what happened.

A Rating of Nonpromotable in a Management Development Job

Many companies have sophisticated management development programs designed to evolve a strong group of general managers for the business. Often labeled "fast-track programs," they are filled with young managers who are hired explicitly for such development. In these companies it is generally understood that entry into middle- and senior-level managerial slots occurs solely through the management development program.

A number of these programs are characterized by an up-or-out policy, especially at the lower levels. A person who does not appear to have the potential to advance will be encouraged (or required) to leave the company in order to keep the lines of advancement open for the next generation of managerial talent. Indeed, in some companies, such as the large accounting firms, almost all professional jobs are on an up-or-out basis. From the start, the need for continual advancement is understood by the employee.

When companies have explicit career ladders along which a manager or a professional person is expected to advance, a rating of "nonpromotable" triggers the termination decision. Although the specifics will vary from situation to situation, policy should require that:

1. The length of time in grade before being assessed for promotion be specified. In most jobs, some time is required before a person can be considered fully trained and experienced at the current level of responsibility. It is only after this period that it makes sense to begin assessing potential for future advancement.
2. The records clearly demonstrate that those performance characteristics that might jeopardize advancement have been called to the person's attention with ample time to improve.
3. A rating of "nonpromotability" be accompanied by a description of specific reasons for this assessment. These reasons should relate to performance objectives or describe behaviors.

Such policy guidelines provide for maximum documentation of the problem areas that led to the negative assessment. They also help keep conflict to a minimum, increasing the number of instances when things go smoothly. Furthermore, they eliminate the possibility of managers' making emotional terminations by forcing managers into a reasoned process to support their decisions. Given the traumatic nature of the termination process for both the person being dismissed and the organization, anything less should be unacceptable.

Finally, such guidelines do not hamstring managers in dealing with subordinates. Flexibility can be built into the process. As noted above, if performance appraisals are given annually, this does not mean that three years are required for discharge. The point is that managers should be forced to deal with the problem rationally and in a manner that provides subordinates with ample opportunity to understand their position.

Other Reasons for Termination

People are dismissed for reasons other than poor performance, and corporate policy should also be oriented toward keeping these instances within specific limits. Following are some of the reasons for termination that are not performance-based but that should be addressed in policy statements.

Reorganization and Retrenchment

Often business conditions make it necessary to restructure an organization, and some employees are displaced. Termination policy should recognize that such circumstances can occur.

Recognizing that reorganization or retrenchment may result in terminations in no way alters a company's desire to provide job security whenever possible. Rather, it acknowledges the obvious. We know of one large insurance company whose top officers made repeated speeches about its commitment to lifelong job security. The history of this company was to disavow termination as a matter of corporate policy, with the exception of severe job negligence. When in 1977 severe financial difficulties required a staffing cut of 800 employees, the incongruity was enormous. Recent corporate speeches had promised job security on the one hand while drastic personnel cuts were taking place on the other. The company's recruiting and managerial credibility took years to recover.

As we pointed out in Chapter Three, companies are well advised to be cautious in their statements about job security. In 1985, an appeals court in Connecticut ruled that a case brought by a professional-level employee terminated by a Hartford-based insurance company should be heard because of the company's statements regarding job security, which the employee maintained had led him to pass up other job opportunities in the past.

Recognizing the possibility of termination is not the same as advocating it. Few, if any, corporations can guarantee total job security, especially in the economy of the late twentieth century. Management can, however, state clearly that maintaining employment is a key corporate objective while acknowledging that it retains the right to dismiss employees when, in management's judgment, business conditions require it.

Ethical Misconduct

Willful violation of laws is a reason for termination. So, too, is misrepresentation, either of the employee or some aspect of the employee's work. Such acts must be confronted, since failure to hold the employee accountable gives tacit approval of the behavior.

As with all terminations, dismissals on this basis should be well documented. Unless criminal behavior is involved, most firms give the employee the option of resigning. References must be worked out carefully. Unless guilt is legally established, the company may be liable for any accusation that prevents the person from obtaining future employment. Therefore, when responding to reference checks inquiring why such employees left the company, most companies simply verify past employment.

Failure to Conform to Conditions of Employment

All organizations have policies and procedures designed to control variation in personal work habits. Policies pertaining to attendance, lateness, break periods, and security are examples. Usually these vary by job classification.

Any employee who regularly fails to comply with such regulations is a candidate for discharge. The key guidelines here are that standards be applied consistently to all employees in a given job classification, that a specific and sequential disciplinary procedure be followed, that a rule be enforced immediately upon violation, and that the employee be warned that continued failure to comply will result in dismissal.

Counseling the Marginal Professional Employee

A division of General Electric recently made a major effort to revise its performance appraisal system.[1] Subsequent to this effort, the division implemented a performance enhancement program, with guidelines to be followed by the manager of any employee whose performance was noticeably deteriorating or whose most recent performance appraisal indicated a failure to meet acceptable performance standards. Essentially the guidelines establish a pattern of effective performance counseling, which is to be followed for a specific period of time (usually three months). Key components of the program are:

- Development of an overall performance improvement plan with a specific start and end date.
- Establishment of specific objectives and actions to be taken on specified dates.
- A schedule of interim reviews (usually a month apart).
- Discussions of all critical incidents.
- Review of the program between the manager and the employee-relations manager.

The purpose of the program is to make every effort to bring the employee's performance up to a satisfactory level. It is recognized that correcting a performance problem requires a dedicated effort, and managers are expected to take all possible steps to insure an employee's successful completion of the process, including counseling, training, and behavior change methods. If, at the conclusion of the counseling period, performance is not fully satisfactory, the manager meets with the employee-relations manager to determine jointly which of a number of options should be chosen. These include extending the program, transferring the employee to another job, demoting the employee to a lower-level job, or terminating the employee for cause. It is both the goal and the experience of the program to date that only a few cases have resulted in termination.

Programs such as this are designed to prevent terminations if possible. In the process, they create a link between the performance appraisal and the discharge process that can generate positive action toward an ineffective employee (an issue considered at length in Chapter Five). By the same token, such programs help to insure proper documentation and due process prior to the discharge decision, should such an outcome prove necessary.

Policy's Role as Referee

Earlier we stated that most managerial terminations are the result of personality clashes: a subordinate does not get along with the boss. We advocate that companies establish policy guidelines for managers that require performance- or organization-based reasons for termination. Will such guidelines control the reasons that underlie most terminations? And to what extent can a manager expect to demand a comfortable relationship with a subordinate? The two issues are related.

At the managerial level of an organization, personality often plays a decisive role in determining effectiveness. Indeed, stripped to its essentials, the manager's hiring decision boils down to two basic questions: (1) Does the applicant have enough experience and expertise to do the job? and (2) Can I work with the person? Once the hiring decision is made, the elusive difference between effectiveness and ineffectiveness often depends on the match between personal style and job environment (including the boss's style).

Policy guidelines do not change this reality of organizational life so much as referee it. Corporate policy should require that superiors relate issues of style to issues of substance. The problem is one of translating personality (for example, overaggressiveness) into specific behavior (failure to consider customer problems) that results in poor performance (loss of sales). Corporate policy can and should put pressure on managers to make the connection between style and performance. In the absence of this type of connection, questions must be raised about the legitimacy of a termination.

A boss has the right to expect the personal style of a subordinate to contribute to the legitimate goals of the work unit. When a subordinate's personality traits lead to disregard of the boss's directives, dismissal becomes a reasonable consideration. However, to expect total congruence of personality is not reasonable. By placing brakes on impulsive termination decisions, policy can force managers into constructive reasoning about the substance and depth of their complaints about subordinates.

Complementary to the requirement that the termination be job related is the requirement that it not be for discriminatory reasons: that is, based on sex, race, national origin, religion, or age. Affirmative action programs already reinforce this principle. Termination policy should restate the company position.

Managerial Review

Once a decision is made to let someone go, corporate policy should require that it be reviewed at the next level of management before the termination interview takes place. The need for keeping a superior informed of this type of decision might appear obvious, yet time and time again outplacement consultants find instances in which a manager became emotional and fired someone on the spot. A policy of managerial review provides an opportunity to determine whether the termination is appropriate.

For example, in one case we observed, Frank, a manager new to the company, was a bit overzealous in wanting to make good. He began changing policies and procedures almost immediately, often borrowing from what had worked elsewhere for him without appearing to give much thought to his new situation. His aggressiveness caused several employees to resist, and he decided to fire a couple of them. Because the two employees had a history of acceptable performance, the manager's superior, George, assessed the situation carefully. He counseled Frank to soften his approach for a while. Somewhat skeptically, Frank agreed. The superior kept in touch with the situation and arranged for Frank to discuss the situation with an organizational development consultant who had extensive experience with the company. With time, the people involved became acclimated to the new situation. Things began to function smoothly, and Frank learned something about how to initiate change.

In subsequent interviews, one of the employees Frank had wanted to dismiss made the following comments: "When Frank first came on board, he was like a bull in a china shop. I think he realized he had to back off a little. A lot of his ideas are good ones. I've learned a lot from him."

The other employee commented: "We had our differences early on. He was trying to do everything like the company he came from. Things have settled down now, though. I think he's more confident, more relaxed. He's done some good things. I think we get along fine now that we understand each other."

Frank himself remarked: "Early on I misread a few people. I tried to force everything. George [Frank's boss] helped me see that. I took a second look at some of my people; worked with them instead of against them. Some people I had doubts about turned out okay."

The point of this case is not to suggest that managers should not be allowed to terminate subordinates. In fact, under exceptional circumstances, a manager can be given the right to dismiss subordinates without review, although this should be a specific exception to policy. The point is to suggest that requiring managers to review possible cases of termination with their superiors before the termination occurs can help avoid hasty and unnecessary terminations.

Finally, the person in the personnel department who is responsible for termination policy should be involved before a termination occurs. This person can be trained to insure that the termination is consistent with corporate policy, that the proper support package is prepared, and that the manager is counseled on how to handle the actual termination.

The Support Package

Beyond specifying the grounds for termination, corporate policy should set guidelines for the nature of the support package given to the dismissed employee. The support package is important, since the person will have to rely heavily on it while searching for new employment. Generally, a good support package has the following ingredients:

- *Severance pay and benefits*. Our research demonstrates that considerable variation exists in current corporate practice involving severance pay. Although many companies give lump sum severance payments, we recommend an agreement to allocate monies on a monthly basis, just as if the previous salary and benefits were continuing. We will explore the rationale behind this principle below. Suffice it to say that the company wants to represent itself as paying the person to find a job. Severance payments are best not viewed as some sort of corporate financial booby prize but as limited assistance for the former employee during the transition period.

- *A letter explaining severance arrangements, which the employee can take at the time of termination.* This letter, cleared by corporate counsel, should spell out in unambiguous language the nature of the financial arrangements. Remember, people are typically not thinking clearly during the termination interview. Details of the arrangement are often not grasped. It is not at all uncommon for discharged employees to be unaware of the status of their financial benefits. Since calling the former boss is awkward, these people often just hope for the best, many times to their detriment. The termination letter is a document to which they can refer.

- *People specified who can be used as references.* The person being terminated should be told what these people are prepared to say regarding the reason for the termination and past performance. In this way, what is said to potential employers will be consistent. More importantly, it is clear just whom the individual can use comfortably as a reference, a detail that is often overlooked during terminations.

- *Specific secretarial arrangements.* Practices vary, from offering no support, to having a secretary continue to take messages for a specific period of time, to providing complete secretarial support. We recommend that a secretary be made available who will type resumes and letters as well as take phone messages. At a minimum, this arrangement should continue until the person's severance payments expire. The secretary can be a member of the company's staff or from an outside service. In either case, the extent to which the terminated employee can rely on this clerical help should be spelled out. Corporate policy in this area should be decided upon and the guidelines specified. Otherwise, considerable variation in practice is likely to evolve. Such variation could encourage a charge of discrimination.

- *Outplacement counseling.* Increasingly, companies are providing outplacement counseling by either a specialist in the personnel department or an outside counselor to help discharged employees in assessing their situation and organizing a job search. Such counseling can range from specific training in job search skills to psychological assessment, assistance in evaluating the events that led to termination, and career planning. In our experience, such counseling can be one of the most important elements of the support package, often preventing the employee from making mistakes that squander other parts of the severance package. Later chapters explore this type of counseling in more detail.

Instituting the Program

The starting point in developing an effective termination program is to gain corporate agreement on the issues we've outlined. The development of a set of policy guidelines should be preceded by a review of past terminations. This analysis should look at:

- Grounds for terminations, both those based on performance and those based on other factors.
- Documentation for each termination and whether it was adequate.
- Names and titles of those who reviewed the terminations.
- Support packages that were provided.

Such an analysis can bring to the surface issues that need to be dealt with on the policy level as well as specific termination practices. Periodic review can help assess compliance with corporate policies once they have been put into effect. Compliance reviews can also pinpoint areas of weakness in policy and identify steps that need to be taken.

Role of the Internal Specialist

If policy is to be converted into practice, a person or persons must be assigned specific responsibility for termination practices. In general, this person will be accountable for maintaining compliance with corporate policy. The job contains several more specific functions, however.

The internal specialist also serves as a point of contact with the corporation for the person who has been discharged. Inevitably, even when there is a letter spelling out severance compensation, benefits, and other issues, questions arise. Terminated employees are often confused about whom to contact at the company with these questions. Typically, they do not feel comfortable about going back to the boss. As often as not, they are uncomfortable with the personnel department in general. There is a need for someone to be specifically designated as the individual's contact.

When the company provides internal outplacement counseling as part of the support package, this becomes part of the internal specialist's role. If outside consultants are used for this purpose, the internal specialist is the best coordinator for their services.

Counseling managers on how to terminate employees is another aspect of the internal specialist's role. Earlier we recommended that corporate policy require the personnel department to be notified before the termination interview is conducted. This notice gives the internal specialist the opportunity both to review the documentation and support package material and to discuss how the manager plans to conduct the termination interview. The specialist can lend expertise on such matters as timing, location, and structuring of the discussion; in short, sharpening the skills of the manager who will do the firing.

Who should the internal specialist be? One large New York bank has a psychologist filling an outplacement counseling role. He also refers people for outside counseling when that best meets their needs. This work is his full-time responsibility. Another organization has a professional career counselor who does some outplacement counseling work but primarily works with people who are dissatisfied with their jobs. These types of human-resource positions are only starting to emerge. In the future, they may well dominate the one-on-one consultation aspects of personnel work.

Smaller companies and field locations find that having this type of resource specialist is not always feasible. In these instances, the function may have to be part of a more general personnel manager's job. Nevertheless, such an individual will have to have basic counseling skills in order to do the job effectively. In the future, such skills are likely to be a basic requirement for a personnel manager.

In our experience it is best not to combine the duties of outplacement counselor and recruiter. One obvious reason is that the two functions inherently conflict. A company may be recruiting at the same time it is discharging people. To have both groups of people in the same area, waiting to see the same person, creates problems.

One example of these problems came up during a consulting assignment. The $12 billion organization had one division undergoing a staff cutback; almost 400 people were being displaced. The division's recruiting manager was assigned to supervise the outplacement of these people. While one of us was in a meeting with the recruiting manager, a ruckus started in the waiting room—a person screaming at the receptionist. When everything calmed down, the recruiting manager explained that this had happened four or five times after a person who was being outplaced learned that temporary help was being hired to cover certain jobs.

Another real dilemma is whether recruitment managers have enough time to spend with employees who have been fired. Terminated employees need time to explain their problems and concerns. Furthermore, managers facing the probability of having to fire someone require considerable consultation time. Unless the company has a freeze on hiring and no recruiting is taking place, the recruiting manager seldom has enough time to spend on terminations.

We have also observed that people who are geared to recruiting are generally different from those who are geared to counseling. By and large, the recruiters with whom we have dealt are motivated to go out and find the best possible people and sell them on the company. They are not psychologically oriented toward listening to the problems associated with the termination process. We are aware of several recruiting managers who had outplacement counseling responsibilities assigned to them for long periods of time and were so unhappy about it they resigned. More than a few told us they were leaving because "dealing with the problems of termination is not my thing."

We mention these problems because there seems to be a tendency to combine the recruitment and termination functions. This may be because both functions deal with issues related to the labor market. Often the reasoning is that a recruiter should know where the jobs are. Also, during a period of staff reductions, recruiting slacks off, so this is a way to balance the recruiter's work load. But, as we have seen, the two aspects of personnel work are not as closely related as some people think. Of course, in a plant setting, a personnel generalist often has to assume this role along with other duties.

Characteristics of the Outplacement Counselor

What are the characteristics of an effective outplacement counselor? As with many professional positions, there is no one ideal "type" for this emerging job. However, it is possible to describe some desirable characteristics of people filling this role.

They should be mature and secure. They don't have to be

outgoing; it is more important that they be confident about their skills and abilities.

They should be mature in the sense that they have insight into the reasons people fail on the job and an understanding of how people who encounter difficulty in one situation can often succeed in another. This characteristic is important if the counselor is to keep a balanced perspective. In addition, the counselor's experience must command respect from both management and the people being displaced. Otherwise the counselor will be unable to establish the type of relationship with both parties that is necessary to be effective. Young, inexperienced people in the position of outplacement counselor tend to encounter continual resistance as they attempt to fulfill their role. Often they end up leaving the company. The area of termination is not an easy entry assignment.

Outplacement counselors should be well trained in career counseling. In addition to having fundamental counseling skills, they must understand the career assessment process and have the skills necessary to help the terminated person sort out his or her current situation. These skills can be learned from universities as well as career guidance consulting organizations.

We are not necessarily talking about a person with a Ph.D. in counseling, but rather someone who has received appropriate training. For example, many displaced employees seek dependency, and are more than willing to let the specialist assume responsibility for them. A pitfall confronting the counselor is the tendency to say such things as, "I will help you find a job," or "Don't worry, we will assist you in finding a job quickly." These are commitments that neither the company nor the counselor can meet. In fact, it is the discharged person's responsibility to find a job; the counselor is there to provide skills that can facilitate the job-search process.

An outplacement counselor should have a good knowledge of the job market, the job search process, and the employment process, especially at the executive level. One of the things a fired person is looking for is practical advice—what mistakes to avoid and what steps to take. Here again the mature person has an advantage. He or she can blend outplacement training with experience to provide credible support to the dismissed person.

Note that most people think they know how to find another job and believe they can counsel others on how to do so. Most of these people would advise getting a resume together and mailing it to search organizations, placement agencies, and corporations.They would be mistaken. There are certain techniques and approaches to finding another position that are mandatory, and if one is going to manage outplacement counseling one should be well trained in these approaches.

Outplacement counselors should enjoy working with people under duress and should have an authentic feeling for people. Many people say they enjoy working with people, but in reality, most people find it difficult. The outplacement counselor must feel secure with other people. This is not a job for a lay psychologist, and outplacement counselors must be clearly aware that their role lies elsewhere. Rather, they should be people who listen well, can give direction and advice, and are sensitive to the trauma that the terminated employee is going through.

People who get into this work often feel sorry for the person who has been fired. This is a natural human response to someone who is in trouble. Feeling sorry, however, does nothing to help the discharged person and frequently results in the counselor becoming depressed too. Empathy, rather than pity, is required. It takes a strong person, with the goal of helping the terminated employee find a new position rather than a new life, to be successful at outplacement counseling. Counselors must avoid getting too close to the person who has been terminated, if they are to help. They must also understand the limitations of their ability to help. The counselor cannot make the person successful.

Although many companies look for a psychologist to fill this role, such professional training is not mandatory. Within the framework of the general characteristics mentioned, people from a wide range of backgrounds have proven to be effective outplacement counselors. Those with corporate experience rounded out with a personnel management background, counseling training, and career assessment skills are capable of performing very effectively.

Management Training in Support of Policy

Corporate policies are limited in their impact if managers are not trained to implement them. In the area of termination, this training is of two kinds. The first is of an informational nature. Managers must be knowledgeable about corporate policy and understand the mechanics of applying it. For example, if it is company policy to require three poor performance appraisals before termination, all managers must be aware that an incomplete performance appraisal can prevent or delay an attempt to terminate someone. Also, managers must have a working knowledge of what constitutes a legitimate reason for termination.

The second type of training is in skill development. Managers must be capable of conducting a reasonably effective termination interview. Knowing how to organize the discussion and retain control of the meeting are issues of managerial skill. Being able to open the interview properly, handle defensiveness, and close the discussion are also matters of skill. In Chapter Six we discuss these skills in some detail.

Many of these skills are basic to the managerial process, including selection interviewing, job coaching, and performance appraisal. Others are specific to the termination process. Time should be allocated in management development programs for training in these skills. The skills can be reinforced by the internal specialist when termination makes them necessary.

After the Employee Is Gone

So far our discussion has focused on issues that lead up to or support the termination. Once the employee leaves, however, the company still has an involvement. Two concerns in particular are the provision of references and the effect of termination on the discharged person's co-workers.

References

With the Freedom of Information Act, reference-giving has become more sensitive, since applicants may ask to see submitted references. A reference that unfairly damages the terminated employee's job search can land the company in court.

Therefore, it is important that company references be submitted only by people who have been previously identified to the dismissed person. All inquiries about the terminated person should be referred to these people or to the specialist in the personnel department. In fact, as a matter of policy, all reference inquiries about employees who have left the firm should be referred to the personnel department unless the manager receiving the inquiry has previously agreed to provide a reference.

The content of the references should be discussed and specified at the time of termination, and references should not deviate from the content agreed upon. By law all that is required is that former employers confirm the fact that the person in question did work at the company during the specified period of time. Any other information is not required and may harm the organization that released the employee. However, it is good practice to agree on the answers to two questions at the time of discharge: What kind of employee (or manager) was the person? What happened to cause the person to leave? Refusing to address these issues in references can place the person in a prejudicial light and hamper his or her job search.

What Kind of Employee Was the Person? When answering this question, we suggest keeping statements positive. This does not mean the reference should be unnecessarily rosy or misleading in any way. Rather, strengths, not weaknesses, should be highlighted. The kind of environment in which the person is likely to perform well should be described, rather than situations in which the person is not likely to do well.

For example, if a person has had difficulty in getting organized, you do not have to say that he or she has poor organizational skills. Rather, the reference should describe either a strength or a situation that won't expose the person's weakness. Perhaps it could say that this person works best in spontaneous and unstructured environments.

Why Was He or She Let Go? This question is more difficult to answer. In sensitive instances, we recommend a statement to the effect that "we agreed to disagree." Phrases such as "We let her go" or "We terminated the relationship" generate a range of negative images in the minds of prospective employers. A company should instead use such phrases as "Both employer and employee agreed that a change was advisable." It is best to avoid the issue altogether unless it is explicitly raised or unless the reason does not reflect on the person's behavior (for example, a staff reduction). In an especially difficult circumstance, indicate that only the employment will be verified.

Exhibit 4.1 is a sample letter of recommendation. Notice that it verifies length of employment and scope of responsibility. It also highlights the person's special strengths: the ability to improve technical knowledge and organization and control on an operation.

Although it mentions that Harvey left the company, the reference avoids placing fault or blame. It states only that Harvey and his boss disagreed. That disagreement is left for the new employer to discuss with Harvey. The letter concludes by indicating that the writer remains appreciative of Harvey's abilities and past contributions, which is true.

Harvey had been dismissed because he never really accepted a reorganization of the company and was continually battling over old issues. His failure to cooperate completely with associates was undermining his effectiveness as a manager.

Exhibit 4.1 Sample Letter of Reference

Mr. Jerome Brown
XL Corporation
New York, New York

Dear Mr. Brown:

I am writing at the request of Harvey Wilson in support of
his candidacy for the position of director of manufacturing
with your firm. I am pleased to learn of the possibility that
Harvey might be associated with your organization.

Harvey was with us for nine years, during which time he
was promoted twice. He worked under me for five years as
general manager of production. Harvey's particular
strengths include an ability to organize and control a
rapidly growing operation. He personally developed and
implemented many of the operations procedures that
allowed us to retain control of our diverse production
operations. His knowledge of process technology is second to
none and he earned the respect of his subordinates. At the
time he left us, Harvey was responsible for nine plant
locations, all of which employed between 500 and 1,000
people.

As you know, Harvey left us three months ago. There were
several changes occurring in our business and we agreed to
disagree. It was a difficult time for all of us, but he left with
my respect for his abilities and accomplishments.

From what he has told me, I am confident he can make a
contribution to your company.

                              Best wishes,

                              John Simpson
                              Vice President

If the reasons for the dismissal are such that the company cannot be comfortable following these guidelines, the agreement with the employee should be that the company will only provide verification of employment.

We cannot recommend too strongly that the whole subject of references be thoroughly discussed with the employee before he or she leaves the premises. Our counselors find that for over 40 percent of the people who have extended difficulty in finding new employment the problem can be traced to poor references.

Co-workers

When a person or group of people is severed from an organization, one of the most overlooked items on management's agenda is what to say to the employees left behind. It's as if management breathes a sigh of relief on the day of termination and tries to overlook the hard feelings and mistrust of the employees who stay on.

When someone is dismissed for cause, the manager doing the termination should inform other employees in the work unit; for example, "John will be leaving the company effective June 2, and we wish him the best in future endeavours." This can be done orally or by memo. The manager should neither encourage nor discourage inquiries about the termination. If some people are upset, the manager can privately ask whether John's leaving has bothered them. Otherwise, the initiative can be left to the employees.

If involved in a private discussion about the dismissal with associates of the discharged person, the boss should be willing to talk, but stress that he or she cannot, with integrity, share information of a personal nature. Obvious job failures can be pointed out. Management should also stress that the problems had been frequently discussed between the manager and the dismissed employee and that the employee was aware that if certain changes did not take place termination would occur. Depending on the agreement that has been reached with the dismissed employee, management's response to inquiries from other employees should reflect the position that "we both agreed John was ready for a change."

Management's comments should be honest; there is no need to lie about the situation. On the other hand, the details of the termination should remain the personal business of the employee. Most people recognize a person's right to privacy and will respect management for guarding it. If it is clear that the severance was on friendly terms, the manager should respond to any inquiries by commenting that, although significant disagreement existed, "We made what we feel is the right decision for both parties."

The concern most employees have is whether those discharged were treated fairly, and especially, whether they knew that their performance was unacceptable. This reflects their own concern about job security. Essentially, management's position should be:

- Any decision about the person's future was not made abruptly but was the culmination of many discussions with the individual.
- Not all the facts are known to others, and management does not feel it appropriate to go into detail.
- The manager is willing to discuss with any employee his or her own job situation.

Occasionally, dismissed employees will complain to their peers about how badly they were treated. If confronted with such complaints, management should simply point out that a significant difference of opinion existed, that factors other than those the person is citing were important considerations, and that employees have been hearing only one side of the story, the other side of which management does not consider it appropriate to tell.

Managers should emphasize that what is important is not

what happened to the dismissed employee, but the job performance of other employees. In discussions with other employees, the manager should ask if they are comfortable in their own positions, if they are unsure about where they stand, or if they have been unfairly treated. If the answer is no, the manager should indicate that this is because their performance is satisfactory and they have good communication with their boss. If employees hesitate or give a yes answer, the manager should attempt to identify what can be done to improve the situation.

The manager's goal is clear: to impress upon subordinates that the manager has, and wants to maintain, an effective working relationship with them. That is the appropriate concern. Comparison with the discharged person is not relevant or appropriate other than to stress that the termination was not a surprise to the person involved.

If more than one person has been terminated, the first step is to tell the remaining employees when the work-force reductions are over. Management should explain the reasons for the cutback thoroughly. If there is a strong possibility of future cutbacks, that, too, should be noted. The key to maintaining credibility is honesty.

We know of one organization that for more than ten years found it difficult to obtain or maintain new talent because of the way it dealt with a series of work-force reductions between 1967 and 1969. The company had to pay extra to recruit good people because of its reputation. Recruiters were often told by potential employees that they were not interested because "the word is you can't be sure of where you stand."

Interestingly enough, even when employees know there is a possibility of future cutbacks, most stay on. Lack of management credibility can hurt an organization more than a frank presentation of even bleak prospects.

Once the terminations are concluded, managers should initiate discussions with remaining employees. The concerns most people will have are job security and future prospects at the company. These issues should be addressed directly and not left to the rumor mill.

Criteria for Successful Termination

The methods described above are the key to terminating in a manner that minimizes the cost to both the company and the person involved. The following checklist summarizes points made in this chapter. As such, it constitutes a working set of criteria for successful terminations.

- Sufficient grounds for dismissal consistent with corporate policy:
  —Not trumped up
  —Well documented
- Well written and effectively communicated appraisals preceding the termination (if performance based):
  —Three or more
  —Acknowledged by the employee
  —Specific performance indicators cited
- Termination review:
  —By next level of management
  —By the personnel department
- Terminating manager trained in termination procedures:
  —Understands company policy
  —Understands how to structure the termination interview
  —Has skills required to conduct the interview
- Sufficient support package:
  —Severance payments in line with company policy
  —Reliable references identified and agreed upon
  —Secretarial support
  —Benefits written out in severance letter
  —Predetermined contact for communication with the company

   —Counseling available on how to find employment
- Follow-up:
  —Consistent references
  —Employees notified that the person is leaving

Endnote

---

[1]R. J. Butler and L. Yorks, "A New Appraisal System as Organizational Change: GE's Task Force Approach," *Personnel* (January–February 1984), 31–42.

5

Coaching the Ineffective Employee

ALTHOUGH TERMINATION IS OFTEN NECESsary, under most circumstances a manager's first responsibility is to improve the subordinate's performance. Efforts at coaching performance should occur even when there is some skepticism as to the person's ability to improve. Consider, for example, the case of John Strauss.

John Strauss was director of a division that provided professional services to other companies. Although the market for the type of services John's division provided was growing, the size of his group had remained the same for several years. Also, his division had not expanded the range of services it offered clients, and several high-potential young staff members had left the organization.

As part of its corporate growth strategy, the parent corporation purchased an independent firm that was a competitor of John's group. As part of the merger agreement, the president of the purchased firm was to become the senior manager over John's division, and both staffs were to be integrated into one unit. John was to remain in place, although in a subordinate position to the person coming in from the outside.

Fred Eliot, the person who was brought in over John, was charged by top management with establishing a growth pattern in the division comparable to that experienced by his firm when it had been an independent operation. Both Fred and corporate management viewed John Strauss as a weak and ineffective manager.

At the time he took over the division, Fred believed it was unrealistic to expect significant improvement in John's performance. John was set in his ways and comfortable in his slot and, despite obvious anxiety over having been placed in a subordinate position to Fred, did not appear about to change his behavior to any great degree.

In deference to John's seniority with the firm, Fred decided to identify projects that were both meaningful for the growth of the division and would permit John to demonstrate that he was capable of contributing to the company. These special assignments would have the added benefit of not reducing John's work to the same level as that of his immediate subordinates. On the other hand, Fred resolved that if John did not perform well on these assignments, other arrangements, including the possibility of dismissal, would have to be made.

Fred gave considerable thought to which projects would be especially suited to John's talents. He wanted to assign work that would be challenging and important but not impossible. Once he had decided on the specific tasks he wanted John to undertake, he arranged a meeting and the two sat down to review John's assignments for the coming year.

Fred was very specific about what he expected. For each job assignment, he stated exactly what was to be accomplished and the date by which he expected John to have completed the work. John complained that some of the projects were not the type of thing he had done in the past and that they were not part of his job. Fred made it clear, however, that John's assignments were important to the division and reflected his professional experience. He also made it clear that these were the kinds of responsibilities he needed John to assume. Prior to sitting down with

John, Fred had already reviewed the assignments with his boss, and he was confident of support from higher management.

Thus, when John complained about certain aspects of his work, Fred listened to him, asked him precisely what his concerns were, attempted to identify realistically what kinds of support John would need to get the work done, but made it absolutely clear that he expected John to meet the specified level of performance. Fred also indicated that he planned to sit down with John in five weeks to review the progress that had been made on his assignments.

Five weeks later Fred sat down with John for a progress review. As it turned out, John had not made much headway on any of his assignments. Several of them had not been started at all, while an inadequate effort had been made on others. Fred informed John that his progress was unacceptable and began exploring why more had not been done. At the end of the discussion, Fred again told John that it was important that he meet his job objectives and indicated that in about four weeks they would again meet to discuss progress.

Four weeks later, it became clear that John had still not made much progress. Fred once again listened to John's reasons and again specified interim objectives he wanted to see achieved in each of the areas on which John was working. These interim objectives were to be met in three weeks.

When John failed to meet most of his interim objectives, Fred said that he was unhappy with John's performance to date and that significant improvement would have to be forthcoming in the future. He also reviewed the notes from each of their meetings, commenting that John was compiling a very unimpressive performance record, and told John that continuation of such poor performance would result in termination.

Fred called John's attention to the many changes that were being made in the division, the new services that were being added, and the opportunities for existing staff to take on increased responsibility for the growth and advancement of the division. Fred indicated his hope that John would be able to make an important contribution to these changes and pointed out the relevance of John's projects to what was happening. He expressed hope that John would recognize his opportunity to become an important part of the division's future. At the conclusion of the meeting, interim objectives were set for the next three weeks.

At the end of three weeks, John had still fallen short of his objectives. This time Fred told John that his lack of progress was creating problems. Consequently, Fred was going to assign some of the projects to other staff members. Once more Fred reiterated his hope that John would improve his performance, and again he set specific interim objectives for the activities that remained.

At this point, it had become clear that John was not making any effort to improve his performance. When he once again failed to meet his interim objectives, Fred indicated that he was going to talk the matter over with senior management and then make a decision as to what should be done. He told John that his failure to make progress on his objectives was moving him closer to being discharged.

In discussions with management, the decision was made to give John a last chance by assigning him to a special project that needed to be done, one that required significant professional experience.

Fred sat down with John and explained that, although he had made no progress on previous job objectives, he was being given a special assignment of importance to the organization. Fred told John that management viewed this as his last chance to prove he could perform in the new climate of growth that was being established within the organization. Failure to perform would mean dismissal. Again, Fred set interim target dates so that John would have a timetable with which to gauge his progress in completing the project. The project was one that should have taken close to four months to complete. Fred indicated that he would be sitting down with John within two weeks to monitor how much headway had been made.

Again John failed to make any significant progress on his new objective. In fact, after two and a half months, Fred informed senior management that, if the project were to be completed, he would have to assign somebody else to work on it. Management decided to allow John the full four months to complete the project, but at that time John had not come close to completing the project and it was assigned to someone else.

Fred then initiated termination proceedings and John was discharged from the organization.

John's performance was in marked contrast to that of Susan Newburg. Susan was a member of John's staff and, like many of the people who worked under John, she had not given evidence of superior motivation or ability. In fact, when Fred came in, he was uncertain what real potential existed within the division. He suspected that many of the high-potential people had already left. He resolved, however, to go through a similar process with all members of the staff.

As he had with John, Fred sat down with Susan and outlined specific performance targets and assignments he wanted completed. Once again, each of these assigments was described in terms of the specific end result expected and a timetable was set for completion. In many respects, the activities Fred assigned Susan represented a departure from the types of assignments she had been given in the past.

When Fred sat down for a progress review with Susan, however, it was evident that a lot of progress had been made. In fact, Susan had invested a significant amount of energy in her assignments and was ahead of the specified timetable. The longer Fred worked with Susan, the more it became evident that the activities assigned to her were not ambitious enough. Her positive attitude caused her to be given increased responsibilities. Within a year and a half, she was promoted to a new job that had opened up within the division. Susan's outstanding performance was representative of the kind of improvement noted in many members of the staff.

Although Fred's work with John did not have a happy ending, the process he went through with John represented a professional approach to the problem. The key element of Fred's approach was a continuing effort to establish a clear understanding with John.

Clarity is an important element of the job-coaching process. It is vitally important that the person being coached have a clear understanding of the boss's expectations. These expectations must also be fair and consistent with what is expected of others within the organization. Fred was careful to establish specific objectives with John, to state exactly what end results were to be achieved and when they should be achieved. These objectives then became the means of discussing and assessing John's current performance.

This process helped to insure that John was getting the message about how Fred viewed his performance. As the process continued, Fred was careful to make sure that John understood the potential results of not performing. Early on, when no progress was evident, he began emphasizing to John that his performance was being documented and that, if progress was not forthcoming, this documentation would provide the basis for discussions with management about his future.

Fred made it clear to John that his continuing with the company was contingent upon his performance. By the same token, Fred took pains to emphasize the opportunities opening up within the division and make it clear that, if John did perform, he could redeem his reputation and become a candidate for advancement. In other words, it was made clear to John at every point in the process that there was a risk attached to not performing, as well as an opportunity to be realized if he improved his performance.

It was hoped that John would take advantage of the opportunity and make an effort to improve his performance. Unhappily, this was not the case. However, because Fred took such a thorough approach to the coaching process, when the distasteful decision to let John go was being considered, it was clear that it was the correct decision for the organization to make. John had been given every opportunity to perform and had not chosen to respond. Not only that, there was written documentation that John was aware of the stakes involved. Therefore, although Fred found it unpleasant to inform John that he was being let go, his ample evidence of nonperformance allowed him to handle the interview comfortably and in a professional fashion.

The same process revealed untapped potential in the case of Susan Newburg. Here the ending was much happier and resulted in her turning into a strong performer.

The Coaching Process

The coaching process has two critical components: setting specific objectives and holding frequent progress reviews.

In their seminal research on coaching at General Electric, Meyer, Kay, and French observed: "One of the most significant findings in our experiment was the fact that far superior results were observed when the manager and the man together set specific goals to be achieved, rather than merely discussed needed improvement."[1] In explaining this finding, they noted that "specific plans and goals seemed to insure that attention would be given to that aspect of job performance."[2] Their research also provided strong evidence that day-to-day coaching, rather than comprehensive annual appraisals, is most effective for improving performance.

Subsequent research over twenty years has generally supported these conclusions. Goal-setting and frequent feedback are not panaceas, but performance rarely improves in their absence.

Setting Specific Objectives

Today, many organizations have some form of management-by-objectives (MBO) process as part of their business planning or performance appraisal efforts. In the absence of a formal MBO system, managers can still sit down and specify the exact criteria against which they expect a subordinate to perform.

When specific objectives are set, the subordinate knows exactly what is expected. Furthermore, the manager has a benchmark for reference in future discussions about the subordinate's performance.

As we have repeatedly stressed, the existence of specific goals is an important precondition for effective termination. The confusion or uncertainty that often characterizes the reaction of subordinates when they are told they are terminated is created by the absence of specific objectives against which they were expected to perform. A rich literature on setting objectives exists, and we will review the points especially important to the job coaching process.

Objectives should be characterized by three elements:

- They should specify end results.
- They should specify the exact extent of achievement the manager expects.
- They should be tied to a timetable.

By *end results*, we mean *what should be observably different* as a result of the subordinate's performance on the job. All too often, employees expect to be evaluated on the basis of how much effort they are putting into the job rather than what they are accomplishing. This is especially true of people who are weak performers. It is critical that the manager make it clear that certain outcomes are expected and that the subordinate will be held accountable for these outcomes.

Failure to write objectives that are directed toward end results will involve the manager in arguments with the subordinate about how the job is going and will not make things much easier if eventually the subordinate has to be dismissed. For example, "improve the security in the plant" is a poorly expressed objective. Whether or not security has improved is often debatable. "Eliminate theft of equipment and parts valued at more than $5.00 during F.Y. 1987" is considerably more specific.

Part of specifying the end result is quantifying it to the extent possible. For example, it is one thing to say that a subordinate is being held accountable for an increase in business volume in his or her particular region. It is another thing to specify that the individual should achieve at least a 6 percent increase in business volume. Quantitative terms include percentage of increase, real-dollar volume increase, and percentage of critical incidents.

In the absence of quantitative measures, objectives should be written in such a way that it is clear whether the person has achieved the objective or has not. For example, in a staff function where the individual is being held accountable for preparing certain reports or studies for use in the corporation, the objectives should specify not only that the projects or reports be completed, but that they be accepted and used by critical managers within the organization. Thus, it is not just the completion of the report but acceptance by relevant line managers that constitutes successful accomplishment of the job.

Managers should specify the time frame within which they expect the objective to be achieved. This may be any amount of time: a month, six months, a year. When the manager begins to consider termination, the objectives should permit ample opportunity to demonstrate improvement—usually four to six months. The important point is that the employee know what the completion date is so that the work effort does not drag on, mired in repeated arguments about how much progress is being made. When a final target date is established, it becomes possible for the manager and subordinate to identify benchmarks indicating how much progress has been made and to assess whether or not the subordinate is making enough progress to be able to complete the job by the required date.

In summary, when dealing with a subordinate whose performance has not been effective in the past, setting exact objectives is an important part of the coaching process. These objectives should be expressed in terms of end result, quantified when possible, and include the time in which the job is to be completed.

The literature on MBO emphasizes the importance of manager and subordinate agreeing on the objectives to be reached. Clearly, the extent to which there is mutual agreement about objectives influences the motivation of the subordinate. In practice, however, it is often difficult for a manager and subordinate to agree on which objectives are reasonable in terms of the resources the subordinate has available. Disagreements of this sort are even more likely when managers deal with subordinates whose past performance has been weak; these people are going to be threatened by the objective-setting process and are probably already seeking excuses for their poor performance.

Therefore, the manager should make every effort to set mutually acceptable goals. However, if the manager has listened and given serious thought to the subordinate's arguments, and there is still disagreement, the manager should unhesitatingly insist upon setting the objectives. We should recall the Meyer, Kay, and French conclusion that "while subordinate participation in the goal-setting process had some effect on improved performance, a much more powerful influence was whether goals were set at all."[3]

In communicating goals or objectives, managers should call the subordinate in and state that they wish to set specific performance objectives for a given period of time. The manager must make it clear that it is critical for the subordinate to achieve these objectives.

If the manager is seriously displeased with the subordinate's past performance, this displeasure should have been recorded in recent performance appraisals. At the start of the objective-setting process, the manager should clearly indicate that, as they have previously discussed, the subordinate's performance has not been up to standard. The manager should state that, in order to get the subordinate back into a position of making significant contributions to the work unit, the manager wants to make absolutely certain that the subordinate understands exactly what is expected, and for this reason is going to set specific objectives for the subordinate. The manager should state that the subordinate must meet these objectives in order to continue within the organization.

As each objective is shared with the subordinate, the manager should ask whether or not the subordinate feels the objective is reasonable, what problems the subordinate expects to encounter in reaching the objective, and what advantages and resources the subordinate can bring to bear in meeting the objective. During this part of the discussion, the manager should listen carefully to what the subordinate says. Based on what the subordinate says, the manager should either make the adjustments warranted or insist on the objective as it was specified.

How many objectives should the subordinate be given? In our experience, a few is better than too many. These objectives should be for aspects of the job the manager regards as critical to the performance of the work unit. If the subordinate is overloaded with objectives, it becomes unreasonable to expect them all to be accomplished.

What do we mean by a few? Obviously, this is a discretionary matter. In some instances, one or two is a reasonable number of objectives if they represent a significant effort on the part of the subordinate. In other cases, more may be warranted. Remember, once these objectives are set, they are going to be the primary measuring stick for determining whether or not the subordinate's performance is improving and whether termination is necessary.

From a developmental counseling perspective, people have a limited tolerance for negative feedback. This is especially true of individuals who are not performing well. In all probability they have their defenses up and are already failing to accurately perceive how poorly things are going on the job. They may be willing to accept the need to improve in one or two areas. In a few instances maybe a third. But four or five? Probably not. At some point they start rejecting the negative feedback, unable to tolerate what amounts to total rejection by the supervisor. Further, once this total rejection is perceived, the person is likely to reject all the negative feedback, including the first points made.

Apart from the strain on the ego, personal change usually requires a substantial amount of effort, especially when work habits are involved. Attempting to make multiple changes diffuses effort instead of concentrating it and, in the process, probably helps guarantee that no progress will be made. For these reasons, developmental counseling is most effective when it focuses initially on a few critical areas and moves on to other objectives if and when progress has been made.

Holding Frequent Progress Reviews

Frequent progress reviews accomplish three things. First, they serve as a continual reminder that reaching the objectives is important to the person's career with the organization. Without frequent reinforcement, people often manage to ignore the fact that failure to meet their objectives could result in being fired.

Second, progress reviews provide an opportunity for the manager to recognize positive movement toward objectives. If the subordinate is striving to meet the objectives, the manager can be supportive, which can encourage further progress.

Third, if progress is not forthcoming, the manager can listen to the reasons for lack of performance and attempt to get the subordinate on track. In this sense, the review becomes a problem-solving session.

Whether or not the subordinate has made progress, holding frequent reviews permits the manager to remain in control of the progress. At every review, the manager should discuss each of the objectives, with the reason for progress or lack of it, and make suggestions for improvement.

The manager should take notes during these meetings so that there is a record of what was discussed. This may be a record of the subordinate's progress and development. If not, these notes become a record of the manager's efforts to elicit improvement.

As long as the subordinate makes progress, the manager should be supportive, focusing the conversation on the progress that has been made. If progress does not occur, however, the manager should be sure to do three things:

1. State the effect of future failure. Stress that failure to improve will result in termination.
2. State the effect of making progress. Stress that demonstrating competence and meeting performance objectives with concrete results will result in the manager's satisfaction.
3. Set interim objectives to be met by the next progress review. These interim objectives further clarify the progress expected and set up the next review discussion.

Progress reviews should continue until the subordinate meets the objectives or until it becomes clear that the objectives cannot be met in the remaining time.

The process outlined above is a thorough attempt at coaching the subordinate's performance. Unfortunately, in our experience, it seldom characterizes the year before a termination. All too often, it is business as usual between boss and subordinate until the boss decides not to take any more. Or objectives are set, but the boss doesn't follow through with the progress reviews. By taking the steps described above, a manager can be sure of being consistent with the policy guidelines suggested in Chapter Four.

Two Case Studies

Recently, one of the authors was approached by a senior executive of a large organization (we'll call him Andy). He was having problems with his division, especially with two of his managers.

The first was his director of construction projects, Sam, who had responsibility for a large and complex department. Among other things, Sam's responsibilities included contracting for all architectural work, for which he had professional qualifications. These activities were actually to be supervised by his manager of architecture, who was to report to Sam. Another of Sam's subordinates was the manager of facilities layout.

Sam was out of the office much of the time inspecting projects, meeting with architects, and generally keeping heavily involved in the architectural side of his department. In the opinion of his boss, Sam's frequent absence from the office prevented him from giving direction to his department.

Meetings with senior executives of the operating divisions were often attended by Sam's facilities manager instead of Sam, leading many executives to ask cynical questions like "What does Sam do, anyway?" Problems and crises would be communicated directly to Andy, leading to meetings between Andy and Sam's subordinates, with Sam conveying an apparent lack of involvement.

This behavior left a power vacuum, which Sam's facilities layout manager was more than willing to fill, since Sam's absence gave him visibility and access to senior executives throughout the company. This manager did little to dispel the notion that he made decisions with almost complete autonomy.

The second situation involved Andy's purchasing manager, Dick. He was young and inexperienced when promoted into his current job, although Andy believed in his potential. The past year had been a disaster, with fixtures often failing to arrive at construction sites when workers were scheduled to install them.

Further, Dick often seemed unable to report the status of placed (or supposedly placed) orders. As the problems mounted, Dick became increasingly withdrawn and at odds with his staff. Generally well liked before his promotion, he had gained a reputation for being unreliable, often not keeping his staff informed of problems. Soon they tired of defending him, as subsequent events indicated he had been wrong on a number of issues.

As vendor deliveries became an increasing problem, Andy assigned a specialist to help Dick, over his objections. This person was able to stabilize the situation, although Dick cooperated in only the most perfunctory manner. His open resentment soured the specialist on him, and upon returning to her normal assignment she was openly critical of Dick and predicted that the old problems would soon reappear.

Andy's comment to the author was, "I'd like to do some team-building to help these guys get their departments under control. If I have to fire them, I will, but they have many positive qualities. I'd like to try to turn them around." As he spoke, his frustration was evident.

The author suggested that he talk with the managers in question, both of whom he knew from management training programs conducted in the organization. Interviews would also be conducted with other personnel within the division. The purpose of the interviews was ostensibly to discover the perceptions various members of the division had regarding its functioning.

It became readily evident that Sam was immersing himself in the architectural work of his department. He was good at it and enjoyed interacting with the architects. His architecture manager was a good architect but had little experience in this particular industry. Although Sam claimed to be planning to develop his manager of architecture to accept more responsibility, it was clear from his behavior this would not happen for some time, if at all. Sam reviewed everything because he enjoyed doing it. Indeed, his architecture manager was not even aware that he was supposed to be developing industry expertise. In an interview he stated, "I was hired over several candidates. Later, I asked Sam why he selected me when I didn't have any experience in this industry. He told me I would bring a pure eye to the job. He's the expert regarding the industry and I rely on his judgment. I worry about the steel and bricks. Together we're a team." It was clear from his comments that he was not making any effort to develop his own judgment on industry-related questions and believed Sam wanted it that way.

Sam treated his facilities manager like a colleague rather than a subordinate. He seemed not to want to be interviewed without this manager present, twice inviting him to interviews at which there had been no indication that anyone but Sam should be present.

It was also clear that Sam had not been getting much direction from Andy. They had fallen into a pattern in which it was business as usual until Andy's frustration built to the boiling point and there was an explosion. Sam would absorb the punishment, and things would return to normal until a month or so later, when another explosion would occur. If Sam had any awareness that something was seriously amiss in his relationship with Andy, he hid it well. This, to Sam, was just the way things were.

Dick, on the other hand, was under enormous pressure. He claimed his problems were behind him, although no one else in the division believed it. His attitude, they maintained, was just another cover-up. In fact, it became clear that he had no credibility with his associates. Too many times he had said in a staff meeting that something had been done and then left the meeting to do it. People did not believe him, and indeed it was difficult to ascertain to what extent he really had gotten a system in place to ease his problems. It should be noted that these attitudes surfaced without the author specifically asking for them. When asked about the problems in the division, the comments invariably got around to Dick's credibility, although some people were more direct than others.

Dick too had suffered from lack of direction, given that Andy's strengths were not in purchasing. While many of Dick's problems were of his own making, this had not helped.

Over lunch the author told Andy that neither team-building nor any other indirect third-party intervention was likely to help the situation. In fact, it would probably confuse the situation by failing to address the problem of managerial direction.

In Sam's case, Andy needed to sit down with him and specifically address the issues that were bothering him, with specific examples and a discussion of the consequences for the organization. Sam should then be asked to produce a plan for correcting the situation, to be monitored on a weekly or biweekly basis. Further, whenever Andy observed a critical incident relevant to the plan, he should mention it immediately. There could be no guarantee that Sam's behavior would change, but in the absence of such a systematic approach, change had no chance of happening.

Dick's case was even more difficult. His past behavior had compromised his credibility and it would take an enormous effort to restore it. Again Andy would have to force the issue, allowing him no excuses.

Andy's reaction was one of mild disappointment. Somehow he had hoped that a third party, in this case a consultant, would take over the burden of controlled confrontation with his subordinates. On the other hand, he recognized the basic truth of the message: that a third party would only confuse the communication between boss and subordinate, and that unless he managed his key subordinates more effectively, a consultant's work would be merely cosmetic and consume energy needed elsewhere.

This situation is not atypical. Few executives are good people managers. The executive in question had an outstanding international reputation in his professional field. He was often consulted by colleagues in other organizations. He had been recruited by the C.E.O. to turn around an unprofessional division, and it was widely acknowledged that he had done so. During a period of rapid growth, his division was for the most part making its expected contributions although not without its share of problems. He was a sensitive man who, when angry, could be quite tough. Such periodic outbursts are not a substitute for systematic performance counseling and discipline, however. On a personal level, he was cultured and charming.

Further, he recognized the need to do what the author was suggesting. His remark was telling: "Okay, I'll do it. Why you have to lead a grown man step by step, though, I'll never know. He should be smart enough to figure it out." He was smart enough to know the answer. To his credit, he did not continue to hide behind his wish and rationalize away his obligations. He was prepared, if reluctantly, to confront the issue head on.

He did ask that the author be present at the initial meeting to facilitate the communication process. "If I don't say it right, tell me. If I cut him off or don't listen to him, tell me, and if he just agrees and doesn't react, help get him going." Knowing the people involved, the author judged that this would be helpful rather than inhibiting, and agreed to participate if the other parties agreed.

First, however, the author needed to give feedback to both Sam and Dick on the outcome of the interviews. As part of the feedback, the coaching process would be set up.

The author told Sam that, from the interviews and from conversations with his boss, it was apparent that Sam needed to clarify his role with his boss, who was unhappy with how he was structuring his time. Furthermore, in the author's judgment, by abdicating certain aspects of his job he was undercutting his own potential effectiveness in the organization. Was he aware of Andy's concerns? "No," he replied. He knew Andy wanted him to spend more time in the office, but that was difficult since he needed to check on the jobs. The author then suggested that Andy and Sam discuss the situation directly.

Dick was told the extent of his credibility problem. It was especially crucial that when he did not know the answer to a question he say so and tell people exactly when he would get back to them. If something had not been done, he should say so and state what he would do to correct it. Further, if he said that something was on order he should give all the details, including invoice numbers, shipping modes, everything. Overkill was necessary. People did not believe him anymore; only his behavior would rebuild his credibility. Further, he needed to incorporate ideas from others into his systems to rebuild past relationships. His one asset at this point was the continued support of his boss. His biggest liability could be his own ego. Dick also agreed to a mutual meeting.

On the day of his first coaching meeting, Andy was nervous but committed to the process. It was obvious that he had given considerable thought to what he was going to say and had carefully worked out his comments.

In his meeting with Sam, he gave specific examples of what concerned him. He also made it clear that, while he thought Sam was a good manager of architecture, he did not need him for that job—he needed him to manage the department. Andy pointed out the importance of many of the meetings Sam was missing, defined exactly what he meant by visibility, and stressed the necessity of leaving many of the architectural problems to his manager of architecture.

The author said nothing except late in the discussion when a question arose about how to develop a plan for giving the manager of architecture more autonomy. The presence of a professional third party seemed sufficient to structure the proceedings, and as the discussion continued it was clear that Andy, once motivated, was quite capable of conducting such an interview. They ended the discussion with Andy asking Sam to decide whether he really wanted to do the job in question and, if so, to work out a plan of action with very specific objectives. They would meet again in exactly one week.

After the meeting the author told Andy he thought the message had gotten through. The point had been clearly made and specific changes discussed. "We'll see," Andy replied.

The discussion with Dick was similar in structure, although different in focus. Dick could no longer try to bluff his way through. "Dick, you won't fail a second time, because I won't let you. I'll step in sooner. But if I have to you won't like it," was Andy's comment. Dick needed a system and he needed to control it. Further, specific behavioral changes were in order, and the ones described above were restated. In future, Andy told him, he would give immediate feedback, either positive or negative, whenever a specific incident occurred. He also wanted a regular update on the status of the department.

The following week, as we prepared to meet again with Sam, Andy was bracing himself to give the same message again. Sam took the initiative, however. The past weekend had been a very difficult one, he said. He had thought a lot about what had been said. By Sunday night, however, he had worked out in his mind how he was going to approach the problem. He had set a specific time each week to review the week's events with his manager of architecture, making suggestions and critical comments. He would use this meeting as both a coaching session and a control vehicle. Sam had already informed his manager that in the future he should handle communications with the outside architects and the internal drafters. Toward that end, Sam had moved the files of drawings out of his office into a central area.

He had informed his facilities manager that he would be accompanying him to any meetings at which important coordination issues might be raised. Indeed, he had attended one the previous day.

Andy was visibly impressed with Sam's approach and made comments to that effect. During the subsequent discussion, Andy indicated that in the future he would channel any problems from senior management directly to Sam. Sam was to communicate the resolution directly to the executive involved, keeping Andy informed on an as-needed basis. The meeting adjourned with another follow-up discussion scheduled in two weeks.

Dick had missed a weekly staff meeting the day before, which, given the current situation, was not an advisable move.

He had called in, however, and his voice had a sense of urgency about it. Andy voiced his disapproval and told him not to travel on staff meeting days without his prior approval. At our meeting, Andy told Dick he was assigning another manager to work with him to audit his current system. While it was clear Dick did not welcome the arrangement, he agreed to it. The subsequent discussion covered how the other manager would work with Dick, and it was decided that reports would be presented jointly by the two of them. The author reiterated the need for Dick to build bridges to his peers and suggested that he view the audit as a collegial effort and not be defensive.

Two months into the process, both managers seemed to be making progress with Sam making the most visible advances. Organizations are systems of interdependent behaviors, with a change in one person's behavior creating reactions in the behavior of others. Sam's facilities manager was not initially pleased as his boss began taking initiatives that closed the vacuum he had been filling. He went to Andy to ask what was happening, and Andy simply replied that he wanted Sam to assert more direct authority over these matters and that he should raise any questions with Sam himself.

A key test of Sam's managerial ability would be to reassert himself in a role he had previously left to a subordinate by default. Sam was frank about his intention to have more face-to-face communication with senior management and to be the source of contact on problems without day-to-day involvement in the details of facilities design. So far his actions have backed up his words and, at present, a new equilibrium seems to have established itself. Andy feels Sam's entire operation is running better, although as the division grows he sees limitations on Sam's potential for handling more senior-level responsibility. It does not appear that Sam will grow into broader responsibility but will remain a functionally oriented manager.

Dick has been doing a better job of communicating with his associates. His defensiveness is still evident in his personality, but he seems to be making strides. His boss is hopeful but continues to pay close attention to Dick's department and give Dick prompt feedback.

At present, neither manager is a candidate for termination, although a short while ago their boss was preparing himself for such an outcome. The executive in question was quite capable of executing the coaching process but had to overcome the reluctance to do so. The keys were communicating in precise terms what was unsatisfactory and the possible consequences, specifying exactly what was expected, including action steps, and frequent reviews.

Endnotes

---

[1] H. Meyer, E. Kay, and J. R. P. French, Jr., "Split Roles in Performance Appraisal," *Harvard Business Review* (January–February 1965), 126.
[2] Ibid., 126.
[3] Ibid., 126–127.

6

The Termination Interview

N O MATTER HOW THOROUGH A COMPANY'S termination policy may be, it can be rendered largely useless if managers do not conduct effective termination interviews. It is the quality of the interpersonal exchange during the interview that determines the impact on the person being dismissed.

There is no easy way to conduct the interview. Firing someone is an unpleasant experience. Even when people know their past performance has been poor, being let go is likely to generate defensiveness. Furthermore, very real economic and social problems confront the unemployed person. At the same time, for managers doing the firing, the feeling of playing God with someone's career is likely to be unsettling.

A question we are often asked is, "What if the manager can't do it?" Sometimes the organization feels that the boss is likely to lose control of the termination interview. Perhaps he or she is overly apprehensive about the termination or has been close to the employee on a social level and just can't deal with the issue. Personal biases might make it easy for the manager to lose self-control. In the final analysis, managers are seldom hired for their termination skills.

If the organization feels the manager is unlikely to be effective in the termination interview, or the manager feels he or she can't do it, either the manager's superior or a personnel specialist should sit in on the interview with the manager. In effect, the two of them should conduct the interview as a team.

The manager of the person being terminated should always be present, however. This is the person who should initiate and carry the burden of the interview. The other person is present only to give support and to be certain the termination is clearly communicated.

There is no way to make the termination interview a pleasant experience. The goal is to make it as constructive as possible, make sure the essential points are covered, and protect the integrity of the company. A corollary to this is that the interview should proceed in a way that minimizes the awkwardness for the manager doing the firing. Fortunately, skills can be learned and procedures followed to help achieve a calm, constructive interview.

Preparing for the Interview

Preparation is essential to an effective termination interview. Proper preparation helps the manager avoid the critical mistakes that typify spur-of-the-moment, angry terminations.

Our discussions of corporate policy in Chapter Four and corrective coaching in Chapter Five have suggested many of the critical elements of preparation. Prior to initiating a termination interview, the manager should already have taken several steps in regard to the subordinate's poor performance. Unacceptable performance appraisals should have been given. Specific objectives should have been set, discussed, and monitored during a carefully calibrated review process.

In the absence of satisfactory performance, the manager must assemble the documentation that justifies the termination and should be thoroughly familiar and comfortable with this material. The decision should be reviewed with a more senior manager and the proper people in the personnel department, and the terms of the support package should be stated clearly in a letter.

Next, the manager can focus attention on the interview itself. Timing is an important consideration. In current practice, a disproportionate number of terminations occur on Friday afternoon or before a business trip. The desire to put off an unpleasant task and to escape once the task is done seems to explain the popularity of this kind of timing.

Generally, we believe individuals should be fired early in the day and at the beginning or middle of the week. There is a scarcity of good research on the relationship between the timing of a termination and the recovery of the employee from the initial shock, but we have observed that most people benefit from a period of time in which to collect their thoughts and prepare to explain their situation to their families. They need time to sort out what has happened, possibly asking questions of the contact within the company. Late-in-the-day and end-of-the-week terminations tend to preclude this, placing additional pressure on the employee.

Nor do we recommend that the termination take place just before the boss goes on a trip, because it creates an impression of abandonment and retreat. While out of the office, the boss cannot respond to the reactions of others to the termination or to any unanticipated problems.

A manager conducting a termination should prepare an opening for the discussion and give thought to the proper structuring of the interview. A model to help the manager in planning and conducting the interview is provided later in this chapter. Prior to meeting with the subordinate, the manager should have reviewed each step of the model.

Anticipating Reactions to Termination

In planning for the interview it is helpful to anticipate how the employee might react. Being terminated is a shocking and stressful event involving significant loss. People react to such blows differently based on their personality and other factors. Predicting how a given person might respond is tricky at best, although if a manager has observed the person's reaction to some similar high-stress loss situation (which usually is not the case) the person is likely to exhibit the same defense mechanisms. Being knowledgeable about the kinds of reactions experienced by other people who have been terminated, however, can help the manager avoid being caught off guard and misreading what is happening. The following reactions have been observed by our counselors.

Normally Defensive but Pragmatic

This most common reaction involves a degree of defensiveness, anger, and other characteristics of a normal grieving process combined with an obvious concern for pragmatic issues. This last trait indicates that the person understands what is happening and is preparing to deal with the situation in terms of his or her best interests from a career point of view.

The subsequent reactions of such individuals will be strongly shaped by whatever conclusions they arrive at following an attempt to assess their next career steps. They may be upset, but they are not likely to act impulsively on their anger or frustrations.

If there is a "normal" reaction to being terminated it is characterized by expressions of anger, hurt, and disappointment. But very quickly the terminated individual moves to practical questions, like "What is the company going to do for me?" and "What kind of support services are going to be provided?" These people may have anticipated the termination and already gotten themselves sufficiently together to ask for protection and assistance.

Almost always these employees exhibit some hurt by telling the manager that they disagree with the action. The manager may in turn feel frustration over the fact that the employee seems unable to clearly understand the problems that caused the termination. These employees may also express disappointment in the company and the ways it has changed in recent years. Nevertheless, they are primarily concerned with survival and about what will be done for them.

When the boss has done a good job of appraising past performance, the employee has been forewarned that his or her performance has not been consistent with management expectations. In that case there is a minimum amount of surprise connected with the termination, although the fact that performance has not improved usually indicates that the employee has not been able to internalize and utilize past feedback. Therefore, defensiveness should be anticipated.

Managers should be cautioned that even when they think they have done a good job of counseling, the employee is still shocked when the termination actually occurs. This is true for two reasons. First, even when the boss thinks performance problems have been clearly delineated in performance appraisals, the more serious problems have often been unconsciously downplayed in order to avoid unpleasantness. Therefore, the employee is still largely unaware of just how serious the problems are. Second, the employee may have blocked out the negative feedback or, in essence, avoided hearing what was said about inadequate performance. We know, for example, that many psychologically healthy people seem to exaggerate positive feedback about themselves and minimize or discount negative feedback. Also, many people tend to convince themselves that termination won't happen to them and, inevitably, when confronted with the reality of being let go, feel some form of shock even though considerable dialogue about poor past performance has preceded the interview.

Nevertheless, when they have been repeatedly counseled about performance and know they've missed job assignments, most people are aware of impending termination even if they seek to avoid recognizing it.

Anticipatory

The anticipatory reaction is a variation of the normal reaction. In one unusual instance, the employee was so sure he was going to be fired that he avoided coming into the office. Expecting to be terminated, he kept traveling or calling in sick. Eventually an outplacement consultant had to go to his home to tell him that he was being terminated. As things turned out, there was little trauma connected with the discussion. On the contrary, there was a certain amount of humor. The employee laughed about being a hard person to find; he said he knew he was going to be fired and was just trying to postpone the inevitable. When the consultant arrived at his home, his family was out shopping and the interview went smoothly. He found a better position within three months.

Fortunately, not all anticipatory reactions are so extreme. However, they share certain characteristics. These people expect termination but hope to delay it. Often, they try to avoid the boss in the belief that "out of sight is out of mind." Typically they have accepted termination as inevitable, so there is no dramatic effort made to improve performance.

When the termination occurs, these people generally acknowledge that they expected it and may even seem relieved. Protest is limited to statements that they don't think it was entirely their fault or "It's a shame we couldn't work together." The interview typically proceeds in a straightforward, unemotional way, with the terminated person concentrating on the particulars of the support package and other arrangements relating to the problem of what happens now. The clarity with which employees deal with these arrangements is a good clue that they are not experiencing shock.

Aggressive/Hostile

When feelings of hurt and anger are especially strong, the defense mechanisms of aggression and hostility may appear. They may take one of two forms: argumentative or violent behavior.

Argumentative

These people will argue with the manager, strongly asserting that the problems were not their fault and accusing others of unfairness. They may make threats about what they will do to get back at the company. They may talk in terms of lawsuits or going public with embarrassing information.

When confronted with this reaction, a manager should not get defensive, but listen to the employee and ask questions. The objective of the manager should be to allow the person to vent these feelings. Above all, the manager must avoid making promises, with such statements as: "We'll try to do something for you" or "I'll help you find a job." Such remarks reinforce these people's belief that they have been mistreated.

Whenever a person being terminated threatens legal action, the manager should simply acknowledge that it is the person's right to do so. However, the manager should also state firmly the belief that documentation will support management's contention that it was within its rights in discharging the employee. In short, the manager should recognize the employee's right to pursue legal recourse without encouraging it. Basically, the manager should listen and not intensify the person's anger by arguing.

Violent

Some people's argumentative response may be so intense that it is best described as violent. Such loss of control is relatively rare in managerial situations, although it does occur. This response is characterized by screaming, shouting obscenities, or even threatening physical harm to themselves, the company, or the person who is firing them.

Again, the objective of the manager should be to allow these people to vent their feelings. Rather than argue or defend the company, the manager should ask questions. What makes him feel he is being mistreated? How could her career have been handled differently? Usually, the person will calm down in the process of talking about the situation.

One of us was involved in a situation in which the terminated employee threatened to shoot his boss. After a period of outplacement consultation, he even threatened physical harm to the counselor. Such cases are rare, however. In fact, violent verbal reactions occur in a distinct minority of instances. Usually, the terminating manager is needlessly anxious about a violent overreaction on the part of the subordinate.

People who react violently usually get over this reaction rather quickly. A day or two later, after having time to think about the situation, they usually realize it is not to their advantage to do something that will render them unemployable or cause legal problems. They then begin to channel their anger into productive energy. This is what happened to the person described in the preceding paragraph. He used his hostility to good advantage by channeling it into an energetic and creative job search. However, it is wise for a manager to exercise caution when confronted with a violent reaction, both during and following the interview.

Withdrawal/Denial

Another kind of person reacts by withdrawing or refusing to deal realistically with the predicament. Since these people offer no resistance, the manager doing the termination will often feel relief and tend to hurry the interview to its conclusion. This is seldom in the best interests of the employee, who has not realistically begun to accept the situation.

We have observed four distinct variations of this general reaction.

Quiet

When informed that they are being let go, many people are
so stunned, and their ego is so damaged, that they appear to have
everything under control. They imply that they have anticipated
the news for a long time and that they are almost happy about
the decision (making this reaction difficult to differentiate from
the anticipatory reaction). The manager who is doing the termination is deceived into thinking that it has gone quite well.

Individuals who react in this way are often the ones who do
the most damage to the organization and/or themselves. They do
not vent their feelings and instead lie to themselves for as long as
they can, but eventually reality penetrates. Their reaction could
come two weeks or a month later. All of a sudden something
explodes inside them and they become extremely distraught. The
point here is that when someone is reacting abnormally "well" to
bad news, the outplacement counselor should be on the alert.
The individual who seems to take the news in good fashion is
probably covering something up. It is more normal to be hurt in
constructive ways than to keep feelings bottled up and pretend
that nothing is wrong.

When dealing with this type of response, the manager must
ask questions to make sure that the fired individual is actually
hearing the bad news. There is a tendency—and a desire—on the
part of management to think the person is okay. These quiet individuals can thus deceive the terminating manager as well as
themselves.

Disbelieving

At the opposite extreme from those who anticipate being
fired are those who look as if they don't believe what they're
hearing. These people say nothing and look as though they are in
a state of shock.

Of all the reactions, this can be the most frightening to deal with. The boss needs to try to keep the conversation going, to draw out these people. Some sort of reaction—perhaps negative, or at least accepting—needs to be elicited before the end of the interview. If the terminating manager cannot obtain a response of this type, an appropriate person in the personnel department should continue the discussion with the employee.

It is important to avoid sending the person off in a state of disbelief. By not facing up to the reality of the situation, these people hope the nightmare will go away. It is in this condition that people may do themselves harm.

John Fredericks is a typical example. John had worked at his company for twenty-five years and held so many different positions that he was known as a jack-of-all-trades and Mr. Company Man. After this length of service, one might imagine that he was well established with his superiors, peers, and subordinates. Management styles change, however, and John eventually found himself out of step with the current approach of top management.

More specifically, John kept telling management that it was wrong in the way it handled certain business problems. Whether he was right or wrong in the long run will probably never be established. However, his superiors decided he was no longer part of their team and could not be counted on to implement key programs with enthusiasm; therefore, he had to be dismissed.

In the termination interview, John was told the news abruptly. The boss's exact words were, "Your services are no longer needed." John sat there and just stared at his boss. His only comment during the hour was, "You can't do this to me; I won't allow it." He did respond with yes and no answers, but never engaged in dialogue.

The company had not done a good job of documenting problems and counseling John prior to the termination interview. However, the day before the termination interview, it had arranged for outplacement counseling services to be made available by an outside firm. The counselor met with John immediately after the interview.

It took the outplacement consultant no less than six hours of counseling to get John to begin talking freely about his feelings and anxieties. Some of these anxieties centered on the fact that he did not know what to say to his friends or peers. After twenty-five years, money and advancement up the corporate ladder were no longer motivating forces. Status and relationships, both on the job and in his community, were his primary concerns. John was deeply troubled about what to say to save face in the outside world and within the organization. The counselor dealt with his fears by helping John with a carefully worded explanation of why he was changing careers and leaving the company.

John's case demonstrates several elements common to the disbelief reaction. A failure to document specific problems and review them systematically with the employee before firing contributes to a climate in which dismissal is the farthest thing from the employee's mind. Couple this with a harsh or aggressive manner of breaking the news, and conditions are created that intensify the employee's disbelief. Although John's case was somewhat extreme, it typically takes a significant effort to get the discharged employee to talk under these circumstances. Therefore, the termination interview can last for a considerable length of time.

Often, the interview needs to be supplemented by skilled counseling. As with John, these people are usually in shock over the threat that termination poses to some aspect of their lives. Until the counselor succeeds in bringing that threat to the surface and resolving it, the discharged person is unlikely to accept the reality of being fired.

Lack of communication between management and the subordinate often leads to a reaction of disbelief, but adequate communication does not always preclude such a response. Many simply dismiss the possibility of being fired, believing that management will continue to tolerate them. For example, Jay, a training and development manager, persisted in organizing certain programs in the face of opposition from his immediate supervisor. Jay was convinced that his approach was correct and believed it was his responsibility to proceed despite direction from his boss to the contrary. To make matters worse, Jay's management style was considerably at odds with his superior's.

When his boss fired him, Jay was shocked, although he had been warned that if the two couldn't get together, a change was going to be made. Jay kept saying that he was doing the job the way he felt it should be done and to the best of his ability.

At eleven-thirty that night, Jay's wife phoned his boss to ask if he knew where Jay was. Jay wasn't home and had not called. In fact, it was two days before Jay went home, still not sure what had happened or what to tell the family.

This would probably not have happened if the manager had taken the time to discuss Jay's feelings. The manager should be prepared with a number of questions to probe the person's feelings, plans, and desires. The objective is to get the person to respond. People who will not speak should receive professional help.

Euphoric

People who respond to termination in an upbeat, almost festive manner can be termed euphoric. They sound almost happy to be let go. They seem positive they can handle what is happening to them. Managers should view this reaction with some scepticism.

People reacting this way are typically so geared to responding to the boss's direction that they go along with being fired just as they might go along with any other directive received from a superior. In essence, they are saying that whatever the boss wants is all right with them.

These people usually have no idea what the next step should be. Unless told to leave the premises, they may continue to sit at their desks without making any preparations for leaving, even though they have been told that they are discharged.

Unfortunately, this disorientation can be intensified if the boss misreads the euphoric reaction. Relieved at the person's seeming acceptance of the situation, the boss often keeps the interview brief, focusing on the termination package and paying no further attention to the person's psychological state. Yet this person is exhibiting one of the reactions most in need of counseling support.

A case in point was Janice, a 37-year-old woman referred to us by the corporation that was terminating her. She seemed extremely happy about the situation. In fact, she was bubbly, excited, and a pleasure to work with. It took her no less than two and a half years to find another position. In essence, nothing that was offered was interesting or real to her. On top of this, when she interviewed with potential employers, she created the impression of not being serious about finding a job. Her counselor's job was to get her to calm down, to describe herself in business terms, and to set out clearly defined objectives for finding her next job. It was a long, arduous process.

These are difficult people to work with because it is hard to make them face reality without crushing their spirit or hurting their drive. Virtually all dismissed people go through cyclical periods of feeling high or low. They get excited about the possibility of moving to a new job and then hit a low period in the job search process. Euphoric people don't have the peaks and valleys of the normal candidate but tend to stay on an unrealistic high. However, if they do come out of their euphoric state, they tend to crash into depression and can be difficult to get back to a level at which they can energetically look for a job.

Escapist

Once told they are no longer with the company, people with escapist reactions want to leave the office immediately, although sometimes they will go back to the work unit and begin talking to others about the problems they are having with the boss or company.

The manager must try to keep these people in the office and initiate a dialogue on exactly why they are being let go. Every effort should be made to continue the discussion and help them vent their feelings. It is especially important that the manager communicate the details of the support package. We know several instances when people with this reaction placed undue stress on their families because they left before understanding the terms of their terminations. Typically, the boss lets them leave, relieved that the problem seems to be solved.

It's helpful if a personnel officer can spend some time with these people after the interview with the manager is over. The personnel officer can get them off the premises, go out and have a cup of coffee with them, and continue to discuss their feelings. If this is not done, the escapist is most likely to vent to others— co-workers, family, other people in the industry, perhaps even the press. If an outplacement counselor has been retained, the counselor can play such a role.

Guidelines

These reactions have been observed by most outplacement specialists. Trained in dealing with the situation, they are capable of recognizing how the person is reacting, retaining their poise, and continuing the interview. For the line manager, the problem is more severe. Under the pressure of the termination interview, it is easy to become defensive, forget to analyze what is happening, and lose control of the conversation. When a company designates a specialist in the personnel department to assist the manager, the likelihood of adequate follow-through increases, since the specialist is more familiar with terminations than other managers and thus has become more adept at handling them.

Review of the possible reactions should be part of the preparation of any manager about to initiate a termination discussion. In the interview itself the manager should remember the following guidelines:

- Continue the interview until the person appears to be talking freely and calmly (if somewhat tensely) about the reasons for termination and the terms of the support package.
- Avoid becoming defensive about the termination. Encourage the person to talk.
- Beware of any reaction in which acceptance, either passive or enthusiastic, could lead to an almost immediate conclusion of the interview.
- Try to avoid letting the person storm out of the office.
- Don't make any promises or apologies. Stick to the content of the support package.

Committing these guidelines to memory will help the manager remain in control of the interview regardless of the terminated employee's reaction.

What to Cover in the Interview

As we have stressed repeatedly, the manager should establish specific reasons for the termination. The manager should stick to these reasons, no matter what the subordinate's reaction. A termination interview is not a counseling session in which managers are obligated to listen open-mindedly for the possibility of hearing something that might change their assessment of the situation. Such discussions should have preceded the decision to discharge the person. Rather, the purpose of the interview is to tell the employee about a nonreversible decision. The manager is listening in order to help the subordinate accept the decision, not to obtain new information.

The problems should all have been discussed before. Even if

the subordinate does not accept the manager's reasoning, the only proper position for the manager is, "Well, I'm sorry that we disagree. However, I think it is important that you know why we are discharging you and how we saw your performance."

Above all, the manager should avoid giving fictitious reasons for the termination. This may seem obvious, yet managers often give reasons that are easier to present than lack of performance. We encountered one person who had been let go three times in five years. No one had given him serious feedback on his problems, and he was under the impression that he had bad luck in choosing jobs. His outplacement counselor was the first one to help him identify and work out his problems.

People need to know why they are fired; otherwise they have no opportunity to avoid making the same mistakes in the future. Giving them concrete reasons helps them digest what went wrong. Management does a person a severe disservice by not giving specific reasons.

There should be no question but that the decision is final. Throughout the interview, the manager should make it clear that the issue facing the individual is "What do I do next?" and not "How do I get my job back?" The manager should be especially careful neither to apologize for the termination nor to promise to see what else is available in the company. These are common mistakes that tend to cloud the issue and often lead people to believe there is a chance of saving their jobs. The manager's posture should be, "We have discussed these problems before, and management has already looked at the option of placing you elsewhere in the company. Our decision is that it is in the best interests of both of us for you to go elsewhere."

Along these same lines, never suggest that the company (or the manager) will help the person find another job. Remember, a major hurdle most people must clear when they are terminated is to get moving and look for work. Well-intended efforts to soften the blow by promising to help out tend to delay acceptance of the new situation by the terminated employee. Thus, such efforts are really more damaging than helpful. A cardinal rule is that the manager should not make any commitments to help beyond those contained in the support package.

Avoid platitudes as well. Never say something like "This really is not the worst thing that could happen to you." On this day it seems like the worst thing that could happen, and it certainly is high on anyone's list of unpleasant experiences. "Things will work out for the best" is no better. Indeed, no one knows how they are going to work out. Platitudes come across as patronizing and do nothing to help the person deal with the immediate problem.

It is important that the support package be discussed *and* understood. The manager should make an outline of the support package before the interview and refer to these notes to be sure each point is reviewed with the person being terminated. Do not go into great depth, as the person will not "hear" much of what is said. But each point should be covered verbally and included in a written explanation for the person to take and review later.

Once suitable preparations have been made, the problem is to conduct the interview. It is helpful if the manager has a model to help structure the discussion.

A Model for the Interview

Experience indicates that managers tend to make certain mistakes during the interview that create unnecessary difficulties for either the manager or the person being let go. To the extent that a manager can avoid these mistakes, the termination interview is more likely to go smoothly. Even more importantly, the manager is less likely to jeopardize the company's legal position.

Below we suggest a model approach to handling the termination interview. The sequence of the steps is important; taking them out of sequence can undermine the effectiveness of the discussion. Furthermore, underlying each step are certain skills and procedures that can facilitate the interview. It is worth the manager's time to develop these skills, since many of them are applicable to a variety of other managerial situations as well. In this sense, they are general management skills.

Step 1. Get to the point.
Step 2. Describe the situation.
Step 3. Listen: Don't get defensive.
  • Open-ended questions.
  • Restatement.
  • Expanders.
  • Silence.
Step 4. Discuss the support package.
Step 5. Specifically define the next step.

Step 1. Get to the Point

When terminating someone, managers often find it difficult to get to the point. Frequently, they are so evasive that it is several minutes before the person being fired begins to realize what is happening. An opening line such as, "Would you like a cup of coffee? I don't know how . . . How is it going on the line?" is characteristic.

Managers frequently make small talk about the kids, last weekend's big game, the state of the economy, or some other remote topic in an effort to delay the actual firing. This small talk is often rationalized as an effort to put the employee at ease, but the real reason for it is the manager's own uneasiness. Uncomfortable, perhaps even a little fearful, the manager is still seeking to put off the inevitable.

Sometimes managers try to ease into the topic gradually. Thus they begin by making indirect comments, such as "Things haven't been going well lately" or "How do you feel about the job you have been doing?" Subconsciously they are hoping the employee will take the hint and quit. Unfortunately, all too often employees seize the initiative by voicing a strong desire to improve or asking how they can do better. Now the manager is in a bind, because doing better is no longer an option; the person is being fired.

For example, a partner in a large public accounting firm was given the task of terminating a staff person whose performance did not merit continued association with the firm. The partner began by stating that the staff person's evaluation on his last job assignment was not good. The staff person responded that he was not satisfied with his performance either and hoped to do better on the next engagement. Next, the partner commented that this had not been the first time his job performance had been rated as inadequate or below average. At this point, the staff person stated that he, too, had been concerned with the way his career was going and he was glad that someone in the firm was going to have a thorough discussion with him about what he could do to improve his performance. At this point, the partner gave up and suggested that they both give it some thought and that the staff member talk to the partner in charge of the office.

A basic principle of any activity is that the more severe the problem, the more important it is to get to the point and not indulge in evasive tactics. Firing someone is one of the most severe problems. Therefore, it is imperative to get directly to the point. The longer the manager procrastinates, the greater the false atmosphere that is created, making it more awkward to present the real purpose of the meeting. Furthermore, the longer the manager delays telling the employee the true purpose of the discussion, the more chances there are that the conversation will take a turn that puts the manager on the defensive.

When the individual enters the manager's office, the manager should give him or her a moment to get comfortable, then annouce the decision.

Step 2. Describe the Situation

The manager's uneasiness about the termination interview can lead to an overkill situation in which the manager seemingly wants to devastate the person being let go. Apprehension that the employee will resist the termination often leads the manager to decide that a good offense is the best defense. The result is an unnecessarily brutal termination. On the other hand, a manager may be so vague about the termination that it is not even clear that the person is being dismissed. One approach is as bad as the other.

In informing the subordinate of the termination decision, the manager should describe the situation, not attack the person. In describing the situation, the manager should be very specific. The interview should begin with a statement like the following:

John, I am really very sorry but I am going to have to let you go. Production in your area is down four percent, and we are continuing to have quality problems. Several of your supervisors are still unaware of key operating procedures. We have talked about these problems several times in the past three months, and the solutions are not being followed through. We have to make a change.

Or perhaps the opening might go like this:

Mary, I have to let you go. In the past, we've talked about your inconsistencies in carrying out our policies in the shop. Yesterday, you failed to discipline two of your people for being fifteen minutes late from lunch. People are talking instead of working, and attendance remains a problem. I have to make a change.

What do both of these openings have in common? First, the manager begins by informing the subordinate of the termination decision. Sometimes subordinates will interrupt at this point and ask why. Usually, however, they will listen, somewhat in a state of shock. In either event, the manager should continue. Second, the manager describes the reasons that led to the decision, in very specific terms. The manager gives at least three examples of problems and reminds the employee that these have been discussed repeatedly in the past. Finally, the manager reaffirms the decision to fire the employee.

Notice that the manager does not attack the subordinate personally. Comments such as "You are too careless" or "Your lack of effort is responsible for your removal" have been avoided. These are judgments about the person's character that are virtually impossible for the person to accept. They are also highly subjective judgments that can be difficult to defend. For example, stating that someone has "exhibited almost total disregard for our reporting system" is going to generate considerable defensiveness, certainly much more than the comment "During the last six months, each of your management reports has been at least three days late." The latter is the objective basis for the termination.

Descriptive statements are more effective because they make it easier for the subordinate to focus on the reasons for the termination. They avoid the unnecessary conflict generated by inferences about the motivation behind poor performance.

Stating things descriptively is a communication skill that can be learned. With practice, any manager can do it. In preparing a descriptive opening, the manager can use the following questions as guidelines:

• *What are the actual events that led to the termination decision?* What has the manager actually observed, measured, or experienced that has led to the individual's termination? If the reasons are performance based, it is obviously helpful for the manager to be able to refer to specific performance objectives. But regardless of why the individual is being discharged, the manager should be able to present specific examples of the problem. For example: "Reports have been late," "Production has not improved to agreed-upon levels," "You have received three poor performance appraisals."

Even integrity problems can be presented descriptively. For example: "You reported that you visited our distributors in the northeast section of the state, but subsequently they asked when you were going to visit them and said they had not seen any of our people for over six months." Or, "You reported that you audited our inventory figures, but the data were never collected."

All of these examples have focused on actual occurrences, thus providing a substantive basis for the termination.

• *How frequently have the events been observed?* How many reports have been late? How long has production been below acceptable levels? How many complaints have been received? When the manager can specify the number of times problems have been observed, the statement becomes even more descriptive and substantive. Thus, the manager can state, "Five times in the last six months, your monthly management reports have been late by more than a week. On three occasions, we discussed this problem."

Notice that the manager states both the frequency with which the problem has occurred and the number of times the manager and employee have already discussed it. Stating the frequency with which the problems have been discussed helps to document the seriousness of the problem further.

• *What, if any, were the observable consequences?* In considering this question, the manager is trying to identify what additional problems have been created by the employee's actions. For example, perhaps the failure to do timely reviews of a parts inventory has led to shortages on the production floor. Perhaps several key customers have complained about lack of responsiveness to their problems.

By answering these three guideline questions, a manager will develop specific descriptive statements that tell the individual, without any personal attack, why he or she is being let go. At the same time, the employee will have no doubt about the purpose of the interview.

To summarize, the manager should get directly to the point in a descriptive fashion. In fact, the termination should take place in the first few minutes of the interview. Once this is done, the manager can focus on the person's reaction.

Step 3. Listen: Don't Get Defensive

No matter how descriptive the opening is, the most likely reaction will be one of shock, disbelief, or defensiveness. As discussed earlier, these reactions can take a variety of forms. For the manager, the most important thing is to avoid arguing.

The first priority is to get the employee talking about the termination. This is because:

- The more the individual talks, the easier it is for the manager to determine which of the many possible reactions is occurring.
- Listening to dismissed employees is basic to insuring that they have a reasonable understanding of their position.

Sometimes, getting the person to talk will be easy. For example, individuals having either a euphoric or violent reaction typically express themselves verbally. Other times, this task will be harder. Disbelief and escapism are two reactions in which individuals may not express themselves other than by shaking their heads or seeking to leave the office.

When a fired individual reacts verbally, the manager's principle concern should be to listen, encouraging the person to express feelings as a first step toward focusing on the reality of the situation. The manager's principal problems are to avoid becoming defensive and to avoid saying something that might undermine the objective rationale for terminating the individual.

For example, if discharged employees begin to blame their failure on the manager, it is easy for the manager to retaliate with judgmental and subjective comments that are not germane to the objective reasons for the firing. Such statements undermine the entire termination process by providing fuel for the fired employees' belief that they were treated unfairly, that the boss "had it in for them." For these reasons, it is important that managers keep their input to a minimum while letting discharged employees talk.

If dismissed employees close up, however, the manager's problem becomes one of drawing them out. Here the boss has to use interpersonal skills to get them talking about the situation, because only by talking are they likely to come to terms with it.

The following communication skills are particularly important at this point:

- Open-ended questions
- Restatement
- Expanders
- Silence

Open-ended Questions

An open-ended question is a question that cannot easily be answered with a yes or no. Open-ended questions begin with the words *what*, *how*, *where*, or *when*. By contrast, close-ended questions are easily answered in a yes or no fashion. Close-ended questions typically begin with the words *can*, *do*, *did*, *are*, *has*, *would*, and *could*.

Because open-ended questions cannot easily be answered with a yes or no, they generally elicit a broader response. Apart from this, open-ended questions minimize defensiveness on the part of the respondent. Close-ended questions tend to force the respondent into a position of deciding whether to come down on the positive or negative side of the yes/no question. This decision can be threatening. Often respondents feel boxed into a corner. Open-ended questions make it easier for them to explain their position.

For these reasons, open-ended questions are generally more effective during the exploration stage of a sensitive discussion. They are particularly effective when trying to elicit reactions to being terminated. Asking questions such as the following can help generate constructive dialogue:

- "What were your reactions when last month's figures showed no improvement?"
- "How did you feel after our last talk about this problem?"
- "In retrospect, what could you have done differently?"

The questions should be linked directly to the dismissed employee's situation. The point of this step is not to generate idle conversation, but to help the individual talk about what happened.

Unfortunately, most questions asked in our society are close-ended. Listen to conversations in the office; you'll see that most questions are phrased in a close-ended fashion. This is fine for casual conversation, but it gets in the way when managing tense employer/employee communications. The problem for the manager in learning to use open-ended questions is to overcome bad habits. One way to do this is to practice phrasing questions in an open-ended fashion until the skill is developed.

Restatement

Restatement is the practice of rephrasing a key point the other person has just made. This serves several functions in a termination interview. First, it allows discharged employees to present their thoughts and ideas without having to argue with the boss. Second, it is a way to express interest and understanding and to encourage the sharing of feelings. Thus, restatement tends to facilitate the discussion in a nonadversary fashion. Finally, when the dismissed person is upset and verbally attacking the manager, restating can help the manager avoid a defensive reaction. For example:

Fired Employee: I tried my hardest. We both agreed that a joint effort was going to be required. I don't think I ever got full support for my program.

Manager: (restating) Under the circumstances, you feel you have done everything possible.

Fired Employee: Certainly, for example . . .

Notice how restatement helps the manager respond to the fired employee's accusation in a nondefensive manner while encouraging the continued ventilation of feelings.

Restatement is best used when individuals are emotionally involved in what they are saying. Under these conditions, restatement is an unobtrusive way to help them express their feelings. It is one of the most useful of listening skills; it is also one of the most difficult to learn. Therefore, as with open-ended questions, conscious practice is required, prior to participating in a termination interview, if a manager is to become skilled in using this technique.

Expanders

As the fired employee is talking, the manager should express interest and understanding by maintaining good eye contact, occasionally nodding the head, and occasionally saying "Uh-huh" or "I see." These gestures are referred to as expanders because that is what they do; they encourage people to expand on their comments.

Silence

It should go without saying that if the object is to listen, the manager should be as silent as possible, yet in our experience, this is easier to say than to do in a termination interview. The tension and nervousness that characterize the situation tend to make most managers talk too much. In an effort to control the conversation, they dominate it. In the process, they undermine their effectiveness.

There are two times when silence can be used effectively. One is right after asking a question. All too often, managers continue talking after asking a question, suggesting the answer they want to hear, asking additional questions, or even going off on another train of thought. This, of course, defeats the purpose of asking the question in the first place. It takes skill to ask a question and pause, waiting for an answer. Our advice to managers is to be aware of how often you do this and strive to improve.

Silence is equally helpful after the other person has been talking. Often a pause, accompanied by an expectant look, will encourage people to continue to talk. Simply giving them an opportunity to expand on what they have been saying is one of the most effective listening skills. Once again, the tendency to dominate the conversation can defeat this simple but important technique.

Managers should remember that the termination interview is not a problem-solving session. The time for that approach between boss and subordinate was in the months preceding the termination decision. Any further attempts at identifying the cause of the problem imply that another chance is in order. In the absence of extraordinary new information, such an implication at this point is inappropriate. Termination should only take place after other attempts at solution have failed and the manager is convinced that a change is necessary. If questions exist, the manager should not have proceeded this far with the termination process.

In response to the employee's questions, the manager should state that the decision regarding the termination is final, the problems have been discussed before, and the employee needs to be most concerned about what he or she is going to do next. For example, consider the following exchange:

Fired Employee: Look, I don't think anyone can do the job better. I've been working hard on the problems. I know the operation like the back of my hand. This doesn't make any sense.

Manager:	John, the decision has been made. For nine months we've been meeting at least once a week on this matter. Whether or not someone else can succeed remains to be seen, but I feel it's our best approach to make a change at this time. You need to be concerned about the future, not the past. Make sure your next move is a good one.
Fired Employee:	Frank, this thing requires time. I wish I could get you to see that. Don't be unreasonable.
Manager:	(using restatement) You feel that with time the problems would be resolved; that we are treating you unreasonably.
Fired Employee:	Hell, yes. Remember, I have a lot at stake here too.
Manager:	I think your feelings are natural, but I also think we're doing the right thing. Time will tell. You need to be thinking about your next step now.

Notice that in the above dialogue the manager is not arguing with John. Rather, he is focusing attention on the fact that problems exist, that other attempts to solve them have not worked, and he is confirming the decision to let John go. In doing this, he reiterates that John needs to be planning ahead to find his next job.

In conducting the interview, there is nothing wrong with allowing fired individuals to talk about what they might have done differently as long as the manager does not imply that they might have another chance at the job. The posture should be one of agreeing that hindsight can be useful to future efforts. Discussing problems of the past can also help fired employees realize that a change may be in their own best interest as well as the company's. The goal of the listening step is to get the employee to talk freely about the situation and to focus immediate concern on the future, not the former job.

Sometimes, after venting their feelings, discharged employees will focus on the issues themselves: "Well, right or wrong, my problem is what happens now. Are you just throwing me out on the street?" Other times, managers can facilitate this process by summarizing the conversation: "Although we disagree on whether this is the correct solution, it's the one I have made. Let's talk about what happens next." That is one way to help the interview along. Another approach, and one that is often effective when a person is experiencing disbelief, might be: "Accepting the decision I've made, what problems do you have?" Such people often have specific concerns that need to be dealt with before they can accept the fact that they have been fired.

Obviously, none of these approaches is a substitute for more thorough counseling, which can help employees understand what went wrong and what their future problems might be, but this kind of help is best given by a third-party outplacement specialist. The manager and employee have not been able to resolve their problems in the past. It is most unlikely that the termination interview will result in any new insights.

Remember, the purpose of the termination interview is not counseling. Rather, it is to communicate the decision that has been made and, as much as possible, to encourage the employee to accept it. If at all possible, dismissed employees should leave recognizing that their energies need to be directed toward finding new employment and understanding their exact status with the former employer.

Step 4. Discuss the Support Package

Once the employee seems prepared to discuss the fact of termination, the manager should review the elements of the support package. It is best for the manager to make an outline of points to cover, to be sure that important areas are not omitted.

Severance payments, benefits, access to office support people, and how recommendations will be handled should all be explained. The manager should answer all questions about the specifics of the package, but no promises or benefits beyond those in the package should be implied.

If the discharged individual tries to negotiate other arrangements, the manager should simply state that the package cannot be negotiated. The manager should avoid promising to "look into" anything. This merely complicates the termination process further. Only when the manager cannot answer specific questions about the support package should the manager make a note of the question and promise that the company will get back to the employee about it.

If, after the interview is over, the manager feels that something can legitimately be added to the support package, it can always be discussed with the appropriate company officials and, if it is approved, the former employee can be notified. However, the manager should avoid creating such obligations during the termination interview. This is important, since managers are often inclined to make such promises.

At the conclusion of this step, the manager gives the discharged individual the letter spelling out the support package that is provided. A termination interview should never be unnecessarily prolonged. Once it is clear the employee understands the situation, and the essential bases have been covered, the manager should bring the discussion to a close. Typically, the discussion will last approximately twenty minutes, although managers conducting such discussions should not schedule their time tightly.

Step 5. Specifically Define the Next Step

People who have been fired are often disoriented and unsure of what to do next. For example, there is the awkward question of where to go. Do they go back to their desks for the day, clean them out and leave, or simply leave the premises and have their personal things forwarded?

These questions point up the advantages of having the employee meet with an outplacement specialist immediately upon leaving the manager's office. The specialist can help employees deal with their feelings in a way that, by the nature of the situation, the boss cannot.

Meeting with an outplacement counselor privately gives dismissed employees a place to go to collect their thoughts and plan their next steps. They can decide whether to get their belongings and what to tell their families. They can begin planning what they are going to do the next morning. Because of the critical nature of the hours immediately following the termination interview, we strongly suggest that an opportunity to meet with a specialized counselor be provided.

When such help is available, the manager can indicate that the company is providing such assistance at no cost to the discharged employee and that the counselor is prepared to meet with the employee now. Employees almost always accept the counseling, and the manager can then introduce the employee to the outplacement specialist.

In the absence of such counseling resources, the manager is less able to facilitate the employee's next step. However, three points should be emphasized.

• *Discuss where they should go upon leaving the manager's office.* This should be discussed in some detail, since they are most likely to be confused about what happens now. We suggest that the manager give employees the option of leaving immediately or remaining for the day and organizing their personal things. Most people opt to spend a few hours collecting their possessions and their thoughts before leaving the office. An exception to this approach must be made when the employee's past behavior suggests he or she might do something to damage the company or be actively disruptive with other personnel. But in general, forcing the employee off the premises does little good for the company or the individual, and does not sit well with peers when they hear of it. Forget about waxing eloquent on the subject of teamwork after having a security guard escort a former member of the team out the door. Still, this is how many organizations handle discharged people.

• *Remind them of their company contact.* Repeat the name of the person the discharged employee should contact about questions concerning the support package or references. The name of this contact person should also be included in the letter describing the severance package. This provides a minimum level of psychological support.

• *Advise them to avoid precipitous action.* Suggest that they develop an action plan before getting in touch with friends and valuable industry contacts. Remind them that their support package means they will not starve tomorrow. Encourage them to consider their options, develop a resume along with a job search plan, and then start making their availability known. Beyond this, there is little the manager can do. At this stage, the interview should end.

The termination interview is always difficult; however, the above approach can make it as professional as possible. A worksheet to help the manager prepare for and structure the termination interview is presented in Exhibit 6.1.

Exhibit 6-1. Worksheet for Preparing a Termination Interview

Before the interview, fill out this worksheet to prepare yourself.

1. How many discussions have been held with the employee about the problem? _____ Are they documented?
2. How many negative performance appraisals exist? _____
3. Has the termination been discussed by management and personnel? _____
4. Has a letter describing the support package been written? _____

   Do you have an outline of the key elements of the support package? _____

5. Have you reviewed the possible reactions? _____

6. GET TO THE POINT. Opening line: _____

_____

_____

_____

7. DESCRIBE THE SITUATION. Three examples: What events are causing the termination? How frequently have they been observed? What were the observable consequences? _____

_____

_____

8. Details of the severance support package: _____

_____

9. Next step: _____

_____

_____

Some Difficult Questions

It is extremely important to provide correct and consistent answers to questions posed by discharged employees. Consequently, a manager's questions about benefits, unemployment compensation, or other support package items should be referred to a professional in the personnel department who is familiar with the case. Other questions often raised are presented below along with some examples of answers. Before a firing, managers should review the policy aspects of these questions with their superiors and the personnel department. The answers below make certain assumptions about company policy and are not appropriate for all corporate situations. However, anticipation of such questions, along with review and clearance of the answers, is basic preparation for the severance discussion.

Question: What recourse do I have?

Answer: Employees are always free to use the open door process (or other appeal process), but since this decision has been made with the concurrence of upper levels of management and with a thorough review of the history of the situation, any appeal process pursued is unlikely to alter the outcome.

Question: I want to talk with Mr. X (the manager's boss or higher).

Answer: Of course you are free to make an appointment to see him, but I must tell you that he's fully aware of the decision and supports it.

Question: How can you do this to me after all these years?

Answer: This decision was made for the specific reasons I stated earlier, all of which I have discussed with you previously.

Question: I don't want to talk about this without my lawyer.

Answer: You are, of course, free to have a legal representative contact us. However, our present commitment is to help you get reestablished as quickly as possible in something that makes sense for you, with the least disruption to your career and family. We strongly suggest that you keep appointments with the personnel representatives and the outplacement assistance counselors. (Lawyers who contact the manager should be referred to the office of legal counsel without comment. Simply say "As a matter of policy, I have to refer you to legal counsel.")

Question: With a company this big, I can't understand why I can't be moved someplace else.

Answer: Before this decision was made, all other options were given careful consideration. Given the specifics of the situation, we are confident this is the best decision.

Question: Can I continue to work for a period of time?

Answer: No. We feel it is in your best interest and the company's that you use your time to explore employment opportunities outside the company.

Question: Will you write a letter of recommendation for me?

Answer: By policy, the company limits the release of personal information to external requestors. Personnel will provide you with information regarding the type and amount of information that you can elect to have released and will work out an agreed-upon letter of recommendation.

Question: May I take my salary continuance in a lump sum?

Answer: No. Salary continuance is provided as a means of helping you over a transitional period during which it is hoped that you will find alternate employment.

Question: If I find another job, what is the status of my salary continuance?

Answer: When you find new employment, you are required to notify the company. Since salary continuance is intended to be a transitional payment between jobs, it will cease when you obtain new employment.

Question: Can I be rehired? Can I be redeployed?

Answer: You are not eligible for rehire. You should concentrate on finding employment outside the company.

Statement: You're not going to get away with this; I'm going to get even with you!

Answer: I'm sorry you feel that strongly, but I want to re-emphasize that we are committed to helping you begin the process of reestablishing yourself. I strongly urge you, regardless of your feelings now, to keep the appointment with the outplacement consultant.

Once again, it is important to emphasize that this imagined dialogue is presented for purposes of illustration and to help prepare managers for the kinds of questions that might be encountered. In answering similar questions, the themes that should be repeatedly communicated are:

- This decision was not arbitrary but the final result of a deliberative process that has been reviewed by management.
- We recognize your rights but regard the decision as fair and final.
- Beginning now, we think you need to be concerned with finding future employment elsewhere; that is the constructive area in which to expend your energies.

7

What Is Outplacement Counseling?

FOR THE PERSON WHO IS DISMISSED, THE TERmination interview is the beginning of a personal ordeal. Searching for work can be one of the most ego-deflating experiences in life. Unfortunately, this ordeal is often intensified by a lack of knowledge about the job search process. Mistakes and lost opportunities unnecessarily extend the period of unemployment, and if the individual has difficulties of a personal nature, the problems are compounded. To ease the departure of discharged personnel and their transition to a new situation, many companies are beginning to recognize the need to provide systematic support beyond the termination interview. Increasingly, companies are looking to outplacement counseling as a vehicle for providing this support.

Outplacement counseling (OPC) is systematic training for people who have been fired or otherwise terminated, in the techniques of securing appropriate new employment. Contrary to popular misconception, outplacement counseling does not assume responsibility for placing the discharged person in a new job. It is solely a counseling service whose purpose is to provide advice, instruction, and a sounding board to help the dismissed person organize and execute a job search program. We hope that by now the possible value of such counseling is evident to the reader.

The pyramid shown in Exhibit 7.1 represents a step-by-step approach to obtaining a new job. Usually, questions emerge as a person wrestles with each step in the process. The outplacement counselor is a resource to help the individual think through the answers. Indeed, providing direction through a systematic approach is an important contribution of the counselor.

Internal vs. External Specialists

In choosing to offer outplacement counseling as part of the severance package, management has to decide whether to use outside consultants or internal specialists. As with any service, there are advantages and disadvantages associated with both options.

Most external consultants are experienced in a wide range of industries, and in many companies they enjoy a level of credibility that is not granted to the internal specialist. As one personnel director remarked: "The history of this company is such that involvement of consultants is a signal that a new program is being taken seriously by management."

When handling sensitive outplacements, outside consultants can often get management to agree to conditions that an internal specialist might suggest but be reluctant to push. Furthermore, since external outplacement consultants are not employees of the company, it is often easier for them to gain the confidence of the dismissed employee. The outside consultant is often viewed as less biased in the whole process.

Many internal specialists, on the other hand, have won considerable respect for their expertise within their organizations. Moreover, there are specific advantages to internal specialists. They can respond readily to the needs of their organizations. As

Exhibit 7.1 Approach to Finding a New Job

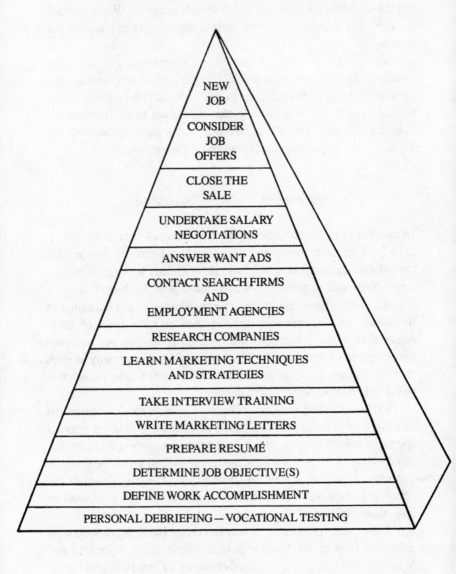

NEW
JOB

CONSIDER
JOB
OFFERS

CLOSE THE
SALE

UNDERTAKE SALARY
NEGOTIATIONS

ANSWER WANT ADS

CONTACT SEARCH FIRMS
AND
EMPLOYMENT AGENCIES

RESEARCH COMPANIES

LEARN MARKETING TECHNIQUES
AND STRATEGIES

TAKE INTERVIEW TRAINING

WRITE MARKETING LETTERS

PREPARE RESUMÉ

DETERMINE JOB OBJECTIVE(S)

DEFINE WORK ACCOMPLISHMENT

PERSONAL DEBRIEFING — VOCATIONAL TESTING

company employees, they can often spot problem areas in termination practices that might elude outside consultants. Usually,
their expertise is based on the establishment and maintenance of
corporate termination policies in advance of termination interviews. By contrast, outside consultants are seldom retained much
before an actual termination is to occur. Thus, they can have
only a minimal impact on the events that preceded the decision
to let the person go.

Many companies use a combination of internal and external
specialists. Internal specialists develop and maintain corporate
policy in this area, often in collaboration with outside consultants. They also handle much of the OPC work within the corporation. External consultants are employed for special cases,
such as the termination of senior executives or employees with
particular problems.

OPC as Part of the Support Package

Whether internal or external experts are used, an outplacement
program should be part of the support package offered to the
person being let go. The manager firing the employee should explain that the company offers an outplacement service should the
employee choose to use it. The financial benefits of the support
package should remain the same regardless of whether or not
counseling is accepted. In our experience, virtually everyone
chooses to use OPC.

The manager holding the termination interview should describe the general scope of the outplacement services at the conclusion of the interview, and a counselor should be available to
meet with the dismissed person immediately afterward. Thus, the
next step after the termination interview is getting together with
an OPC counselor.

The availability of OPC takes some of the pressure off the
manager dismissing the employee. Knowing that counseling is

available, the manager is less likely to make ill-advised promises or similar mistakes. Furthermore, the next step becomes a structured one—meeting the counselor—and therefore less awkward. Finally, the counselor takes over from the manager the task of helping the person think through or vent feelings about the company. Thus, OPC is particularly relevant for the more difficult reactions, such as avoidance, which the average manager is unlikely to deal with adequately during the termination interview.

Identifying the Client

For the outplacement counselor to be effective, the discharged employee must be the client throughout the counseling process, even though the company terminating the employee is sponsoring the service. True, the company absorbs the expense, but the counselor's first professional concern is with the discharged employee who is the recipient of the service.

One of the counselor's most important tasks is to clarify this relationship with the employee being let go. It is critical that the individual believe that the counselor's suggestions are intended solely for his or her benefit.

For example, one outplacement client believed that the counselor's job was in part to support the company's reasons for terminating him. Thus, he continually resisted feedback from the counselor regarding personal characteristics that might hinder his job search. Most of the counselor's suggestions were met by quiet resistance. Finally, after one rather severe criticism, the client shot back, "Look, you have to say that because they are paying you to." At this point, counselor and client confronted the issue head on. After a half hour of discussion, the matter was resolved, and matters went more smoothly in later sessions.

Another client suspected that the counselor's job was to direct her away from certain competitors. Once again, the depth of her suspicions only became evident after a couple of meetings with the counselor. As the client remained distant, showing little enthusiasm for what they were discussing, the counselor finally confronted her directly, saying, "I don't feel that you're convinced this process will help you. Let's talk about how you feel toward what we're doing here." Eventually, the client said, "Look, some of your ideas make sense, but you're working for the company, and I have to watch out for my own best interests." In the ensuing discussion, it became clear that she felt the counselor was advising her to consider a range of alternative career possibilities in a covert effort to steer her away from the competition. Once the problem was on the table, the counselor pointed out how many people in similar jobs moved from her company to the competition every year (and vice versa). Her company had little to gain by attempting to influence her job search, and if it had, there were more direct methods, such as placing her previous performance in the harshest possible light, which would be more likely to work. Gradually, the client came to trust her counselor.

Usually, problems of this nature can be resolved during the initial meeting as long as counselors clarify their role and answer questions in a straightforward manner. Experienced outplacement counselors are sensitive to the need to establish relationships of trust between themselves and the individuals being terminated. An external counselor may have an advantage over an internal specialist in this respect. When a terminated employee is especially paranoid about his or her former company, an outside counselor often can gain the person's confidence simply by not being one of its employees.

Intense mistrust is often fueled by the discharged person's imagination. Having been rejected, discharged employees often rationalize their unconscious feelings by believing the company must protect itself from them. They see themselves as powerful and capable of harming the company rather than weak and vulnerable. This skewed perception is a source of psychological comfort as well as an outlet for hostility. The counselor's job is to enable them to move beyond such irrational beliefs and channel their hostility into constructive action—finding jobs in which they can succeed. For this relationship to work, the counselor's efforts must be persuasively directed toward the client's best interests.

Of course, in developing policy and practice as well as in counseling managers on how to conduct termination interviews, the outplacement counselor's client is management. But in all meetings with discharged employees, the counselor's primary consulting responsibilities are to those particular individuals.

Thus, the outplacement counselor must recognize changing responsibilities in moving from one consulting arena to another within the same organization. This is a skill all management consultants (internal or external) must have if they are to sustain relationships on any sensitive project.

What Constitutes an Outplacement Program?

A complete outplacement program includes a variety of services that meet the needs of both the company and the person being let go. Depending on the circumstances of termination, some services may be more valuable than others. But the capacity to deliver them all is characteristic of a true outplacement service.

Pretermination Consultation

The outplacement specialist usually comes into the picture too late in the termination process. Ideally, this specialist can offer advice long before the decision to dismiss someone is final, principally by helping the manager consider all the available alternatives and by making sure that the approach taken is objective and consistent with sound corporate policy.

In such a role, corporate outplacement counselors function as advisers to operating management on human-resource problems. They become a resource that management can use in reviewing its problems with poor performers, a difficult area of personnel practice, that is as important as recruiting, fair employment, affirmative action, compensation, and training and development.

All outplacement counselors have encountered cases in which, had things been handled differently, termination might have been avoided. To be effective, the OPC specialist must be viewed by managers as capable of providing valuable input on human-resource development from a perspective broader than termination issues alone.

Whenever possible, the OPC specialist should work closely with the senior personnel officer in establishing corporate termination policy and procedures. Although ideal, involvement in such issues is not the norm. More typically, OPC counselors enter a situation when the events leading to the termination have not been well managed. In fact, the counselor is being asked to "pick up the pieces" that are expected to fall as a result of the termination.

Often individual circumstances complicate the termination problem: the subordinate is especially argumentative, is a member of a protected class, or has considerable seniority with the company. Perhaps the manager who has to do the firing simply has cold feet and needs some extra support.

Usually what each of these situations has in common is that the OPC specialist doesn't become involved until it is too late to influence prior performance counseling with the subordinate or to monitor compliance with corporate policy. Placed in a crisis situation after most of the significant decisions have been made, the specialist's job is to help management avoid or minimize the negative consequences of a less-than-ideal set of circumstances.

At that point pretermination consultation is limited to:

- Reviewing the support package and pointing out any areas that might have been overlooked (such as failure to specify references—a typical one).

- Attaining agreement that the OPC counselor will approach management later with any request for adjustments in the support package that might prove important to the person being terminated (while cautioning management against agreeing to changes during the termination interview itself).
- Reviewing the reasons the manager intends to give for firing the subordinate, making sure they are as descriptive and specific as possible.
- Preparing the manager to conduct the interview.

In pretermination consultation, the OPC specialist tries to insure that the person being let go is treated as professionally as possible by management and that managers avoid falling into typical traps that will complicate the process. Achieving these aims is a vital part of the OPC service.

Vocational and Career Path Counseling

People who have just been fired have one overwhelming problem: to find another job. Right at the start of the job search process, they have to settle several questions. They have to define the type of job they are going to pursue and the geographic location they are willing to accept. Indeed, if they are to take full advantage of a basically negative situation, they should examine their careers carefully and perhaps redefine some of their career goals and job objectives. This is a good time to do a thorough self-assessment and to decide on any changes they want to make.

This may be the first time they have ever given thought to the direction of their career. Outplacement counselors frequently encounter people who in college decided to major in a given area, fell into their first jobs pretty much by chance, and began pursuing whatever career ladder those jobs seemed to afford them. In fact, most studies indicate that this is the typical pattern of career choice. An employee has often been drifting for some time before being terminated.

Today, there is a growing literature on career development that reflects our increasingly sophisticated understanding of the career process. Thus the outplacement counselor should be capable of providing the dismissed employee with appropriate career guidance.

Management Style Counseling

Often managers are fired because their management style is so inflexible that they encounter continual problems with subordinates, superiors, or peers. Failure to receive constructive feedback on this problem can lead to a pattern of job losses, with each job loss directly traceable to the individual's management style.

Outplacement counselors should be capable of addressing this issue. When they are not, they should have access to others who are in a position to offer assistance.

At this point, the outplacement process overlaps with aspects of management development work. There is reason to believe that a person's management style is not something that can easily be altered, especially in a short period of time. However, it is incumbent on the OPC counselor to make managers aware of their problems in this area so that they can attempt to address their weaknesses in the years ahead. The counselor can do such things as:

- Create awareness of the problem.
- Focus on a few critical behaviors.
- Create understanding of favorable environments.

Create Awareness of the Problem

Management style inventories can be used to help managers see how their style comes across to others. These are typically completed as part of a total assessment package. While psychological assessment instruments are discussed with the client by a licensed psychologist, management style inventories can be utilized by both the psychologist and the counselor working with the client. They are especially helpful if the data can be coupled with specific examples of the consequences of the manager's approach on the job. These need to be developed from the manager's past performance record and can be made available to the counselor by the manager's previous boss. Anything discussed, of course, must be consistent with what was presented in performance reviews and the termination interview.

Focus on a Few Critical Behaviors

Although the outplacement process is not designed to generate major changes in behavior, it is often possible to identify one or two critical behavior patterns that, if controlled or altered, can make a difference in future job performance.

For example, one OPC client whom we'll call Jim was too rigid in his thinking. He always viewed issues in "either/or" terms, not dealing well with ambiguity. Once his mind was made up about some issue, he resisted the efforts of others to point out possible alternate courses of action. Since he tended to arrive at a decision early in a discussion, his subordinates saw him as arbitrary and close-minded. His superiors viewed him as impatient and argumentative. More to the point, his decisions often rendered his department ineffective. Ultimately, these personal characteristics cost him his job.

Initially, Jim resisted feedback from his counselor about his behavior, preferring to see himself as decisive rather than opinionated and rigid. Gradually, with the help of examples, he came to accept that his decisiveness was getting him into difficulties. Working with his counselor, he agreed to a strategy in which, once he had made up his mind, he would assume that for some reason he was blocked from following that particular course of action. What would his backup strategy be? It wasn't easy, but gradually he trained himself to look at another point of view. The end result was a less arbitrary approach to issues.

In similar ways, counseling oriented to behavior change can help outplacement clients avoid repeating some of their past mistakes.

Create Understanding of Favorable Environments

Apart from attempting to alter certain pronounced aspects of management style, the outplacement process should help managers understand their strengths and weaknesses. For example, someone with a tendency to overcontrol people, while striving to prevent this tendency from becoming extreme, can also work toward finding a job situation in which the characteristic is more likely to be a strength than a weakness. The situation might be one in which strong control over a disorganized department is required.

Psychological Assessment

A licensed psychologist should be available in case of need and to provide psychological assessment. Follow-up research with our clients indicates that help based on psychological assessment is one of the most valuable aspects of the OPC process. Indeed, such assessments have become increasingly standard in outplacement programs. All our individual clients take a battery of psychological assessment tests and have an interview and a feedback meeting with a licensed psychologist. The results of this process are coordinated with the counselor as appropriate. Also, when appropriate, subsequent sessions may be held with the psychologist.

Job Search Expertise

The heart of the outplacement counseling process is helping a person learn and execute the mechanics of an effective job search. This means that OPC specialists need extensive experience in resume planning, development, and circulation. They must also possess expertise in interviewing techniques. The job seeker should be able to turn to the counselor with questions about any of the many dilemmas that confront those in the process of looking for a position. The needs of the employee in this area are discussed more fully in Chapter Eight. Working together, the counselor and terminated employee can forge an individualized marketing strategy.

Secretarial Services

A major need during a job search is secretarial support. A job seeker must have access to someone who can type letters and resumes and take messages. Doing these things personally generally wastes valuable time and often gives potential employers an impression of poor organization. If the company has not arranged for such support, the outplacement service should provide it.

Job Development

One of the changes in OPC practice during the 1980's has been the establishment of job development efforts by the outplacement firms. Firms actively solicit job listings through various sources. These are then organized into a "job lead bank." It is important to recognize that the firms are not functioning as recruiters. Such activity is still regarded as a conflict of interest. Nor do reputable firms guarantee jobs for the simple reason that only the clients themselves can successfully complete a job search. Indeed, it is getting the person to accept responsibility for their employment search and preparing them to execute it effectively which is at the heart of the OPC concept. What the firms are doing is providing information which is a valuable asset to the job search process.

Access to Data Bases

Like many fields, OPC has been significantly impacted by the application of information technology during the 1980's. Today outplacement counselors no longer just tell clients how to use information to their advantage and encourage them to search it out, but provide on-site access to many important data bases. The result has been the automated job search. With the availability of information processing technology has come a myriad of valuable data bases including those on industries, professional contacts, job markets and sources of capital funding. For example, a client interested in starting his or her own business can learn where and what funding is available and even initiate the process without leaving the office.

In one instance the C.E.O. of a corporation suddenly arranged to travel to Connecticut on a Saturday morning to meet with a senior level client who had been identified as a strong possibility for heading up one of the company's operating divisions. This all fell into place late in the day on Friday. Obviously the client was anxious to make a very favorable initial impression. Through such data bases the client was able to access a wide range of information such as press reports, financial information and biographical material on the C.E.O. and other senior officers. He was well prepared for his meeting at 10:00 A.M. the next morning with the C.E.O.

The impact of these systems has been two fold. First, job candidates are making stronger presentations during their job searches than in the past. Second, for competitive reasons professional OPC firms must supplement counseling with technological access to these data bases in their offices.

Continuous Access for the Counselee Until Placement

The job-search process consists of a series of operations. It is clear that employees can use support for more than the first few days after the termination. Of course, the first few days call for the most active and intensive support. During this time, a structured counseling program can provide clients with significant insights into both their past job performance and the nature of the problems that now confront them.

However, beyond this early learning process, clients have a continuous need to be in touch with a counselor in order to ask questions that relate to their marketing strategies or the process of finalizing a job. Indeed, the lack of someone to talk to who is knowledgeable about these kinds of issues is often a major problem confronting an unemployed person.

This being the case, the extent to which periodic conversations with a counselor are provided largely determines the helpfulness of the outplacement support. Although the discharged person will need less extensive help from the counselor once actively looking for work, the program should allow for continued availability of the counselor. This type of continuing support is most easily provided by external consultants.

Continuous Feedback to Management Until Placement

Even when employees have been dismissed, most managers find themselves wondering what progress they are making toward finding a job. Having gone to the effort of arranging for outplacement support, management can reasonably expect to be informed of the ex-employee's status. This has the advantage of satisfying the organization's need to assess the value of the outplacement counseling.

8

Counseling the Terminated Executive

F OR THE AVERAGE EXECUTIVE, UNEMPLOY-
ment and searching for a job are rare experiences. Many
managers never encounter the problem; others face it only
once or twice in their careers. Leaving one company to join another does not count, nor does soliciting job opportunities while
solidly employed. The problems and pressures confronting the
discharged executive are more extensive, more intense, and very
different from those experienced in either of the other two situations.

Therefore, it is reasonable to expect a manager to be naive
about the details of conducting a job search when he or she has
been terminated. The problem has not come up before, or if it
has, not recently.

On the other hand, corporations are regularly besieged by
managers looking for work. They hire people on a regular basis.
Typically, formal systems are in place that give the companies an
aura of sophistication and competence often markedly lacking in
the approach of the applicant. This contrast is magnified by the

fact that the job-seeking executive is more anxious about being hired than the corporation is about making an employment decision. Thus, even the most experienced managers often appear naive and amateurish as they enter the job market.

Problems apart from the job search process can exacerbate the situation. If there have been problems at work, these difficulties can have an unsettling effect on other areas of an executive's life. And work performance can, of course, be the result of domestic troubles. Either way, problems on the job often indicate difficulties in an individual's personal life as well.

Moreover, the terminated executive is often in a state of shock. As noted in previous chapters, the executive may or may not receive emotional support from family members. In either case the situation is awkward for all concerned as the executive tries to protect a damaged ego. Typically, questions of self-worth are seldom far from his or her mind.

If the termination was not well handled, the executive is probably confused about what went wrong on the job. Anger, resentment, or bitterness can find expression in counterproductive ways. In short, the need for counseling goes beyond "how to find a job."

Two Case Histories

Harry was a general foreman in a large production facility who had been on the job for more than fifteen years with very little training. There was a change in management and Harry was discharged. In typical fashion, he was fired on a Friday afternoon.

When he arrived at the counselor's office on Monday morning at ten o'clock, Harry was noticeably shaken; in fact, he was physically shaking and he stammered throughout the interview. For two hours he went on about how the company was his life and how he never thought he would be fired. He continually stated that he would never get another job.

As so often happens, the outplacement counselor had had no opportunity to work with the firm prior to the termination. The firm contacted the counselor on the day before the firing, with the termination process already set in motion. It appeared that the new management felt Harry represented an old philosophy that had prevented the company from growing. In essence, Harry was a symbolic figure, and getting rid of him meant getting rid of "old" attitudes.

The termination had completely destroyed Harry's self-confidence. Coming from a situation that provided little training or development, he was convinced he would be uncompetitive in the job market. Even if he were hired, Harry felt he would be unable to make the grade. That was how he interpreted his being singled out by the new management's "housecleaning."

In truth, Harry was not the most attractive job candidate. But he had fifteen years of experience. What he needed was help in targeting his job opportunities and in selling himself. And first, he had to see that he had something to sell.

It took thirty hours of counseling before Harry felt prepared to face a job interview. During this counseling, Harry came to understand that in a production situation he had many strengths. He was strong technically; he could deal with other supervisors effectively; and he had a strong record in cost control. He was also capable of learning new techniques and functioning in a different environment.

After eight months, Harry found a job both he and his counselor felt he could handle. During those eight months, he received sixty-three hours of personal counseling. This substantial effort proved to be the deciding factor in rebuilding his confidence to the point where he could go out and find a job. Harry's belief was that counseling helped him hold his life together during this crisis. Four years later, he was still employed and happy with his job.

Jane's story is somewhat different. Jane was a high-level executive with an Ivy League background. She was fired from her job after a decline in her job performance over a period of three years. After pretermination counseling, she was terminated on a Thursday afternoon and met with the outplacement counselor immediately afterward. The next day she started her formal outplacement counseling program.

During the first week of counseling, Jane mentioned that there had been increasing stress in her home life over the past few years. She felt her family situation was deteriorating, and her unemployment was placing still more strain on the relationship with her husband. There was an element of desperation in her comments. Having lost her job, she feared her marriage was coming apart as well.

The counselor invited her husband to spend time with the psychologist and the counselor working with his wife. Discussions with him uncovered a lot of hostility, much of it centered on feelings of exclusion from his wife's working life. He felt that her career was consuming her, that she was not sharing her life with him. There was reason to believe that the undercurrent of stress at home was contributing to Jane's problems on the job. She was aware of the tension but didn't understand it or know how to deal with it.

In this instance, counseling was directed toward both Jane and her husband. The couple examined their marriage and how they used their time together. Their relationship was reestablished, and Jane obtained a new executive position with an increase in compensation.

In both cases, the fired individual had to overcome obstacles other than the immediately obvious one of finding new employment. Harry lacked the confidence even to begin looking for a job. His previous work situation, coupled with the mishandling of the termination, had destroyed something very basic—his sense of competence. All the years of working in supervision without the benefit of opportunities for development had created in Harry a dependency on the company. Suddenly cut loose, without warning and as a symbol of "what is wrong around here," Harry had no concept of what else he could do.

Jane, on the other hand, was fighting a battle on two fronts. Her career was coming apart and her marriage was floundering. She had little insight into what was wrong in either case. Each was a distraction from the other. Jane had made all the right moves, yet things seemed to have turned out wrong.

Clearly, Harry was in no position to be effective in job interviews. Jane's position wasn't much better. They had to sell themselves, yet unlike the last time they went after a job, they had real doubts about their ability to deliver.

The Role of the Outplacement Counselor

What are the implications for the counselor? From both of these cases, we can see that outplacement counseling is more than simply job search coaching. The termination process can intensify and bring to the surface problems that hinder an individual's ability to find as well as keep a job. But counselors should resist any tendency to play the role of lay psychologist. They should avoid becoming involved in problems that go beyond their expertise. In the emotionally charged atmosphere of a termination, it is as easy to do harm as good.

What counselors need is the sensitivity to perceive the pressures that come to bear on the terminated executive and the willingness to recognize when these pressures are best handled by another professional. Throughout the process the counselor needs perseverance in providing support and direction to the client, even when the job search process seems stalled.

For example, one man—we'll call him Mike—was, at the age of 61, described by his boss as "plateaued out." After his termination was completed, the company decided to provide outplacement counseling in deference to Mike's thirty-three years with the company. Holding the title of Director, Finance Department, at the time of his termination, Mike vowed not to accept retirement.

The counseling process with Mike continued over two years,

during which the counselor and Mike met periodically. During these meetings the counselor made suggestions for using what was becoming a wide network of contacts and discussed methods for turning a seeming disadvantage—age—into a strength. Perhaps more importantly, the counselor helped Mike clarify his reasons for not retiring and identify the type of company that might be most interested in his services. For much of the two years, the counselor was mainly a source of moral support, someone who would intervene when Mike's frustration led to sloppiness in his search efforts. At the age of 63, Mike obtained a job as manager of internal control in a small company that needed his expertise. Three years later, Mike was flourishing, along with his new company.

Except for the age factor, which complicated his situation by eliminating many employment opportunities, Mike's case typifies the role of the outplacement counselor. The counselor recognizes the motivations and needs of the discharged person and provides direction within the framework of these needs. The counselor recognized the importance of Mike's desire to continue working; Mike's work was what Mike knew and how he defined himself. At the same time, the counselor gave Mike realistic advice on the possibilities open to him.

Harry's case afforded the same challenge to the counselor. Harry needed concrete help in defining himself correctly in the job market. He also needed the skills and perseverance to market himself correctly.

In the case of Jane, the outplacement counselor perceived problems apart from the workplace and therefore recommended that Jane and her husband consult a psychologist who was trained to deal with the issues involved. Effective outplacement counselors must be prepared to refer people to psychologists or psychiatrists when problems outside their competence emerge.

The neutral but supportive role of the outplacement counselor is one to which it is sometimes difficult to adhere. Once a relationship of trust is established, it is easy for counselors to delve into areas in which they have little or no training. At the other extreme, a counselor can be so intent at fitting a client into a "packaged" job search process that important issues are ignored. Clearly, the middle ground is marked by ambiguity. In each case, the professional outplacement counselor strives to adjust to the situation at hand, always mindful of the need for using other professional resources.

A Model for Outplacement Counseling

An effective counseling relationship does not happen by chance. The successful counselor works hard at it. As in any area of sensitive interpersonal communication, it is helpful for counselors to have a model that can assist in structuring their relationship with the client. The model offered below summarizes the steps counselors may go through during the course of an OPC relationship.

Step 1. Initial Meeting
- Greeting
- Diffusing feelings
- Establishing trust and confidence

Step 2. Self-Analysis and Job Search Counseling
- Assessment
- Getting organized
- Developing a personal marketing game plan
- Selling one's abilities

Step 3. Monitoring

Step 1. Initial Meeting

Outplacement counselors meet clients in any number of circumstances, although two occur most frequently. First, and preferred, the dismissed executive meets the counselor immediately after the termination interview. This meeting can take place in a conference room or in a private office on the company's premises, removed from the immediate work area of the person being discharged.

The meeting immediately following the interview permits the counselor to deal with the discharged individual's initial reaction to the termination. Many individuals who have just been fired panic and immediately begin calling their friends and industry contacts, even though at this point they are seldom in a position to use these contacts wisely. Thus, all they accomplish is alerting contacts to their distress. Others are more concerned about what to tell friends and family. Making the counselor available right after the termination interview provides a resource when many people need one most.

The second place for the initial meeting is at the counselor's office, usually a day after the termination. This arrangement obviously makes it impossible for the counselor to help during the first twelve to twenty-four hours after the firing. Companies usually make such arrangements in the belief that they simplify the termination process by making it possible to ask the discharged person to leave the premises immediately. However, because it precludes assistance immediately after the firing, we do not recommend this approach.

Increasingly, companies are letting terminated executives "shop" for OPC services. These executives meet with more than one firm, review the services and facilities of each, and select the firm they want to use. The selection process allows the affected individuals to pick the professionals who will help them deal with this difficult transition in their lives. Generally, one immediate consequence of the choice is an increase in the initial level of commitment to the counselor. A drawback, however, is that it precludes any help with the initial shock and requires a traumatized individual to make an important decision while under the pressure of job loss.

It is the on-site post-termination meeting that affords the best opportunity to help the discharged client. Such meetings have, of course, many inherent pressures requiring sound counseling skills. The client typically is still in a state of shock and is confused, angry, and/or defensive. Most clients will at least allow the counselor to help, however, and on some occasions the client will be eager for assistance.

The counselor must be prepared for whatever reactions the client may exhibit. The sponsor company expects the counselor to "handle the situation," which translates into helping the executive "accept" the termination and preventing him or her from doing anything foolhardy or irrational. Essentially, the company's need is to have the aftermath of the event managed and under control.

Greeting (or What Do You Say After You Say Hello?)

The counselor should greet the terminated executive with direct eye contact (implying confidence in handling this emotionally charged meeting), a firm handshake, and a simple "Hello, my name is _____. I'd like to talk with you about how I might be able to help you." Some introductory remarks as simple and direct as these should suffice as an icebreaker.

Care should be taken not to express thoughtlessly cordial greetings like: "How are you?" "It's a pleasure to meet you," or "How do you do?" It's obvious the client is not feeling fine and it's not a pleasure to meet under the circumstances. Also avoid platitudes and weak attempts to comfort such as: "I'm sorry this happened," "You'll get over it in time," "Don't worry, it's probably the best thing," and "Don't worry, you'll probably find another job."

Typically, the terminating manager or the human-resource representative will leave the counselor alone with the terminee. *Feeling* statements or questions are helpful in establishing empathy with the client, such as: "This must be difficult." "You must be upset/shocked/etc.," "How do you feel about what's happened?" "Do you feel like talking about what led up to this?"

Diffusing Feelings

To questions like "How do you feel?" expect angry reactions such as "How would you feel?" "What do you expect?" or—silence. A counselor must be patient and compassionate with newly terminated individuals: they have been rejected, hurt, and stripped of personal and professional security. They feel the loss immediately—as in any grief reaction (loss of loved one, home, or health). For the moment, a crisis has been created by the organization. The counselor's task is to minimize the impact of the shock by providing support and continuity to the client.

The complexity of emotions and thoughts that can result from being terminated is enormous. The shock of termination induces feelings of:

Anger:	"We'll see about this. Does the Chairman know about this?"
Grief:	"What am I going to do now? I can't handle this now."
Disbelief:	"I don't believe it!"
Guilt:	"This is all my fault. I always screw things up."
Relief:	"Thank God it's over."
Acceptance:	"It was going to happen. I expected it."

Experience has shown that shock compounds and complicates human emotions, creating considerable confusion in the client; often rapid-fire thoughts and feelings erupt almost simultaneously. The consultant needs to be sensitive to this complexity and to be mindful that many emotions can be triggered at this time. Such intense feelings are not usually rational, so arguing or telling the client to be logical serves no purpose. Client reactions to the on-site counselor derive from the termination circumstances, so the counselor should not take umbrage at abrupt, curt, or strained conversation.

How does the counselor handle these shocked and typically

irate clients? By earning their trust and confidence. Although shocked, most reach out for assistance. Of course, some are so angry they refuse to listen or flatly reject outside help. The majority, however, are willing to spend time with an OPC consultant, for OPC is perceived as helpful. Nevertheless, the meeting can be strained initially due to the trauma suffered by the client.

Until the client's emotions have been acknowledged and discussed, it is highly unlikely that he or she will listen to suggestions from the counselor or be able to focus on the necessary task ahead. The counselor should be prepared to employ crisis counseling techniques with these clients. Open-ended questions, accepting behaviors, restatement, and silence are the fundamental tools of such counseling.

Early in the meeting, it is usually best to restate feelings. For example, the counselor could make comments like the following:

Anger:	"Sounds like you're so mad, you're going to try and get a hearing."
Grief:	"I know this has upset you. I'd like to help you handle it by putting my professional experience at your disposal."
Disbelief:	"This caught you by surprise and I'm sure you're shocked."
Guilt:	"Blaming yourself for what happened is understandable, but I'd like you to see that it's not constructive in terms of what you have to do in the future—that is, find another job."
Relief:	"Sounds like you've been waiting for the other shoe to drop, and now that it has, you can move on."
Acceptance:	"It's great to see you handle this so well, but I wonder if you have any other feelings about it?"

Restatement helps convey empathy as well as encourage necessary discussion of reactions to the firing. Once these are aired, people are typically better able to assess their situation in a rational manner.

The most difficult client for a counselor to work with is the silent hostile kind who will say, "Okay, go ahead, I'm listening." In fact, these clients probably are not listening to the counselor, but listening instead to their own inner voices talking about how they are going to get even or what a rat the boss is and always has been. Similarly, when the initial reaction is euphoric or escapist, the dismissed person may adopt a posture of indifference. In these cases the counselor should go ahead and describe the OPC program while watching for openings to restate feelings.

Typically clients want to talk about how they feel once they get past their initial defense mechanism. The counselor needs to probe in an effort to get them to open up. One way of doing this is to explore the client's feelings about the event that has just transpired: "How were you treated in the separation meetings?" "How do you feel about what happened?" "Did you have any expectation that this might happen?" "What are your feelings about the company?" If the person initially avoids talking about his or her feelings, the counselor should attempt to overcome this avoidance with additional questions. For example:

Counselor: At this point, what are your feelings toward your old employer?

Client: Obviously, not good. But it doesn't do any good worrying about it, does it?

Counselor: It is often helpful to examine what went wrong. What events led up to your being let go?

Client: Events! Hell, the guy is impossible to work for! He never gives any meaningful direction to his people.

Counselor: You feel he isn't supportive.

Client: It's more than lack of support. . .

Once the client gets talking, there is usually plenty of hostility expressed, hostility that needs to be aired and discussed.

In this diffusion stage the counselor has two purposes. The first is to give clients an opportunity to ventilate and get off their chests issues that can otherwise serve as distractions. If these problems remain buried, they may not only impede preparation for the job search, but also surface at an inappropriate time. For example, one discharged executive felt considerable resentment toward her former employer. However, her initial statement was: "Things were not handled well and I got the short end of the stick, but that's over now and it's not worth talking about." Later, she let her anger come out at a social gathering within hearing distance of some influential people in her area of expertise. She came across as bitter and succeeded only in minimizing their willingness to refer her to contacts.

The counselor's second purpose at this stage is to listen carefully and attempt to identify those concerns that may be intensifying the client's reaction. As we saw earlier in this chapter with Harry, some clients may be afraid that they are not adequately trained to be competitive in the labor market. Family uncertainties or fears about age might intensify this reaction. Some people are concerned about saving face with colleagues and friends. Any of these fears can inhibit the development of a positive attitude on the client's part.

Thus, while the client is letting off steam, the counselor can get clues about genuine concerns. These concerns are critical to the success of the outplacement counseling process. Getting the client to express them is an important step in establishing trust and confidence in the counselor/client relationship.

We have been highlighting methods useful for getting the dismissed person who is closed, withdrawn, or evasive to talk. The opposite extreme is also encountered. One fired manager met the counselor in an agitated state. His opening comment was: "How can they do this? No warning! I was doing my job just like everyone else. Well, they aren't going to get away with this!" He proceeded to talk for half an hour about how unfair his boss was and how he was going to demand an explanation from senior management. After he had quieted down, the counselor told him that senior management was aware of the termination and that although he could request an audience with someone at a higher level it was not likely to change anything. The counselor advised him to treat his current status as a given and went on to briefly introduce the kind of help that was being offered through OPC. At this point the two began exploring the events that preceded the termination. This facilitated a further diffusion of feelings.

How might such a dialogue develop in practice? Following is an example of the greeting and diffusion phase of an on-site meeting.

Counselor: Hello. I'm _____. I'd like to talk with you about some ways I can help you.

Client: (Silence. Sits down, no eye contact.)

Counselor: You look like this hit you pretty hard. Can we talk about it?

Client: There's nothing to talk about. (Pause) I can't believe they did it. Some gratitude after all I've done to upgrade the Accounting Department. (Pause) This is what I get.

Counselor: Sounds like you worked hard and are upset because you feel you're being treated unfairly.

Client: (Silence)

Counselor: Look, I can see you've been hurt by what you just went through, and I can't say I blame you for being damned angry. However, since I would like to be your career consultant and assist you in finding a new position, I'd like to get to know you better. Would that be all right?

Client: Go ahead. What do you want to know? (hostilely)

Counselor: I can't expect you to get over your anger right away—so why don't we talk about why you think you were asked to leave.

Client: I should've left last year when the new V. P. of finance came. The president brought his old buddy in, and we've all had to live with his changes. He doesn't know the first thing about it.

Counselor: Part of what you are upset about is being unappreciated and passed over for promotion.

Client: (Silence) I just don't believe they pulled the plug . . . (chokes and becomes tearful)

Counselor: Nothing hurts more than being told you're not wanted . . . that's a real kick in the pants.

Client: (Silence)

Counselor: Look, I know this has been a blow to you—you're upset and angry—you'd like to get even—that's a natural reaction. However, one of the reasons I'm here is to help you, from this moment on, not to make any blunders regarding a new job search campaign.

Client: Blunders? I must have blundered this entire past year for this to happen.

Counselor: You didn't see it coming?

Client: I thought they were going to thank me for a good job done on our new conversion system. For two months I worked every night until nine to make the system work, and this is the thanks I get.

Counselor: This must have shocked you all the more. On the other hand, something hasn't worked out. How about that side of it?

Client: Bullshit! Not worked out? I wasn't getting the support I needed. They had no idea what I was contributing.

Counselor: And why was that?

Client: (Calms down) I guess I didn't play the politics. It wasn't that way before. When I joined under John

Miller six years ago, we didn't have to curry favor with the boss.

Counselor: With a new regime, things change. I hate to sound so logical when all you can think and feel is resentful. But then again that's my point. You need to handle this as professionally and gracefully as you can, because you do need them for references. And they have agreed to be positive references for you. That's critical to your search effort.

Client: What did they tell you about me?

Counselor: I met with them to arrange to see you immediately after your termination interview. They told me that it had not worked out and that your future lies elsewhere.

Establishing Trust and Confidence

To attain the trust and confidence of the client requires persuasion and salesmanship, which in turn require effective listening, sensitivity, compassion, and counseling expertise. The first step is establishing oneself as a willing listener. This is accomplished through the process we just described. Beyond the diffusion of feelings, the counselor can further establish trust and confidence by exploring with the client how and when to tell others about the situation (spouse, children, colleagues, friends, and neighbors), by describing the OPC program, and by establishing a mutual set of expectations about the program.

The message the counselor should convey throughout is: "I'm someone who sees this kind of situation all the time and who is willing to listen to your problems and share my experience with you."

In describing the services that will be provided, the counselor should give an overview, not a detailed explanation. This is especially true when meeting right after the termination interview, when typically the individual is too distressed and distracted to remember details. What the counselor needs to do is describe a structured program of constructive action to deal with the client's predicament. Counselors usually do this by outlining the major steps of the process and pointing out to the client that they have a place to go during the next workday. The discussion should cover both the types of services that will be provided and the limitations on these services.

The principal limitation to OPC services, which counselors should clearly state, is that they are there to advise the client during the job search process, not to find the client employment. Discharged employees should never be given the impression that it is the counselor's job either to find them employment or make critical career decisions for them.

This point can be made gently: "You now have a new job—finding another position. The process I have been describing can help you do that, but you'll find it necessary to make some important decisions. My job is to work with you and share our experience with you as you go about the task of seeking employment." This kind of statement helps structure the relationship between client and counselor in a healthy fashion.

Equally important is avoiding statements that promise assistance the counselor cannot deliver. For example, one counselor had a tendency to refer clients to a contact in an executive search firm. The implication was that this contact would lead to employment. After a few referrals the contact in the search firm requested that his name not be used again. Furthermore, none of the clients got a job through the contact. Hence, the counselor ended up irritating both the search firm contact and the people sent there. Most counselors learn early that they should not make promises of help in circumstances over which they have no control.

Any questions the client has should be answered directly and honestly. These questions typically relate to the services themselves, the counselor's role, and to how long the client can expect to be unemployed.

The counselor should point out that severance benefits give the client some breathing room, but it is important that the time be used effectively. For example, one client stated that he was going to postpone looking for a job until he had used up a good portion of his severance pay. The counselor responded by pointing out that, while no one could force him to look for a job, the exact length of time required to locate a position was unpredictable and that by adopting such an approach, the client was running the risk of hurting himself. The counselor suggested he first examine the job search process before making up his mind on timing. The counselor recognized that the statement had been motivated by a sense of powerlessness. With continued discussion, the client began focusing on the problem at hand in a more constructive way.

Once the client's feelings have been aired, it is possible for counselor and client to establish a psychological contract. Contracting involves clarifying the expectations of both parties. This process grows out of the counselor's description of the outplacement process and the nature of the counselor's role in it. The counselor makes it clear that he or she can assist the client in developing job search skills, but can't get the client a job. In fact, the counselor's expectation is that the client will view the job search process as his or her current job. The counselor also asks how the process meets the client's expectations. It is especially important that the two discuss the allocation of the counselor's time and the amount of access the client will have to the counselor.

Usually, OPC is loaded at the front end, in the sense that the counselor works intensely with the client during the first week or so after the termination. The counselor devotes this time to getting the client to follow a structured job search program. After this, the client assumes increasing responsibility for the job search, with the counselor providing periodic advice and support.

The counselor should state clearly that, although the expense of the OPC service is being borne by the former employer, the counselor's actual client is the terminated employee. The distinction between the sponsor (the ex-employer) and the client (the discharged person) should be emphasized.

It is critical that the client understand how the process works. Earlier we spoke of the need for the counselor to avoid creating a sense of dependency. Sometimes the client will strive to create dependency and end up using the counselor as a crutch. If this behavior emerges, having explicitly discussed expectations makes it easier for the counselor to confront the client with the behavior.

The client should be made aware that the counselor will periodically report progress in the job search to the client's former employer but will not reveal any confidential information. If the client learned about these status reports during the job search process and was unaware they were being made, the counselor could lose credibility.

If the stress level is high throughout the initial meeting, the counselor is well advised to review contracting issues at the beginning of the second meeting, which takes place at the counselor's office. It is important to be sure that no misunderstandings have occurred.

Step 2. Self Analysis and Job Search Counseling

In Chapter Seven we used a pyramid to illustrate the steps of a thorough outplacement program. With the second meeting between counselor and client, which takes place in the counselor's office, the terminated person begins the process of continuing his or her career.

This starts with a psychological assessment, which can help clients gain insight into their strengths, limitations, and potential prior to organizing a job search or initiating a career change. Most clients find such assessments extremely helpful, often learning how to avoid past mistakes. For years, psychological assessment has been a tool used by corporations to help reduce error in the selection process. Included as part of the outplacement process, this tool can also help those preparing to enter the job market.

Getting Organized

The worst mistake terminated managers can make is to think of themselves as entering an idle period. In reality, they now have a new job; namely, to package and market themselves. If they are to be successful, they must approach this job with the same vigor, imagination, and discipline that would characterize their approach to any other important task.

Becoming impatient and expecting overnight success is the downfall of many a job-seeker. Most positions at the managerial level are not advertised publicly. Some have not even crystallized within the company, and are often triggered by the arrival of the applicant. Outplacement consultants refer to this as the hidden job market. Prematurely jumping into job interviews can keep the hidden jobs hidden and exhaust the job-seeker's opportunities. Moving too soon can alienate colleagues and work against the applicant, who is seldom prepared to look for and recognize choice opportunities. Finding good job situations requires discipline, patience, and a systematic approach.

This advice is more easily given than practiced. The trauma associated with the interruption of employment naturally generates a whole gamut of negative feelings. These feelings tend to recur at different times in the job search. However, to give way to such feelings for an extended period is no more productive than it would be in any job situation.

More specifically, these negative feelings often lead to prolonged periods of inactivity while feeling sorry for oneself. Bitterness can sometimes surface and become a prominent part of one's conversation. Some people try to ride out the storm of early negation by taking a breather for a while and going on a vacation. Others embark immediately on an almost manic period of activity, contacting everyone they know in their industry and sending out numerous resumes in an effort to show they are not taking this lying down. Both bitter withdrawal and manic activity are self-defeating. Now more than ever, a discharged person needs to plan activities thoroughly. It is the counselor's job to help defuse the counterproductive impulses and help their clients plan and structure their time wisely.

Developing a Personal Marketing Game Plan

Just as the success of any business enterprise rests on the ability to market its product or services successfully, so, too, does the success of a person's job search depend on the approach to marketing the talents being offered to prospective employers.

No major corporation would leave its marketing strategy to amateurs. Indeed, companies employ the best talent they can find in order to make sure all the key pieces of an effective marketing strategy are in place. However, most people approaching the job market are amateurs at marketing themselves. They simply have never had to confront the problem of selling themselves before.

But just as there are proven skills in corporate marketing, there are established methods known to be effective in marketing oneself for a job. One of the greatest needs of people entering the job market is access to the kinds of skills that will help them convert their career goals into effective personal marketing game plans.

Some of the elements of a successful marketing strategy are well known to managers. Others are easily overlooked. However, well known or not, the ability to adapt these elements to one's own particular situation and make intelligent choices among the available options requires a certain degree of sophistication.

Helping the client develop a marketing game plan starts with a systematic review of the basic elements common to all successful job searches:

- Preparing a resumé
- Developing a contact network
- Contacting target companies

All three are illustrated in the marketing game plan of Peter Hill.

PETER HILL

Peter Hill was a 44 year-old executive with an extensive background in sales, market research, and finance. Virtually his entire career had been spent with three manufacturing firms. This was the first time he had been discharged from a job.

Like many people, Peter got started in the manufacturing sector because of a good offer when he left graduate school with an M. B. A. Thus, he had fallen into his career. Despite his industrial background, for some time now he had harbored a personal dream of going into retailing and eventually owning his own store. However, he had no real experience in this area.

In thinking about his career objectives, both he and his wife decided it was now or never if he hoped to open his own business. The first step was to try to get a position with a large retail organization in order to learn the business and make contacts.

Recognizing that the switch would be difficult, Peter and his wife resolved to do it anyway.

Preparing a Resumé. The chronological resumé, which lists one's various jobs in reverse order with the most recent first, is the most common. Since that is what most employers expect to see and are comfortable reviewing, the majority of executives seeking work are best served by using it.

However, Peter's counselor suggested a functional resumé. This format avoids or plays down the employment record, and instead features a summary of the capacities in which the person has worked. Since Peter was seeking to radically change his career path, he and his counselor felt he would be better off with a resumé that emphasized his skills and areas of expertise. The functional resumé would also divert the interviewer's attention from the fact that Peter was attempting to enter what was for him a new industry—retailing. Unfortunately, many prospective employers fail to interview job applicants whose chronological resumés indicate that they have not spent most of their careers in a related sector of the economy.

Through conversations with friends and acquaintances working in large retail companies, Peter learned which critical skills were sought after and the type of position for which he would be best suited. His initial goal was to "crack" the industry. Having done his homework, Peter constructed a functional resumé that highlighted his marketing and cost-control skills.

Developing a Contact Network. Contacts are a person's most important job-seeking resource, provided they are developed and used correctly. The majority of people we work with find their jobs through personal contacts.

Since Peter was attempting to change industries, he felt he could not rely heavily on his personal contacts, most of whom were not in retailing. Still, at his counselor's urging, he pumped some of his former associates for introductions to friends in retailing. Most people who are asked to suggest sources of job opportunities will draw a blank. However, systematic interviewing, running down possibilities, and suggesting some possible areas in which the job-seeker is interested are all ways to stimulate creativity on the part of the people who make up one's contact network.

Peter was surprised by the number of leads he got from former associates. By asking them about people in specific companies, he got his former colleagues to recall neighbors, school buddies, or members of professional societies who were in retailing. For example, his former industrial relations manager knew the vice presidents of personnel at two large retailers.

Soon he had acquired from friends, associates, and industry

publications—a list of specific people who could help him in his
job search. Initially, he contacted people with whom he had the
advantage of a personal introduction. His counselor advised him
to approach these people on the basis of learning more about the
industry and not of finding a job in their organizations. This way
he found it easier to get an appointment. Soon he had developed
an extensive set of contacts and had elicited a few hints of interest.

Contacting Target Companies. As his job search became more
focused, Peter began contacting companies he knew had a need
for someone with his skills. His counselor helped him with his
cover letters and taught him how to get past a secretary on the
phone in order to set up a personal appointment.

He avoided wasting time contacting search firms and answering newspaper ads. The larger search firms receive hundreds of
resumés a day, and naturally these have to be screened by a low-
level staff person at a high rate of speed. A fair-sized ad in the
New York Times for a position that is at all attractive commonly
draws five hundred to a thousand replies. Therefore, unless a
person has outstanding qualifications and is a perfect fit for a
given job, merely mailing a resumé to a search firm or responding to an ad is ineffective. Given the nature of Pete's experience,
his counselor advised him against investing his time in these pur-
suits.

In short, Peter had to tailor his marketing strategy to his
particular situation. Four and a half months after he had been
fired, he found a job in retailing—one he felt would provide the
exposure he wanted.

Selling One's Abilities

Once the marketing strategy works and the client is invited
for an interview, the real selling takes place. As any salesperson
can tell you, a good firm lead is helpful, but it doesn't make the

sale. All that resumés, cover letters, and contact networks can do is get you an appointment. Then the real work begins.

The considerable demand for seminars in interviewing skills reflects a growing awareness that how one handles oneself during the employment interview is a critical factor in landing a good job. In fact, in the first few seconds of an interview, perhaps while still getting seated, the applicant will convey some important impressions that often lead the interviewer subconsciously to reach a conclusion. Proper dress, getting rid of outer clothing such as coat and overshoes before coming into the interviewer's office, and meeting with a firm handshake accompanied by a smile are important aspects of the interview process. They help project an image, and that image will work either for or against the applicant.

Once the interview begins, it is important to handle questions effectively. Prior to the interview, the applicant should have given some thought to handling difficult questions, such as "What is motivating you to change jobs?" "Why did your previous company let you go?" "If I were to contact your former boss, what would he be likely to tell me about you?" "What are your major weaknesses?" These questions need to be answered smoothly and believably.

For example, Peter Hill needed to be able to give convincing answers about why he wished to switch from manufacturing to retailing. Peter talked about the flair of retailing, which he liked, about how he felt his previous experience provided him with skills useful in a low-margin business; about how his unique background would provide opportunities for advancement once he adjusted to the retailing environment. He also learned to express concisely how he had adapted rapidly to new work environments in the past. Peter and his counselor role-played interviews on videotape over and over again. From friends in retailing, Peter picked up key words and behaviors that would help him sell himself to an employer.

Equally important is the ability to answer more standard,

positively directed questions. The applicant should be able to give an overview of his or her professional life in one and a half to two minutes. Beyond that, the applicant should have memorized four to six primary accoplishments and practiced feeding these into the interview so that they flow naturally. All of this, of course, requires thorough preparation. It is especially helpful for the applicant to rehearse the interview and receive professional feedback on how he or she is coming across.

Step 3. Monitoring

Once the executive is actively involved in the job search process, the counselor's role becomes one of periodic review and supportive advice. For example, it is important that the job-hunter recognize when a job opportunity is getting serious. Otherwise, he or she may suddenly be called upon to enter into final negotiations or even be pressed for a decision without being fully prepared.

Many job candidates need help in how to approach a potential employer with whom they have had several interviews but with whom they are still not sure where they stand. It is both a pleasant and agonizing experience to have more than one job offer in hand or apparently close. When a job-hunter has three or four offers pending, it almost always seems that the favored company has not made a firm offer while another is pressing hard for a decision.

There are many reasons companies seriously interested in a candidate may take a while to make an offer. Often, hiring someone at the middle to upper level requires groups of people to meet and approve the appointment; the salary committee, the board, the executive committee. Perhaps one of the key people has been traveling, or pressing business matters have made it impossible for the necessary people to get together.

In such a case, if the pressing company is a viable opportunity, the candidate is obliged to lean gently on the lagging company, saying something like, "In order to deal forthrightly with this other company, I feel obliged to give them an answer on their fine offer, but I would really prefer something from you, and I am hoping it will be attractive too. "The counselor should help prepare the applicant to deal with such issues as they arise.

Sometimes an important part of the monitoring step is simply helping the client maintain morale and keep the job search process in perspective. Just as some fired people are fearful about their ability to find work, others are overly optimistic. For some people, the realities of looking for a job come as a shock.

Without counseling, the sense of isolation that individuals frequently experience when they find themselves terminated can be overwhelming. As they go about preparing for the job search, questions keep popping into their minds. They find themselves making decisions without the opportunity to assess the options adequately. Family members frequently have little or no experience on which to draw in attempting to help. Friends may offer conflicting advice, much of which is not reliable. Some friends may even shy away from discussing these matters, simply because they are afraid of giving the wrong advice or prefer not to get involved. It is the job of the outplacement counselor to help solve these very real problems.

Areas of Counselor Support Common to all Cases

There are three general areas other than job search skills in which all clients can benefit from the advice and experience of a counselor: relationships with the former company, dealings with people outside the work place, and career planning.

Relationships with the Former Company

One area a dismissed manager must get firmly under control is his or her relationship with the former company. Although the employment relationship is being severed, the former company is in a position to be of assistance to the discharged manager. Furthermore, since executive circles in many industries and/or functional specialties are relatively small, the terminated manager will probably continue to encounter many former colleagues.

These relationships can be delicate for obvious reasons. The company is often relieved to have the person gone and wants to put the whole matter in the past. The terminated person may express both embarrassment and anger during encounters with former associates. As in a divorce, simple inquiries can be perceived as unreasonable demands, and statements of corporate policy can seem like justification for abandonment.

Judy Gentry was typical in this regard. She was not sure just what kind of a recommendation she would get from her former boss. Her suspicion was that he was never comfortable with a woman in her former job, and she could not see him going out of his way for her. When she encountered former associates, she had a tendency to refer to her ex-boss as "an amateur who was easily threatened." Her former associates said little. Her boss was simply glad she was gone.

In an atmosphere such as this, an outplacement counselor has a vital role to play. In Judy's case the counselor talked to her former boss and obtained agreement on the "official story" of why Judy was dismissed, so that he was able to tell her what kind of recommendation she would get. At the same time, the counselor got Judy to see that her comments were coming across as sour grapes no matter what the truth was about her boss. Few of her associates were likely to introduce her to potential employment contacts when her manner was so bitter.

No matter how clients may feel, it is profitable for them to remain outwardly calm and cool. If they feel the need to go further into the reasons for being terminated with the ex-boss, it is often wise to postpone this until they have calmed down. Nothing is to be gained by indulging in recriminations with a former boss, the personnel department, or anyone else who may have been involved in the termination process.

An important part of the counselor's role is to help the ex-employee recognize this fact. The first step is for the counselor to provide the opportunity for the client to air feelings of frustration in a safe environment. Once this has been done, if the client feels something can be learned from an objective review of his or her performance with the boss, the counselor can try to set up such a discussion with the counselor present. More typically, the counselor and the client assess what happened from the information already at hand.

The behavior of the client toward former business associates can either enhance or hinder job search efforts. Lack of previous experience in this kind of situation can create unnecessary stress and strain on valuable relationships with others if the individual does not receive the proper advice.

Dealings with People Outside the Workplace

On the home front, some executives try to keep their dismissal a secret from their families. Although this has to be a personal decision, it is our experience that it is best to share the situation with family members in a mature way, involving them in the current crisis.

Spouses may find themselves unsure how to react. If they act indifferent, it may appear that they are abandoning their partner in a time of crisis. If they act supportive, their partner may become defensive and resistant. All too easily the spouse can end up in a "no win" situation. Maintaining a mature relationship under these stressful conditions is no easy task.

Of course, many times the family is less than supportive. In our experience, close to half of the executives who have been discharged confront a response on the home front of "Well, what did you do wrong this time?" Hostility and blame are directed toward the individual for this threat to the security of the family. This attitude, of course, places an even greater strain on the client.

The family's task can be lightened if the counselor can help the discharged individual understand the dilemmas that confront family members. For this reason, we invite the spouse to meet with the counselor as part of the OPC process. Frequently, both partners will express feelings of underlying tension in their relationship after the termination. The counselor can help them talk to each other about these feelings and agree on a posture with which each can be comfortable. It is important that the couple come to realize that these pressures are typical and will ease once the terminated person settles into another job. Part and parcel of this mature approach is the client's coming to understand that termination is a temporary setback, not a sign of total failure.

If the tensions that arise after the termination are allowed to inhibit communication between husband and wife, job decisions may be made that create a future strain on the relationship. For this reason, it is imperative that the counselor strive to get both partners to understand that having been fired doesn't represent permanent failure; it happens to many successful people.

As we saw earlier in this chapter, in the case of Jane, sometimes the counseling process reveals personal difficulties that require specialized professional help. Jane was fortunate that her counselor was competent enough to refer her to such professional assistance.

As for contacts with the outside world, things need to be kept as normal as possible. The worst thing someone can do is withdraw into a shell. If the job change comes up in conversations with neighbors and friends, it should be discussed factually, using the same approach that will be used with potential employers, and avoiding bitterness or criticism of the former company or associates. These criticisms seem to get back to the people involved with amazing frequency and can only serve to hurt the discharged person, further.

The counselor may be able to help prepare both the terminated person and the spouse by role-playing how they are going to deal with social and professional contacts. Once they hear themselves explain what has happened and come to understand some of the emotions they feel while talking about it, the couple will be better prepared to deal with the outside world. In fact, once the two of them overcome any sense of humiliation, the discharged person can start to involve contacts in his or her job search.

Career Planning

As early as possible after the termination, the individual needs to begin thinking about his or her career goals and start making decisions that will ultimately influence the marketing strategy.

First, career goals must be assessed thoroughly. A growing research literature indicates that everybody passes through career stages. Often, goals that were attractive early in a career are less attractive in midlife or at a more advanced age. Certain career goals may already have been reached, while others may realistically be unattainable. Thought about one's career objectives is a prerequisite to consideration of the kinds of jobs and labor markets in which to concentrate job search efforts.

In one recent case, a middle-level executive came to realize that making it to a high-level position was not really important to him anymore. He wanted to live comfortably and enjoy his family. In addition, he did not want to relocate. having transferred three times during his career, he was beginning to put down roots and develop a sense of being part of a community. Even more importantly, he came to realize that part of his problem in his old job was that he was working at cross-purposes with some of the younger people who were moving up around him. He resented their progress, yet he was not willing to make significant sacrifices to continue advancing his own career. The result was a destructive resistance toward his associates. With a clearer understanding of his career objectives, he would not make the same mistake again.

The career planning process should include a thorough self-assessment. Not only career goals and job objectives but past strengths and weaknesses in performing the job should be analyzed. What things does the client do really well? What special skills have elicited compliments or have helped advance his or her career? What, realistically, are the client's weaknesses? In approaching the job market, older, more experienced employees have more data on their abilities than recent graduates do and can generally form a more realistic picture of the kinds of jobs at which they are likely to be successful.

Along with the question of what one can do well is the issue of what one really wants to do. Counselors often have clients assess their job history: of all the assignments with which they have been involved, which ones were the most interesting and satisfying?

In our experience, many people arrive at the realization that they haven't been happy for the past six or seven years, simply because their job situation was not one in which they were particularly interested, nor was it leading to relevant career goals. From this perspective, the client comes to realize that perhaps termination was not a wholly bad thing.

The Role of Outplacement Counselor Revisited

Given the uncertainties of the situation, it is important that clients think through each move carefully. When they get into situations that have them puzzled, they are better off asking for time to think it over rather than making a quick commitment. Unfortunately, most people engaged in the job search process do not have anyone with whom to work or plan their strategy. Thus, they are left to puzzle through the proper course of action on their own.

Our sketch of the needs of the terminated executive should accomplish one thing. It should make the reader aware that, once the termination interview has been completed, the problems for the person who has been let go are both substantial and continuous, at least for a time. As the individual gets further and further into the job search process, more and more decision points are reached.

To the extent that the job-seeker makes amateurish mistakes or unfortunate decisions, the period of unemployment is extended unnecessarily.[1] Decisive executives often flounder as they are confronted with the decision-making of the job search process, simply because they do not have an experience base upon which to draw. Continually, they reinvent the wheel. Outplacement counseling is a vehicle for helping the jobhunter through this difficult period of adjustment.

The authors wish to thank Dr. Donald Monaco, Senior Vice President, DBM for his contributions to this chapter.

Endnote

---

[1] See William J. Morin and James C. Cabrera, *Parting Company* (New York: Harcourt Brace Jovanovich, 1982) for a thorough discussion of job loss and search strategy.

9

Outplacement Counseling Problems

COUNSELING CLIENTS WHO ARE FACING stressful situations may lead to interactive difficulties between counselors and clients. If a counselor does not correctly read a client's signals, the outplacement program can become entangled in the client's resistance. Resistance may arise because a client, and the client's family as well, feel threatened by the outplacement process. A life, perhaps several lives, are undergoing close examination in an effort to meet and overcome some critical challenge.

Models of Helping and Coping

Phillip Brickman of the University of Michigan and several colleagues from other institutions have recently developed four models of helping and, based on existing research and experience, have suggested possible consequences for each.[1] Their observations are relevant to counseling in general and outplacement counseling in particular. These models represent assumptions held by the client and the counselor, which also may be embedded in institutionalized programs of assistance. If client and counselor hold different conceptions of the counseling process, conflicting expectations can introduce additional stress into the relationship.

The four models identified by Brickman and his associates are:

1. *The moral model,* in which people are assumed to have responsibility for both creating and solving their own problems. Brickman and his associates write that "the value of the moral model for coping is that it compels people to take an unequivocal stance toward their lives."[2] Albert Ellis's rational emotive school of therapy lies within the assumptions of the moral model.[3] The moral model suggests a direct, confrontative, authoritative approach to helping others—you got yourself into it, you can get yourself out.

2. *The compensatory model,* in which people are not blamed for their problems but are still held responsible for solutions. Thus, people are seen as having to compensate with personal cleverness, extra effort, or constructive use of others for problems and dilemmas imposed upon them.

Many contemporary counseling schools of thought are based on the compensatory model assumptions that people's problems are due to external factors beyond their control, such as:

- Poor upbringing (as a result of alcoholic parents, for example).
- Cultural disadvantages (such as poverty).
- Traumas (such as loss of parents in an accident at an early age).
- Physical handicaps (such as blindness).
- Job lost (as a result of organizational cutbacks).

The role of counselor is then to provide remedial help to assist people in helping themselves. The Reverend Jesse Jackson's message to black communities that "you are not responsible for being down, but you are responsible for getting up" embraces the assumptions of the compensatory model.[4]

3. *The medical model,* in which people are responsible for neither the problem nor the solution. This model is most clearly evident in the traditional role of the doctor with an orientation that holds that patients are victims of infection or physical malfunction and only the doctor can cure the problem. A counterpart to this model is found in the behaviorism of B. F. Skinner who holds that behavior is a function of contingencies that make "it foolish to blame people for their problems or give them credit for their solutions."[5] An advantage of the model is that it allows people to request and seek help without requiring them to accept blame. Its weakness is a tendency to foster dependency.

4. *The enlightenment model,* in which people are responsible for their problems but cannot be held responsible for the solutions because the problems are too difficult for them to solve alone. As Brickman and his coauthors state, in this model "central emphasis is placed on enlightening participants as to the true nature of their problem (which they may not regard as something for which they should take responsibility) and the difficult course of action that will be required to deal with it."[6] Under the enlightenment model, people are required to "accept a strikingly negative image of themselves and, in order to improve, to accept a strong degree of submission to agents of social control . . . It is their own impulses—to eat, drink, lie, cheat, steal—that are out of control . . . To control these impulses, people must submit to the stern or sympathetic discipline provided by members of the community."[7] Alcoholics Anonymous is an example of a program that epitomizes the assumptions of this model.

The Four Models and Outplacement Counseling

A clear understanding of the four models can help counselors recognize when they and their clients are at cross-purposes. The models can also clarify certain aspects of the outplacement counselor's role.

Based on observed results from a variety of settings, Brickman and his colleagues "hypothesize that models in which people are held responsible for solutions (the compensatory and moral models) are more likely to increase people's competence than models in which they are not held responsible for solutions (the medical and enlightenment models). . . It may also be beneficial not to hold people responsible for problems, though the evidence for this is less clear."[8] They also suggest that certain of the models may prove to be more appropriate than others in certain specific helping situations.

The outplacement counseling role rests on the assumptions of the compensatory and, at times, moral models. In a majority of outplacement cases, it is both possible and preferable that client and counselor embrace the key assumption of the compensatory model ("It really was not your fault that you lost your job, but with hard work you can find another one.") In cases of workforce reductions, elimination of redundant jobs, and problems of changing management, it is quite likely that the client has been largely a victim of circumstance. Further, the issue is not so much blame or fault as understanding what happened for purposes of getting the client to accept responsibility for future actions.

Many discharged employees feel shame and guilt, even though their current predicament is largely the result of forces beyond their control. The extent to which our culture assigns personal status and identity based upon work achievements virtually assures such feelings at some level.

A key issue with most OPC clients is making sure they do not assume *too much* responsibility for the job loss. If the counselor assumes that the client has, at most, minimal responsibility for the job loss, and the client feels more responsibility, the resulting communication problems can damage their rapport. The counselor will be counseling from the premise that the client should not feel responsible for his or her predicament, when the client actually wants to feel and does feel responsible.

When such problems seem to be emerging, the counselor should encourage the client to examine what has happened. Some recent research by Shelley Taylor of U.C.L.A. suggests that, when an individual experiences a personally traumatic event, "the readjustment process focuses around three themes: a search for meaning in the experience, an attempt to gain mastery over the event in particular and over one's life more generally, and an effort to enhance one's self-esteem—to feel good about oneself again despite the personal setback."[9] We submit that the counselor can best serve most clients by helping them understand that, whether the problem was caused by them, others, or some combination of both, the most constructive use of energy is in gaining control of the future. The counselor can do this most effectively through listening and dialogue. If the compensatory assumptions of the counselor lead to too little response to the clients' efforts at self-understanding, however, clients may become frustrated over their inability to communicate their reactions to being terminated.

With regard to OPC, the moral model is reflected in an attitude of "You selected the company, you remained in the situation, you behaved in a certain way; don't complain about being fired, but find yourself another job." Some clients want the counselor to take this approach. The counselor may find it a necessary or helpful means of getting other clients out of unusually prolonged states of denial, displacement, or depression. Most clients experience these to a degree, as part of a more general grieving process that characterizes most traumatic events involving personal loss.[10] When adopting a moral model stance, the counselor must be sensitive to the possibility that the client will feel abandoned. Brickman and colleagues suggest that loneliness is a potential pathology associated with this model.[11] For our part, we have observed that executives may present a brave front that often belies their feelings toward their situation.

Counselors must remember that the client's *expectations and needs* dictate one approach over the other. For this reason, it is clearly mandatory for the counselor to get to know the client. Initially the counselor must spend several hours with the client to determine which model will facilitate the counseling process.

In the majority of instances, the client's needs will become manifest as the counseling process unfolds. Occasionally an unusual level of confusion on the part of the client will emerge, and it is in such instances that the counselor can often benefit from the insights of colleagues, especially psychologists on the OPC staff.

The compensatory and moral models are appropriate to outplacement counseling, because they embrace the idea that *the client is ultimately responsible for making use of the counselor's help in securing employment*. In the process, the client's own competence is reinforced.

The assumptions of the medical model are disastrous when counseling individuals seeking help for career or life problems, because they foster dependency by minimizing the need for the client to take proactive, controlling measures.

Some outplacement clients come to believe that being a victim of circumstance entitles them to be taken care of. Hence, they think the counselor should do more to provide solutions to their plight (such as provide job leads). The counselor must confront such thinking in a straightforward manner. Such a transfer of responsibility places the relationship outside the common structure of outplacement assistance and is generally counterproductive. Outplacement counselors can point the way, but the client bears the major responsibility for finding new employment. The counselor should be certain the client understands this well.

Several contemporary theories of therapy espouse the view that, while you are responsible for the problems in your life, you need particular "agents" or methods to help solve them. For some behavior problems, such as chronic alcoholism, overeating, smoking, and gambling, this approach may be viable. For OPC it has little to offer. It too fosters dependency and overreliance on a strict authoritative structure.

Programs that incorporate such an approach may help solve a behavioral problem that has created an employment crisis. In such instances, the counselor might utilize the moral model in encouraging the client to seek therapeutic help concurrent with his or her job search activities.

When confronted with a meticulous, dependent client who wants and needs everything spelled out, the counselor may have to take a very structured "this is the way" approach. Final responsibility must still be clearly placed on the client, however. Within an outplacement program, counselors faced with this kind of obsessive-compulsive personality should probably recommend additional counseling by a staff psychologist.

By keeping these models clearly in mind, the counselor can often recognize early clues to pathology in the relationship and take steps to address them.

Common Counseling Problems

As our discussion has shown, outplacement counseling requires both skill and experience in counseling and knowledge of the corporate workplace and the job-search process. Each case is somewhat unique, and counselors can expect to encounter a number of challenges during the course of their practice.

Generally, OPC counselors find their clients eager and cooperative. However, some clients present challenges that can cause at best misunderstanding and at worst a serious stalemate in the relationship. If improperly handled, the client may become resistant, and the counselor may react in an unconstructive manner.

Three common problem areas involve:

- Incomplete assignments (early phase of the OPC process).
- Network resistance (early to middle phase of the OPC process).
- Long-term assistance (late phase of the OPC process).

Incomplete Assignments

In the early phase of the OPC process, the client has to produce a great deal of data by completing assignments in the following categories:

• Work accomplishments
• Self-assessment
• Career assessment

Completing these assignments is fundamental to future progress. When the client is not prepared for the next appointment, the counselor may respond with annoyance and impatience. This is counterproductive. Instead, the counselor should probe into the emotions experienced by the client.

Keeping in mind the psychological impact of termination (for example, feelings of anger, despair, shock) and some of the associated coping reactions (such as desire for revenge, depression, hurt, lowered self-esteem), the counselor should try to understand the specific reasons why the client is not ready for work. These may include:

• Continued negative feelings regarding termination.
• Lack of rapport and trust with the counselor.
• Lack of motivation to produce (for example, because of long severance).
• Problems involved in a career or life transition (such as separation, divorce, career restructuring).
• Dependency on the counselor.
• Failure to understand the importance of the assignments.

The antidote to low productivity, especially regarding assignments, is one of the first steps in an OPC program, the career background review. The counselor should spend several hours getting to know the client, understanding his or her frame of mind, motivations, habitual patterns and behaviors, strengths, limitations, coping ability, intellectual strengths, and problem-solving ability.

An open relationship in which the client has confidence in the counselor has to be achieved before moving on. Simply put, there are decided advantages in OPC when the client likes, respects, and feels comfortable with the counselor. Later on, the client will be able to handle the possible strain resulting from the counselor's critiques, confrontation, cajoling, candor, and even the counselor's shortcomings and limitations. Spending time getting to know the client is the most constructive way to build a productive relationship. Counselors will see the evolution in rapport as clients loosen up and even smile more. Clients need to trust and respect their counselors before disclosing more about themselves. Failure to complete assignments is a symptom that clients have not yet accepted their counselors. Thus, the symptom needs to be diagnosed and treated.

Network Resistance

Experience as well as common sense about how the world works tell us that one of the most effective avenues to new employment is through "exposure" in a network of personal relationships. There is a high degree of payout in talking to a multitude of key individuals. For the client, networking means hard work, which is often associated with personal uneasiness. When properly organized and rehearsed, however, it can become easier, and even enjoyable. As former clients have discovered, the client is building a lifetime networking system, and equally important, is learning more about his or her field and where the opportunities lie.

There is, perhaps, 99 percent agreement from clients that networking works. There are some who resist, however, often claiming that they "don't know many people." In response, the counselor must often give an almost evangelical talk, to which most clients listen, finally yielding to the counselor's experience and guidance.

Some clients, however, develop a staunch anti-networking posture. Networking is fine and works for others, but not for them, they flatly assert. Among the common excuses given by the client for not networking are:

- "I've been in one company too long."
- "Recruiters are more helpful in my special field."
- "My contacts didn't give other names."
- "It won't work in my situation."
- "I don't want to strain relations."
- "How many times can I go back to them?"

In reality, their resistance is rooted in other dynamic forces, most often one or some combination of the following:

- They want the easy way out (for example, recruiters are seductive solutions, networking takes time and energy).
- They seek to avoid what they perceive as an embarrassment.
- They feel it's demeaning, a way of begging for a job.

The personality dynamics of the network-resistant client often center on poorly developed social and interpersonal skills, which result in an inability to feel comfortable interacting from a position experienced as powerless and without status. These people may well be highly qualified professionals with outstanding accomplishments and technical experience. We have noticed that scientists, engineers, and computer experts typically develop this resistance, since their background and training have often not enabled them to develop social and interpersonal skills, despite the security of their professional role.

Additionally, like the procrastinator, the network-resistant client can have underlying problems which relate to:

- Low self-image
- Low frustration tolerance
- Poor personal problem-solving skills

Helping the network-resistant client requires the counselor to expose the underlying personal anxieties (fear of embarrassment, fear of feeling awkward or inadequate). Then the counselor needs to reinforce the idea that networking will help the client build confidence in an area that has been neglected for too long. In actuality, both the client who ignores assignments and the network-resistant client represent forms of procrastination. Both represent, in essence, readiness problems; the client is holding back due to underlying feelings.

The counselor facing these challenges will be unable to "decipher the code" and understand the underlying motives without an in-depth initial interview with the client and continuing sensitivity to the client's ongoing experiences.

Long-term Assistance

Paul Rhine, a 50-year-old senior marketing executive from a Fortune 200 manufacturing organization, was let go after twelve years of service due to a cutback resulting from aquisition by another company. He was stunned by the termination. That was fifteen months ago. What is Paul doing now? Still looking, stalling, procrastinating, and trying to recover psychologically.

Paul is bright, competent, respected in the business community, and above all, well connected. Although somewhat overly verbal, he is a brilliant analyzer and conceptualizer. Besides, he is charming and affable. The OPC counselor was impressed with all of this and with his willingness to participate in the OPC program. Fifteen months later and no job—some close calls, but no handshake—the counselor had to wonder what was going on.

Can outplacement specialists identify the potentially long-term client? Can they prevent the phenomenon from occurring?

What can be done to restructure the pattern if it does occur with a client?

Practically speaking, a long-term client is an individual participating in an outplacement program who, for whatever reason, has not relocated within a reasonable time frame. Mid- to upper-management clients can be considered long term if not placed within six to eight months, while top executives should be placed within nine months.

The Savard Younger Consulting Group of Chicago conducted a study on laid-off executives and reported the following results relevant to the long-term client:

- The severance benefit was the only variable that affected the length of the job search ("The greater the severance, the longer the search").
- There was no significant correlation between length of search and salary, position, age, or area of specialty.
- Important personal qualities for the job search included high orientation to task completion, ability to think conceptually, low dependency on others, realistic self-appraisal, competitiveness, greater risk orientation, less interest in social relationships, less judgemental attitudes, and an ability to generate goals internally.[12]

Our experience has been that other factors also contribute to the development of a "long termer." These include:

- Extended employment contracts (one to three years).
- Job search campaigns limited to a specific and confined geographic area.
- Delayed recovery from the shock of termination, which leads to remaining in the denial, anger, or depression stages for longer than normal. Often a serious self-image or confidence problem exists.
- Attitudinal/motivational problems. Statements such as the following are symptomatic: "I'm still going to get even,"

"They'll take me back," "At my age, where will I get a job?" "I really don't want to network," "I'm really annoyed you outplacement people don't put me in touch with prospective employers," "I've done everything, I can't go back to my contacts again."
- Poor appearance: overweight, unappealing attire, skin condition.
- Poor attitude toward self-marketing.
- Flat interest profile (no high interests).
- Personal or family problems (separation, divorce, alcohol abuse).
- Introverted, fearful, slow-moving, low-keyed personality.
- Litigious posture.

Any one or a combination of these factors can create a long-term client.

Citing the results of the Savard Younger study to our clients with lengthy severance arrangements lets them know early on that we are aware of this potential problem and how it can affect the results of the job search effort. Gentle reminders are made throughout the process. This usually facilitates matters, but not always. A few clients have their own ulterior motives, including, "I'll take X number of months to benefit by getting the full amount," "I've worked hard, I'll take it easy for a few months," "I've completed the program, mailings have gone out, so now I'll wait for responses," or "It's Friday, I'll go play golf."

Such attitudes are usually counterproductive, since, in the absence of extraordinary luck, a successful job search is the end result of a formal and well-organized campaign. Thus, by the time clients begin to take the process seriously, they have been out of work for an extended period and must now begin to climb out of a second hole, which they have dug themselves.

Where some of the characteristics of a potential long termer are present, the counselor should begin to address them early in the process and attempt to minimize their impact. Little good is served by a "let's wait and see" approach, acting only when the long-term phenomenon has become evident.

Some long termers have difficulties not easily discernible to the counselor. Here we have found what we call the client review process to be helpful. This is a one- to two-hour interview or brainstorming session in which a group of counselors (preferably three or four) meet with the client to review job search activity to date. This review usually covers personal contacts (network activity), recruiter activity, mailings, and marketing strategy. Usually multiple suggestions develop during the meeting as the counselors share their ideas on the problem with the client.

Generally, the long termer's problem involves the approach to the job search campaign. The solution is often a reasonable dose of reality administered in conjunction with a sharp focus on the correction of some deficiency.

It is hard to find a job. However, the conclusion regarding the long-term client is usually simple; the client hasn't persevered or done enough. As in prospecting for gold, attention to detail pays off.

The problems we have described are sufficiently common so that anyone regularly engaged in outplacement counseling encounters them more than once during the course of a year. Anticipating their occurrence is fundamental to understanding the outplacement counseling process.

The authors wish to thank Dr. Donald Monaco, Senior Vice President, DBM for his contributions to this chapter.

Endnotes

---

[1]Phillip Brickman, Vita Carulli Rabinowitz, Jurgis Karuza Jr., Dan Coates, Ellen

Cohn, and Louise Kidder, "Models of Helping and Coping," *American Psychologist* 37 (April 1982), 368-84.

[2]Ibid., 371.

[3]Albert Ellis, *Humanistic Psychotherapy: The Rational Emotive Approach* (New York: McGraw-Hill, 1974) and *Disputing Irrational Beliefs* (New York: Institute for Rational Living, 1974).

[4]Brickman et al, "Models of Helping," 372.

[5]Ibid., 373.

[6]Ibid.

[7]Ibid.

[8]Ibid., 375.

[9]Shelley E. Taylor, "Adjustment to Threatening Events," *American Psychologist* 38 (November 1983) 1161.

[10]Robert B. Garber, "The Psychology of Termination and Outplacement" in *Employee Termination Handbook* (Englewood Cliffs; Prentice Hall, 1981).

[11]Brickman et al, "Models of Helping," 371.

[12]Savard Younger Consulting Group, *Study of Job Charge Factors in the Involuntary Termination* (Chicago: Savard Younger Consulting Group, 1983).

10

Parting Company at the Top: Outplacement and the Senior Executive

BECAUSE OF THE SUBSTANTIAL SEVERANCE packages some senior executives receive, there is a tendency to think that high-level managers have little need for outplacement support. Such a view is at best naive. The shock of termination can be greater for top executives than for middle managers. A counselor at Drake Beam Morin who has worked extensively with senior executives observes: "The higher they are, the farther they have to fall . . . A history of success and years of deep involvement in company affairs can actually intensify the feelings of frustration, isolation, and anxiety that are a natural consequence of termination." Additionally, because of their visibility, discharged senior managers must often deal with their reactions under the glare of industrywide publicity, which starts the grapevine working before they have given any thought to future plans or the nature of their job search.

Close inspection of their circumstances reveals that discharged senior executives are confronted by a complex situation that usually makes them appreciate the help afforded by outplacement counselors. There are many similarities between the kind of help required by middle managers and that needed by senior executives: for example, dealing with feelings of shock, embarrassment, anger, or frustration associated with being discharged; sharpening job search skills that have been dulled by lack of use, often because the executives have been more than a decade with the same company. It is also true that, because of their relatively unique stature and situation, senior people often benefit from a mix of counseling services that differs in significant ways from that targeted to the needs of middle managers. This chapter outlines some of these key differences.

The Uniqueness of Senior Executives

Senior managers enjoy certain advantages but also are confronted with distinct problems during the search for new employment. Consultants familiar with the experiences of senior executives argue that the task of finding new employment is no more difficult for them than it is for middle-level people but that senior executives have to set unique priorities and deal with different issues during the job search. It is this difference that Ernest "Bud" Whitney, who for several years has coordinated the senior executive program at DBM, repeatedly returns to during discussions of the topic.

Three factors tend to make senior executives' circumstances unique:

- *Experience*. They are seasoned generalists who understand how the various functions of a complex enterprise interrelate. Potential investors are willing to trust their judgment on matters of business strategy.
- *Financial situation*. Because of their past participation in executive compensation programs, their net worth may provide them with a degree of financial independence.
- *Broad contacts*. In their role as generalist, they have typ-

ically developed important contacts in a number of areas of the business community. They have access to powerful people who often will assist them on the basis of past friendship and personal respect.

There is yet another way in which senior executives are often unique: they usually have pronounced personal qualities and skills, which provided the impetus for their original rise to a position of leadership. These qualities are typically combined with a high energy level and a desire to influence others that can make them very effective during a job search campaign. One experienced counselor observed of these clients that "once they've dealt with their emotions, they tend to start the search for new opportunities more quickly and push things along more vigorously than many other outplacement clients. They're determined to get back in charge." Their behavior patterns reflect a power drive and a positive self-regard that result in their assuming responsibility for their own self-development.

The outplacement counseling process must channel the psychological needs of these executives to their advantage. More specifically, the requirements of senior executives shape the delivery of outplacement support in at least three ways. They mandate (1) a counselor with similar senior-level experience, (2) use of a staff approach, and (3) availability of a secondary support network of specialists.

Accustomed to taking responsibility for their own development, senior executives require less specific direction than others but want access to individuals with informed judgments about the various options confronting them. The executive's primary counselor must be someone whose judgment the executive trusts, which tends to mean someone with senior-level experience or experience as staff to such individuals. The trust that must underlie the consultant/client relationship requires that the parties see each other as professional equals.

The judgment factor is particularly significant in the senior-level outplacement process. For example, consider the client who, as president of a large division, had just finished liquidating his organization, the job he had originally been retained to perform. Having successfully accomplished his task (for which he had been well rewarded), he was faced with making his next career move. He was torn between seeking another corporate position and pursuing an entrepreneurial opportunity. His pyschological assessment and career patterns indicated that he was well suited to either choice.

He was attracted by an offer to join an investment firm that bought and sold small companies. The four partners each had $10 million to invest; our client was invited to take over the active role of a partner who was retiring. Through his participation he would gradually build up his capital base.

Then a company in another city contacted him about the possibility of becoming its new president. Although the job was in an industry in which he had considerable expertise, he was excited about the opportunity to join the investment group and was about to turn down the new offer when his counselor suggested he at least meet the representatives of the company. He acted on this suggestion.

Following the meeting, he commented that it looked like an exciting job with strong prospects but that he still favored the partnership. Because it was clear he found the job attractive, his counselor suggested that he visit again to explore the specifics of the job.

He returned with a firm offer and the comment, "Now I have a real problem." The client had now developed two very attractive and firm opportunities. To help him assess the two, the counselor asked him what he liked about the investment partnership. The client identified the personal chemistry and the potential for a high return on the risk. The down side was that his net worth was only a little over $800,000 and the risk was significant. That made him a little uncomfortable. He wasn't really in the same financial league as his potential partners.

His counselor suggested he spend additional time with the key people in the industrial firm to get a better feel for the chemistry there. Also, since he had nothing to lose, why not up the ante on that job offer–see if he could negotiate a compensation package that would further increase his net worth with less risk.

When he returned this time, he had accepted the job with a greatly increased compensation package. He felt he could get involved with a similar investment partnership in the future if he so desired. On this visit he had become convinced that the chemistry with the board of the corporation was every bit as good as with the investment partnership.

This was not a big surprise to the counselor, who had thought all along that the company offer might prevail. He had felt it was important to keep the client from cutting off this opportunity before he had thoroughly explored it and carefully assessed its potential. He also wanted the client to realize he was in a position to maximize the potential of the offer. These were matters of judgment on the counselor's part that made his advice of particular value in the situation.

Because of their experience, senior executives are often in a position to consider a wider range of options than are typically reasonable for middle-level managers. General management consulting, a leveraged buy-out of an existing business, and raising capital for a new venture are often attractive possibilities. So too are opportunities for managing an organization in a field different from the one with which they were previously involved.

Weighing divergent options is a task made easier by hearing opinions and judgments from a range of people with different backgrounds and perspectives. For this reason, DBM usually makes a team of senior staff members available to the client for discussion purposes. Senior executives make ready use of this resource. Accustomed to seeking a range of opinions on issues of significance to them, they welcome a staff approach to sorting out career opportunities. While some people might find this confusing, senior executives are used to looking at choices from different perspectives before making basic decisions–a pattern that is especially appropriate given the complex risk/reward calculations they are making.

Given the complexity of senior executive severance arrangements and the executive's future career moves, questions requiring technical expertise frequently arise during the outplacement process. For example, financial analysis is often called for; tax advice, expertise in contract negotiations, and up-to-date experience in mergers and acquisitions or buy-outs may be necessary. No counselor can provide competent help on such a wide range of topics, and, responsibility for obtaining ongoing support in these areas must lie with the client. However, a network of outside experts who can be contacted for initial opinions is often invaluable.

For example, in the area of financial analysis and tax advice, we find that 90 percent of our clients have an ongoing relationship with a professional adviser and thus have a handle on the issues involved in their personal estate. Yet many of them take advantage of the opportunity to make a phone call for a second opinion on a particular isssue.

Career Continuation Opportunities

Data collected on our senior executive clients indicates that the average age hovers around 52, but the range covers the mid-40s to early 60s. Usually, if a potential employer has a choice between a 45- and a 55-year-old senior executive, the younger person will get the nod. Not always, however. Those in their mid-50s have the potential for ten years in a leadership role, plus the advantage of experience, which can make them very attractive candidates.

Additionally, there are in the job market a number of so-called regency positions. That is, an employer has a set of promising executives who are slightly lacking in the necessary experience to assume the top spot; it thus needs an older executive who can lead the organization while these younger executives gain the experience they need. In this situation an older candidate has a distinct advantage. Older senior executives have also proven attractive to smaller firms, who see in them someone who can protect the owner's investment and help the company grow without the tendency to use the position as a stepping stone.

Of those senior executives under age 50, about 60 percent find their jobs through search firms, 40 percent through the networking process. Of those over age 50, only 10 percent find positions through search firms, over 75 percent through networking. These data reflect the kinds of assignments search firms generally get, as well as their preference for presenting younger "comers" to their clients, in contrast to the broader contacts older senior executives have been able to establish, especially if they have had tenure at the top.

Because these clients are highly sophisticated, they quickly grasp the importance of the marketing perspective on which the job-finding process rests, and they easily learn the practical steps of the program. Thus, a principal focus of a counselor's effort is helping the senior executive shape a strategic plan, with special attention given to unique positioning and marketing approaches tailored to the client's campaign.

This is classically illustrated by a 62-year-old client who had held more than twenty jobs in different key areas of the same industry (an industry in which job mobility was very common). His resume made it clear that he was well known in his field. He was really almost the perfect candidate to serve as an industry association president, a job he targeted and in fact obtained.

The Entrepreneurial Option

Because of generous severance packages or their personal reputations, senior executives often have access to the capital resources needed to act on their entrepreneurial impulses. For those individuals seriously considering this choice, outplacement counselors try to help with a "philosophy of informed choice."

Senior executive counselors must work with these clients to shape their plans and assist them in areas where they may not be experts. For example, one top manager who was terminated by a major corporation in his late 50s did not want to join a new company. He had run his own consulting firm in the past, but the operation had not been altogether successful, primarily because he lacked marketing experience. After this client determined that he would attempt to revive his consulting business, his counselor worked with him on marketing topics and even helped him develop a sales brochure. The client's wife joined him in the business, and the two brought in $100,000 in consulting revenues within their first year. Another client purchased a small company using a variety of financial sources and in less than sixty days had sold off needless inventory to retire his debt load entirely.

Only a very small percentage of our senior executive clients end up as entrepreneurs, however. For one thing, there is a high risk of failure, even if everything is done right. "It's impossible to offer any guarantees in this area," says one counselor, "but we certainly make sure that our clients have looked carefully before they ever think about leaping into the entrepreneurial arena."

In Sum: A Highly Tailored Process

Many senior executives benefit from receiving outplacement support. The benefits range from help coping with the very human initial reactions to losing a job, to help tailoring their continuing career path to their unique strengths and experiences.

There are many similarities between the issues confronted by senior executives and other managers. Basically, the kinds of career options are similar, but the specific choices and resources available to the senior executive are unique, as are some of the limitations. For one thing, there are clearly fewer top jobs available and they are more difficult to get. Candidates for them must demonstrate that they can make a significant contribution to the organization's performance. Thus, the care that goes into positioning the individual is particularly important, since each executive may represent a unique resource.

11

Discharging the Nonexempt Employee

MOST RECENT OUTPLACEMENT LITERATURE has focused on managerial or professional employees. Yet the largest number of people fired every year by large corporations are nonexempt workers—both white collar and blue collar. Inevitably these workers suffer the most when a company has cutbacks, and in the absence of a collective bargaining agreement, they are also most likely to be terminated for disciplinary or performance reasons.

Traditional Lack of Concern

Historically, companies have seldom been concerned about assisting nonexempts who are being terminated. Generally, the corporate attitude has been that these employees can go next door and find a job. Since they were never part of the management team, the sense of corporate obligation has been less than for administrative employees.

Finding another job is frequently not as simple as going

down the street, however. Average periods of unemployment range from three months to years, depending on the economy and the transferability of the employee's skills. Secretarial and certain mechanical skills are more easily transferred than those of other nonexempts who, in effect, have skills only within the context of their former jobs. Assemblers are an example. In the general labor market, assemblers are semiskilled or unskilled workers. Usually, the only organization that has a need for Class II assemblers is the company that has just dismissed them or a direct competitor.

Often nonexempts have limited financial resources and are not as geographically mobile as managerial employees. Yet they are the least likely to be provided with a support package. Economists have documented the number of blue-collar workers who have become downwardly mobile in the labor market. Many workers losing jobs in manufacturing industries are finding that the only work available to them is in lower-paying service jobs. Barry Bluestone reports results of a survey of laid-off autoworkers, which found that "these workers earn an average of 30 percent less than they did in the auto industry and 41 percent no longer have any employer-paid health insurance, 56 percent have no employer-paid pension, and 40 percent have no employer-paid life insurance."[1]

The psychological trauma of being terminated is, by and large, the same for a nonexempt employee as it is for an exempt one. We have worked with people who have been in the secretarial ranks for ten or fifteen years and thought the company would take care of them until retirement. These people are often in shock when they lose their jobs as part of a general cutback or are terminated for whatever reason. Many of them fall into what we call the "brittle case" category. In essence, a brittle case is someone who cannot go out and find another job because of the degree of trauma connected with the termination. The shock is such that they feel as if another job will never be available.

Although not every nonexempt has such a severe reaction,

being dismissed generates the same problems that it does for the exempt employee. Learning how to apply for a job, whom to use for a reference, how to explain what happened on the last job, and how to deal with family and peer pressure and one's own reactions of failure and frustration are problems everyone faces, not just managerial personnel.

Termination Policy for the Nonexempt Employee

As with all employees, terminations of nonexempt personnel or we believe that, as with all employees, termination etc. should be guided by strict company policy requiring supervisors to document substantive business reasons for the discharge.

For example, when a worker is abusing company standards, failure to apply discipline undermines the supervisor's ability to maintain control over the work unit. Behavioral scientists recognize equity as a strong need that motivates worker behavior. Advanced by J. Stacy Adams, equity theory maintains that workers continually compare the quality of their inputs and the level of their outcomes against those of their co-workers.[2] Inputs are characteristics the worker brings or contributes to the job (such as skills, education, experience, and motivation. Outcomes are benefits derived from the job (compensation, status, and so on).

Equity theory holds that when workers perceive an unfavorable ratio between their own inputs and outcomes and those of others, a state of psychological tension is created. Workers strive to release this tension by reducing or increasing inputs or outcomes. For example, an employee who perceives that his or her job qualifications are greater than those of co-workers receiving the same pay might produce less work in order to reduce the inequity.

Equity theory has special relevance in the disciplinary process. When one worker violates work rules, as by being repeatedly late for work, a state of inequity is created. Other workers view their inputs (showing up on time) as being greater than the tardy person's. Most of them look for the supervisor to restore equity to the work situation by imposing discipline. Every consultant has heard complaints during interviews about a supervisor who lets people "get away with murder."

If the supervisor fails to restore equity through the use of disciplinary methods, eventually employees will move to restore equity to the situation by reducing their own inputs; they, too, will fail to comply with the regulation. Soon the supervisor finds even his good employees violating the rule. Discipline is a tool for maintaining equity in the work situation. Failure to use it as such leads to more control problems as employees take the initiative to restore equity.

When the employee's behavior is the cause for termination, documentation of at least three warning discussions should be required. When terminating any employee, the supervisor should be required to demonstrate that the worker was aware that his or her current behavior was not acceptable, was told what was expected in the future, and repeatedly failed to meet that standard.

Over the years, the arbitration of labor disputes has resulted in general guidelines in the area of discipline and dismissal. The principles that guide the arbitration process are instructive for any corporate policy aimed at establishing fair employee-relations practices. Some of the more significant ones are briefly summarized below.

1. Termination should not be used as a punitive tool.

Termination is the harshest disciplinary measure available to supervisors. In that sense, it is always punitive in nature. Termination, however, should be the end result of a series of disciplinary measures, and it should never be used as a means of retaliation or to make an example of someone. It is in that sense that we use the term *nonpunitive*.

2. Work standards and performance expectations must be communicated to the worker in a specific and coherent fashion.

While this might seem self-evident, it is amazingly often not the case. Try this little experiment. Ask a subordinate to list the performance standards that he or she is expected to maintain and to rank them in order of importance. Leave the employee alone to do this while you go elsewhere and do the same thing: list your performance expectations for the person in rank order. Then get together and compare lists, with the employee going first. See how well you agree. Remember, this is a test of mutual understanding. Don't get angry if differences are revealed.

The same principle applies to rules. Important rules should be written in the employee handbook, and evidence that the employee knew and understood a rule should exist before disciplinary action is initiated.

3. If a work standard has not been enforced in the past, it is incumbent on the supervisor to warn all employees that in the future the standard (or rule) will be enforced.

By not enforcing the rule, the supervisor has given tacit approval of employee behavior on the job. Thus, employees have every right to expect that the rule will be overlooked in the future. Employees must be put on notice when supervisors change their attitude toward enforcement. Otherwise discipline, including termination, is excessively punitive in nature.

4. Disciplinary procedures must be applied without evidence of favoritism.

Failure to perform to organizational standards should invoke the same penalty regardless of the person involved. When disciplinary sanctions are not invoked for some employees, the disciplinary process is undermined and again takes on an excessively punitive connotation. Because termination is the final step of the disciplinary process, or the harshest form of discipline, any failure in sound disciplinary practice undercuts corporate termination policy.

5. Termination should be part of a progressive process of applying sanctions.

As implied above, termination should be management's last recourse when other disciplinary efforts have failed. Only acts of gross misconduct should meet with immediate dismissal. These include fighting, malicious disorderly behavior, willful destruction of company property, lying, theft, and willful acts that threaten the health or safety of superiors, co-workers, or the general public. Other actions should initiate a progressive process in which the supervisor first counsels the employee and then gives a series of warnings, perhaps even time off from the job, before finally terminating the employee. Even when the supervisor feels there is little hope for change, it is important to go through the entire process, giving the employee ample opportunity to improve.

6. When applying discipline the supervisor should establish with the employee what the employee must do in order to meet the organization's expectations.

As we have repeatedly stated, when working with an employee whose performance or behavior is poor, the supervisor should state clearly what is expected. The employee should be aware of the consequences of failing to improve, but also of how to avoid further disciplinary action and, in effect, get back in good standing with the supervisor.

Although the supervisor may feel that such a change is unlikely, it is always worth the effort to give the individual an opportunity to improve and, if performance does come up to standard, to try to put the current problems out of mind.

7. The employee should always know the consequences of failing to respond to the current disciplinary measures.

When a discharged employee can effectively argue that he or she was unaware of the consequences of failing to respond to previous disciplinary measures, arbitrators have not upheld the dismissal. These arbitration decisions are based on sound industrial relations practice. From the standpoint of fairness and making sure that the lines of communication are not confused, whenever an employee is given a warning or is counseled, the supervisor should inform the employee of the next step in the disciplinary process, especially if it involves a substantial penalty. This should be done even when it can reasonably be argued that the employee should know what that step is. For example, most large corporations publish the steps of the disciplinary process in their employee handbooks. New employees are informed of these steps at the time of employment. Under such conditions, supervisors often feel that employees know exactly where they stand, as indeed they often do. Still, informing employees of the next disciplinary step, especially if it involves time off or discharge, is the best practice for guaranteeing that employees are aware of the consequences of their actions. Failure to do so undermines the concept of fair warning. At the end of every disciplinary session, the employee must be aware of the consequences of failing to improve.

8. The history of the disciplinary process must be documented before the termination is initiated.

Once the supervisor begins the disciplinary process, it is important to document it. The purpose of documentation is not to threaten the employee but to communicate the seriousness of the situation and provide a record of what has transpired. Often documentation itself convinces the employee that the time has come to improve, avoiding the necessity of termination.

At every disciplinary interview, the supervisor should note

the time, place of discussion, problem discussed, employee reaction, and next step to be taken. It is particularly important that the supervisor note what the next disciplinary step will be, along with the required standard for improvement. It should be noted that failure to meet that standard will be cause for further disciplinary action.

The employee should be asked to sign and date the document. If the employee refuses, the document should be witnessed by another representative of management after being reviewed with the employee present. We suggest that three such documents should precede dismissal. The third of these written warnings often involves a suspension period.

The Support Package for Nonexempts

Termination of a nonexempt employee requires a support package (especially when the termination is for reasons other than gross misconduct). The employee should get severance pay consistent with tenure and skill level. This may range from a week's to a couple of months, compensation. It is also good practice to provide a letter specifying whom the employee can use as a reference and what will be said in the reference. This can be given to the employee by the supervisor doing the termination. This information should also be communicated verbally during the termination interview.

Nonexempt employees are just as likely as exempt ones to be in a state of confusion over the termination. They are also likely to benefit from advice on the job search process. Therefore, counseling arranged through the personnel department is a highly appropriate part of the support package.

Today, more and more companies are providing counseling assistance to severed nonexempt employees. This assistance ranges from providing a workbook on how to find another job to offering outplacement counseling with a reputable firm. Although such counseling efforts are generally not as elaborate as the support offered exempt employees, personnel experts are coming to agree on certain topics that are important to nonexempts:

- How to fill out application forms.
- How to be interviewed.
- How to identify jobs to which their skills are transferable.
- Income tax exemption of job search expenses.
- How to determine "what I want to do with the rest of my life."

Nonexempts also need to let off steam and to sort through what has happened. Often this need is as strong as the need for job search skills, although it is less likely to be recognized.

We suggest that a representative of the personnel department be available to meet with employee after the dismissal by the supervisor. The personnel representative can review the events that led to the discharge, provide some hints on what to do next, and generally spend time helping the employee calm down and collect his or her thoughts. If possible, job search counseling should be provided the following day. Such training is more likely to be beneficial once the employee has overcome the initial shock of the termination. The terminated employee is also more likely to ask questions after having a day to think through the situation.

Rationalizations aside, the reasons nonexempts have been excluded from such counseling support have more to do with their status in the workplace than with their needs. Management simply has not viewed them as worthy of such support. Extending such consideration to nonexempts meets very real individual and corporate needs, however. At the same time, it helps break down class distinctions in the workplace, which tend to reinforce an adversary posture between nonexempts and administrative and managerial employees. Increasingly, programs breaking down these barriers are becoming part of enlightened human-resource administration.

The Termination Interview

The termination interview should be direct and to the point. Once the employee is seated in the supervisor's office—the termination should be done in private, not in front of other workers—the supervisor should simply begin by stating, for example, "_____, I am very sorry, but we are going to have to let you go. You missed your shift three times again this month" (or whatever the reason for termination). The supervisor should refer to the previous disciplinary interviews, reminding the employee of the warning that failure to improve would result in termination. The supervisor should not argue with the employee but make it clear that the decision is final.

Next, the supervisor should inform the employee of the severance package. Above all, the supervisor should promise nothing to the employee beyond what is specified in the severance package. The employee should be sent to the personnel department for final counseling or discussion.

The nonexempt termination interview is considerably shorter than the exempt interview for a couple of reasons. First, assuming policy has been followed, the causes are generally more clearcut. The intangibles of the work relationship have less to do with causing performance difficulties at this level of the organization. Second, many first-line supervisors are even less comfortable with counseling than are managers. Nevertheless, the full range of reactions on the part of the employee is possible. The supervisor should be prepared to defuse an emotional reaction, not be intimidated, and avoid arguing. Rather, he or she should remain calm, listen to any initial comments, and restate the facts of the current situation, which are that the employee is discharged. The supervisor should be sure the employee understands the situation and knows where to go next.

It is best for employees to collect their things, go to the personnel department for counseling, and then leave the premises. They need support and time to assimilate what has happened. Returning to the work unit does little good and can do damage if the employee is working around equipment in a distracted state.

As with exempt employees, terminations should not be scheduled at the end of the week or the end of the day. All too often nonexempt teminations occur at five o'clock on Friday for "payroll purposes," leaving the employee to go home in a state of shock.

As with other terminations, when a decision is made to terminate a nonexempt, it should be reviewed by the next level of management and by the personnel manager before any action is taken. This review should concern itself with determining that the above principles have been followed. Here is a checklist that can be used in the review process. Following this checklist virtually guarantees that a termination is fair and can be substantiated.

1. Documentation of just cause:
   • Repeated failure to meet performance standards.
   • Lack of compliance with company regulations.
   • Gross misconduct.
   • Job elimination part of corporate cutbacks.
2. If disciplinary in nature:
   • Is the termination the final step of a progressive process of applying sanctions?
   • Does the employee know what level of performance is expected to avoid termination?
   • Has the employee been informed that termination is the next step if improvement is not made?
   • Was the rule or regulation clearly communicated in advance of the violation?
   • Was gross misconduct intentional?
   • Has each of the above been documented (at least three signed and dated memoranda)?
3. Managerial review:
   • Department management
   • Personnel department

4. Severance package:
   - Payments
   - Contact for recommendations identified and agreed to
   - Counseling by personnel arranged
5. Termination interview:
   - In private
   - Direct, with statement of cause

The Appeal Process

Virtually all labor agreements provide for an appeal process, which affords employees an opportunity to dispute the dismissal. A final step in this process is the opportunity to have the case reviewed by an independent arbitrator. In nonunion companies, the only source of appeal is usually the personnel director or some other representative of management.

The most common form of the appeal system is the open-door policy and/or a step procedure that permits an employee to appeal his or her case to increasingly higher level managers. Open-door policies, which invite employees to register complaints with more senior managers, are fine, and employees should be encouraged to use them, but senior managers should not exaggerate their effectiveness. As one employee told us, "That doorway can seem awfully small." Often too, problems are rooted in rules management has promulgated and may be defensive about. If an employee's complaint centers on the unfairness of a certain role, a manager who helped draft it may be unwilling to admit that it is having unintended consequences.

Some nonunion companies have established a grievance procedure that makes use of a jury or hearing committee. A survey conducted by Maryellen LoBasco of the American Management Association found three types of jury procedures in use by a few companies.[3] In two of the procedures, a representative from the personnel department served as chairperson or hearing officer.

One of the procedures used a jury of three, chosen by the employee, the other a committee of five, three of whom were chosen by the employee. The three members of the committee selected by the employee were chosen from a panel appointed by the president. The third procedure selected the jury through random drawing of two peers and two senior administrative staff. In each case, the jury was used only after a step procedure had been followed and the employee wished to pursue the issue further.

A few nonunion companies provide for outside arbitration as part of their grievance process. We strongly support this practice.

When other nonexempt employees view a colleague's dismissal, it is easy for them to conclude that the company was arbitrary in its judgment. If the supervisor's case is legitimate, well documented, and in compliance with corporate policy, management has little to fear from arbitration proceedings. The more substantial the case, the less likely the employee is to appeal it. Furthermore, a decision in favor of management removes doubt from the minds of other employees about management's fairness. Finally, the availability of arbitration reinforces company policy. It demonstrates management's confidence in its termination policy and places pressure on supervisors to follow policy practices carefully.

Some managers believe that arbitrators rarely uphold a discharge for poor performance. According to Robert Coulson, president of the American Arbitration Association, that's not true. But arbitrators do require proof. When the employer demonstrates that a measurable standard exists and was fairly applied, the arbitrator will find for the company.[4] Coulson also reports a Conference Board study of nonunion companies using grievance arbitration. The companies were satisfied with the procedure and claimed it did not compromise management's prerogatives, nor did the process get swamped with cases.[5]

Having such a policy provides an atmosphere of security for employees and can contribute to a climate of support and trust between employees and management. Above all, it is a practical demonstration that employees don't need a union to protect them from unjust dismissal.

Management is becoming increasingly sophisticated in battling unionization. Indeed, proponents of the "quality of work life" movement in industry argue that productivity gains are possible, while maintaining a nonunion environment, if management recognizes the need workers have for an element of discretion in their jobs and for protection from arbitrary management practices: Fair and consistent discharge practices are an important element in the quality of work life. Establishing arbitration rights for employees can greatly reinforce such practices, while providing workers with a tangible source of protection against unfair dismissal. As Coulson notes "no system of grievance review, short of arbitration, can be entirely credible."[6]

Whatever its form, an effective grievance procedure can often reveal problems early in the disciplinary process, so that it does not reach the point of discharge. Nonexempt employees tend to perceive themselves as more dependent on their immediate supervisors than exempt employees do. Thus, it is important that nonexempt employees be aware of the grievance procedures established by the company and have faith in their fairness.

The practices we have recommended are consistent with our previous discussions of corporate policy. The extent of the benefits may not be as great for nonexempt as for managerial employees, but the basic principles should remain the same.

Endnotes

[1]Barry Bluestone, "Do We Need an Industrial Policy?" *Harpers* (February 1985), 39.
[2]J. Stacy Adams, "Toward an Understanding of Inequity," *Journal of Abnormal Psychology and Social Psychology* (1963), 422–36.

[3]Maryellen LoBasco, "Nonunion Grievance Procedures," *Personnel* (January 1985).
[4]Robert Coulson, *The Termination Handbook* (New York: The Free Press, 1981), 85.
[5]Ibid., 84.
[6]Ibid.

12

Work-force Reductions

RESTRUCTURING, DOWNSIZING, DESELECTING—NO matter which term is used, they mean the same thing: a substantial number of employees terminated at the same time. Often whole work sites are closed down or entire levels of organizations are eliminated. The latter is highly significant, because it reflects a realization on the part of senior managers that their companies are overstructured and that this results in confused communications, poor responses to changing market conditions, and excessive resources diverted into battles between competitive groups within the corporate hierarchy.

The stakes are high for companies engaged in restructuring. More is involved than just savings on salary and overhead costs: coordination costs are also saved and communication efficiencies achieved. As a single communication (for example, an oral request for information) travels five levels through a hierarchy, 80 percent of the original intent and content may be lost.[1] Organizational researchers generally accept the notion that, other things being equal, flat organizational structures have more effective internal communications than tall ones.[2]

A number of factors have resulted in the current trend toward work-force reductions. The high level of merger and acquisition activity is an obvious one: merged organizations usually result in redundancies, especially in staff services. Another factor is the emergence of an intensely competitive world economy, in which the United States is no longer dominant.[3] Since American corporations are generally more heavily layered than their most powerful world competitors. they have borne excessively high communication costs, and the current downsizing in part represents a reorganization of the corporation. Economist David Birch argues that retrenchment is often a clue that a large company is positioning itself for future competitiveness.[4]

The current explosion in technology, especially in information systems, is a more subtle yet most potent influence on corporate restructuring. One of the effects of computers on organizations since the 1960s has been the move toward re-centralization and the trimming of middle management. Improved efficiencies of information flow to top management reduce the need for corporate staff to gather and report data. Moreover, there is less need to delegate authority, since senior managers are able to remain in close touch with local conditions. Since the explosion of information technology in the early 1980s, these effects have become visible on a larger scale. Additionally, new approaches to managing are emerging, such as just-in-time inventory scheduling and out-sourcing of production functions. The result has been referred to as the hollow corporation.

Finally, once a company has experienced a significant work-force reduction, it is often easier to downsize a second time. Management then realizes:

- The extent to which excessive layering is a problem.
- That smaller may be better.
- That the company can indeed live through the pain of such a process.
- That outplacement counseling and related methods make the process less painful.

The net effect of all these changes is that restructurings are, for the foreseeable future, more likely than in the past to be a recurring feature of corporate life, regardless of economic conditions.

Potential Problems

Such retrenchment is not without its problems or liabilities, however. For example, many of the methods that have been developed to facilitate downsizing must by law be available to everyone within the class of employees to which the program is extended. *Window* programs refer to a period of time during which a clearly defined class of employees has the option of accepting a financial incentive package to leave the organzation voluntarily. The period of time during which the offer is in effect is the window. Early retirement programs have similar rules. Unfortunately, many of the employees who opt to leave are precisely those management wanted to stay, and those who remain are exactly the ones management hoped would leave. Also, a delicate balance in the program must be reached: with too generous a program, too many employees may leave, and the company may pay more than necessary; too miserly a program will probably result in too few employees leaving. Miserliness may foster hostility and resentment among employees, who then become candidates for involuntary separation. Hostility in these circumstances cannot be taken lightly given the potential for charges of discrimination and abusive dismissal. This last possibility is a special concern for companies that in the past have made job security a matter of company policy (see Chapter Three).

Less overt, but potentially troublesome, is the realization on the part of employees that loyalty is no longer a two-way street. As corporations make themselves leaner, they also break the unwritten psychological contract with employees that longevity of service is rewarded both financially and with job security. No one knows the long-term consequences of breaking the link between length of service and security but one thing seems clear: employees are less likely to identify with the goals of the corporation than in the past and more likely to look out for their own interests. Companies are going to have to work harder at retaining key personnel who are highly marketable. Since loyalty is no longer rewarded, employees can be expected to seek maximization of immediate financial rewards. The work force is likely to become even more cynical about corporate purposes.

Succession plans are often disrupted by management reductions. In addition, survivors are often demoralized.[5] While some employees may have increased opportunities for career advancement as a result of organizational downsizing, many find fewer slots for upward mobility in the new, leaner organization. In addition, many find themselves with fewer trappings of prestige and more involved in the less glamorous work processes of the company. Furthermore, the loss of mentors for upcoming executives and key personnel, leading to the need to recruit from outside right after a reduction, often causes confusion and bitterness among those remaining. Finally, poor press can make recruiting new talent difficult.

These potential problems mean that careful planning must be done to assure that a work-force reduction strategy is developed for the specific conditions within a given company.

The Steps of Work-force Reductions

Experience with more than 150 work-force reductions has led to the following general model for approaching large-scale downsizings. Of course, the specifics of each step must vary according to the established policies of the company, its industry position, the social and political responsibilities it has to the immediate community, and the forces driving the retrenchment.

Step 1: An Organizational Study

The first step should be a carefully conducted organizational study that considers:

- *The climate within the organization.* What are the likely reactions to the work-force reduction from various segments of the organization? Which employees are likely to perceive themselves as potential winners from a given type of reduction? Which are likely to regard themselves as losers? Is this action anticipated by employees? Or is the action unexpected and will the organization be traumatized? What is the corporate culture, and to what extent can the approach be tailored to the culture?

- *The goals of the organization and its strategy for accomplishing them.* Which components of the organization are fundamental to future operations and which are not? Should the corporation be reducing some areas while building up others? What skills and human-resource assets must be preserved?

- *Succession planning.* How will the reduction impact existing succession plans? What developmental activities should be engaged in immediately following the reduction?

- *Impact on the ability to do business.* How will the downsizing impact the organization's ability to service its markets? How will key customers react? What steps can be taken to avoid inconveniencing them?

- *Reaction of the competition.* What will be the competition's posture relative to key suppliers, customers, and community image?

Failure to consider the basic issues outlined above is likely to make management appear inconsistent and incoherent to important constituencies. Above all, *credibility* is critical during a major work force reduction.

Unfortunately, management often starts cutbacks either

without such a study or before the study is complete. When this happens, it soon becomes apparent to the press, employees, and customers that management has not done its homework. Worse, management is in the position of not moving toward a clear goal. Hence, its actions often seem arbitrary and unnecessarily draconian.

The need to assess the climate within the organization is often overlooked, with unfortunate consequences. Management simply assumes it knows the sentiment of the majority of the work force and is surprised when the reaction runs counter to its expectations. For example, one major chemical corporation assumed that, since it had virtually never fired people in the past, its professional staff was secure and happy. In reality, many were angry and felt locked in. Management was shocked when large numbers of people took advantage of the window program. In another company, the cutback was so totally unexpected that more then ten years later employees still refer to it as "the massacre." Commitment to the organization has been significantly damaged.

It is equally important for key members of the management team to be familiar with the current staffing of the organization and conversant with the impact that the reduction will have on work assignments. Management should track specific responses to the cutback, including how managers are reassigning workloads. In one steel company, for example, lower-level managers "hid" people—reducing the budget but not the payroll. It took some time for management to realize what was happening.

Step 2: Review of Performance Appraisal Data

The organizational study is a review of the company's structure and processes, not an assessment of individuals. Once the organization knows where it wants to go, it has to determine who it needs to get it there. The future plans of key managers should be carefully assessed. Also, if performance is going to be the criterion for involuntary separations, the quality of performance appraisals becomes a critical concern, both from a legal point of view and in terms of making the right choices. As mentioned in Chapter Four, performance should be documented against specific goals. There should also be sufficient descriptive data regarding the abilities individuals have demonstrated in performing their jobs to sustantiate comparative rankings.

Ratings from multiple sources are more compelling than assessment by a single individual, since they help overcome the problem of rater bias. For example, one company undertook a program of having its professional employees rated by peers as well as by current supervisors. The result was a much more substantial data base for decision-making, supplementing the regular appraisal system. This approach has also withstood legal challenges to its validity.

Step 3: Voluntary Separation Incentives

As much as possible, it is best to encourage employees to leave voluntarily. It should be noted that, even when voluntary, leaving a job in which one has had some success and security is potentially traumatic for long-term employees. Uncertainty about the future may spread to those who choose to stay, for they cannot be assured that future involuntary terminations won't be necessary. Viewed from the standpoint of the corporation's best interests, it is imperative that employees be prepared and supported when choosing voluntary terminations. Otherwise, horror stories begin to surround the work-force reduction.

The design of the incentive program is important and must take into account the context within which the organization operates. Key considerations are:

- *Demographics*—especially how the age group is arrived at and defined.
- *Economic conditions*. If the perception is that the local

economy is strong, offering many immediate opportunities (as in Boston in 1986), the impact will be different than if the reverse is true (as in, Houston in 1986).

- *Geographical mobility of the employees.* How tied are they to the area?
- *Cost to the company.*

Beyond the financial structure of the incentive, the way the company manages the termination process will influence who chooses to stay and who chooses to leave. How the package is presented sends certain signals to present and possibly future employees. The extent to which the company provides other kinds of support to its employees in transition also sends a message. Career decision workshops, which help employees objectively assess their options, are one such support vehicle. Outplacement support is another. These activities establish that the company is not merely trying to "buy people off" but is concerned that career transitions be well thought out, with a reasonable degree of structure and planning.

Step 4: Evaluation and Internal Placement

Once the window closes, it is imperative that management immediately evaluate the results against the original plan. Here is where the data from steps 1 and 2 become extremely helpful. What in fact has happened to the mix of necessary skills and plans for succession? Internal placements of remaining personnel should be carried out expeditiously. It is also critical that the remaining individuals be made to feel that their immediate value to the organization is recognized and appreciated. Key employees need to be reassured, for this is still a time of considerable uncertainty among those who have stayed, and top management does not want to risk alienating or losing those it will depend upon in the future.

Step 5: Involuntary Work-force Reduction

Severance packages should be planned, as criteria are developed for selecting those who will be terminated. Generally, the fixed-percentage-across-the-board approach is harmful to the organization. Reductions in each department should be targeted by means of a strategic plan. Clear direction must be given on how people should be selected (by performance or seniority). Outplacement support should be offered, including group sessions of two or three days, conducted by external or internal specialists.

Once everything is in place for step 5, consideration must be given to making the announcement and dealing with the press.

Management needs to establish a theme based on its strategy and then plan a sequence of events that fits the theme. For example, the company may be repositioning itself in the marketplace so that its new cost structure will make its principal products more competitive. This theme can be established in communications that lead up to the main announcement, allowing people to anticipate and mentally prepare for the work-force reduction. This is as necessary for the larger community as it is for employees. Despite management's fears, employees will not abandon ship as soon as they get word of the direction things are going.

Included in the theme is the C.E.O.'s justification for the downsizing. This explanation should be placed within the context of the company's overall strategy. Particularly important is the need to focus on the positive aspects of the reduction, or what the company is trying to accomplish, and in effect show that management is moving toward its goals.

If an error is to be made, it is better to err in favor of communication than the reverse. People should have benchmarks in terms of dates: "By March 2nd, I will know _____." This will help reduce uncertainty. One company, for example, announced that a shutdown would occur on a specific date. At the time of the announcement, employees were told that within a week everyone would know whether they would be asked to leave at the end of the week, stay for a month, or remain until the final close-down. Key public figures, such as the mayor, were informed in advance of announcements to the press. The public announcements included details of the kind of support that would be provided to the work force.

Once the decisions are made, a communication center should be established, and one person should be appointed to handle all public relations. Training programs should be set up to instruct managers in the proper way to handle discussions with employees.

All told, communications are an important part of carrying out a work-force reduction. If a company does all its homework but falls down in its communications, the result can be just as disastrous as if preparations were poorly made.

Step 6: Building Recommitment Among Those Remaining in the Company

This final step in the process is often overlooked by those planning a downsizing. Their assumption seems to be that, once the organization has been restructured and the reductions in staffing completed, those employees who remain will be energized into a highly productive work force. This is rarely the case. Months after the changes have been completed, management may be surprised to find the organization "dead in the water." One divison president told us, "When I walk through the shop, I am shocked at how lethargic everyone is. There is more work than ever to get done, but no one is taking the initiative."

This division head was witnessing what has come to be referred to as *survivor shock*. While it seems reasonable to expect people to respond to a work-force reduction by putting more energy into their work in an effort to make the company competitive, close examination of the dynamics of the situation reveals this expectation to be unrealistic. Indeed, once the formal reorganization has been accomplished, management has only established the basic framework for organizational performance. A program to help those who populate that framework is necessary if the new organization is to be revitalized. The new program must seek to accomplish two objectives: (1) psychologically prepare employees to become productive following the turmoil of the downsizing and (2) provide them with specific skills for performing their jobs in the new environment.

Psychological Support

Most people think of those who have left the organization as the ones with a problem. Conversely, the attitude toward the survivors is, "You don't have a problem, you have a job."

In reality the survivors face a number of emotional issues. Having witnessed what is often a violation of mutual expectations between their peers and the organization, those who remain are often on an emotional roller coaster. They are experiencing anger, distrust, guilt, and anxiety.

A helpful way of understanding the reactions of the survivors is through the concept of the psychological contract. In Chapter Three, we observed that employees often take at face value statements made orally and in company documents regarding job security and lifetime employment. Indeed, many state courts are now treating such statements as legal contracts.

On an emotional level, many employees have come to depend on the organization as a source of security. The expectation, often encouraged by the company, has been that loyalty will be rewarded with job security. Likewise, statements regarding the commitment of the corporation to its human assets have been believed by employees. The work-force reduction calls into question both aspects of the psychological contract. The company is abandoning human assets and declaring that loyalty is a luxury it can no longer afford to reward.

Those who leave the organization experience the trauma of separation and then move on, often with the structured support of an outplacement program. Once they find a new position, there are rituals that signify a new beginning: a formal offer of employment, an official welcome and orientation to the new job, and so on. There are no such rites of passage for those who remain. They are often told that the company is undergoing a new beginning, but with the passage of time it often appears that the company remains the same but with increased work loads and fewer opportunities for advancement. Ironically, the company appears to be doing more for those who leave than for those who remain.

Of course, those who stay still have a job. The objective reality of that fact provides relief from the need to make any immediate change in their situation. Wishing to preserve this option, most seek to blend in and not make waves, to repress any strong negative emotions. Yet almost everyone we have talked with who has lived through such a situation reports having experienced strong negative feelings.

The initial reaction is one of disorientation. After months of uncertainty, employees learn that they will remain with the organization, but they are not sure what that means. If they have been given a new job assignment, it may have no real meaning since the organization has changed so much. Obviously, the larger the downsizing, the more intense this reaction.

Gradually, disorientation can give way to focused anger if people perceive that some of their former colleagues were treated unfairly. There can be excessive concern with who is "on the team" and who is not. As the rumor mill heats up, a growing sense of isolation can develop, and people become unsure whom they can trust. The people who have jobs are not sure they are really the lucky ones. One manager told us, "I think I would have been better off if they had let me go."

This feeling is intensified as stories of those who have done well after leaving begin to filter back. People begin to question whether they should stay. At this point they focus strongly on what their prospects are in the organization. Roughly six months to a year following a downsizing, the company is very vulnerable to losing its most marketable people.

Skill Development

Apart from these psychological problems, it is simply more difficult to accomplish one's job in the new environment, even when focusing on the task at hand. Often procedures and priorities are unclear. Management may have published a new organizational chart, but no functional chart exists. People are not really sure of what their new job entails.

Following a downsizing, management can establish a new formal set of working arrangements. What it cannot create is the informal network of relationships that people build up over the years and come to depend on in order to get their jobs done. For one auto manufacturer, this was a particular problem, since not only specific people but entire units had disappeared. As one engineer remarked, "In the past, when you had a problem, you could go to friends for answers, cut through the red tape. If an old colleague couldn't help you, he would introduce you to someone who could. That doesn't work anymore. Too many people are gone, or relocated."

Many people are faced with establishing a relationship with a new boss who is also dealing with survivor issues. Hence, the single most important relationship to an employee has itself been complicated by the downsizing.

These issues are obviously not insurmountable. The point is that, for an extended period of time, a lot of energy will be misdirected in the organizational system. Further, many of the practical supports to job performance will be disrupted. It is in management's best interests to minimize these effects.

Management must formulate a plan to address the concerns of the survivors as well as those who leave. If the downsizing involves a number of involuntary separations, a key element of the plan is training managers how to respond on the day involuntary separations are communicated. There is a pronounced tendency for managers to schedule such interviews in a highly formalized manner. Once the task is over, managers tend to disappear, either leaving for meetings or withdrawing into their offices, where they occupy themselves with detail work, much of it meaningless. Hence, at exactly the point when the organization is violating what many believe to be a psychological contract, key managers are becoming remote.

Managing Such Situations

One of the most important things managers can do in such situations is be visible and readily accessible. This is one time when walking around is sound managerial practice. Once all the discharges have been completed, unit managers need to schedule meetings with their new team to discuss what has happened and plan future job assignments.

A key decision is how long discharged employees should remain in the work area. Requiring them to leave immediately intensifies the impression that the process is being handled in a cold and unfeeling way. On the other hand, if they remain in the work area for days or even weeks following the downsizing, others are placed in a difficult position. Therefore, those who are leaving should be given a reasonable period of time to collect their things, perhaps until the end of the working day, and then be scheduled for the career center or similar outplacement assistance.

During the months following the downsizing, management must strive to communicate effectively with the members of the organization. These efforts should go beyond speeches and pep talks. Managers should hold "sensing" sessions with employees to identify their real concerns, and these concerns should be acknowledged by management. Upward communication, always a problem in organizations, is especially so following a work-force reduction. People become very political and try not to be noticed. Indeed, how to encourage risk-taking is often a major problem for management seeking to energize the organization. Acknowledging concerns that are expressed is one concrete action management can take toward encouraging self-expression and individual initiative.

At the same time, it is important that management not promise more than it can or intends to deliver. Frankness is the first step in guarding future credibility. All too often, we have heard management promise that the last reductions have been made or, in smaller organizations, that the survivors will be generously rewarded. If later events prove these statements false, as is often the case, the organization experiences extended malaise.

Training sessions that allow participants to express their reactions to the downsizing and to develop the skills they need to perform their new jobs effectively are helpful pieces of a corporate revitalization strategy. Confidentiality of comments made during such sessions is essential. Among the skill development topics that can be covered are: internal networking skills (to reestablish necessary productive contacts within the company), managing the boss, and role clarification.

We hope we have persuasively made our point that the survivors, like those who are leaving, have specific needs that have to be addressed during a downsizing. They are the ones who must reconcile the events of the work-force reduction with their continued commitment to the organization. And after all, it is with them that the organization must go forward.

Two Experiences

That companies are becoming better at the downsizing process is hardly debatable. Following are the experiences of two organizations that went through the process.

A major financial institution, when confronted with the need for a sizable reduction in its professional ranks, involved its human-resource people in the process from the beginning. As one of the human-resource professionals put it, "This was the first time we were ever involved this early in the decision-making process. Usually we are just told that this is what they want to do and that we should make it happen. This time we were called in, listened to, and given the chance to help shape the decisions that were made."

An executive in the company commented, "Involving our human-resource people right from the start was a wise business decision. We're highly visible and we knew that our actions would have a big impact on people throughout the industry. We also knew we would have to go out and recruit again at some point in the future."

A personnel committee was formed, consisting of the department heads of employee relations, compensation, organizational analysis, and employment. The head of corporate communications was also a member. Meeting at least once a week for two months, they developed a strategy, which was approved by the firm's executive committee. This strategy included policy decisions on outplacement assistance, benefits and salary continuation packages, and administrative systems to monitor and process data. A program of internal and external communications was designed. All this work was done in a confidential manner.

Among other actions, the company organized an information and placement center at which other firms could inquire about certain kinds of skills and receive the resumes of appropriate candidates. In fact, the firm made special efforts to communicate to potential employers that capable people would soon be on the market and then made efforts to bring them together.

Once the downsizing was completed, the firm turned its attention to instituting better controls in adding staff. As one person put it, "We need to be more creative in finding other ways to get work done besides just adding people. This industry is too reactive. We need to plan better."

The coordinator of the personnel committee identified three lessons the firm learned from the process. First, thorough planning in the early stages helped enormously. Second, managers needed training in how to handle terminations. Particularly important was training in how to avoid allowing the discussion to turn into a debate. Finally, outplacement counseling was extremely valuable. Too many people fail to realize how difficult it can be searching for a job after a work-force reduction. In our example, many of the discharged employees assumed it was just a matter of going to a referral agency.

The need to improve the termination skills of managers was also observed in a large insurance company. This company too went through a thorough planning process, with key human-resource people involved from the start in a task-force format. One of the positive results of this planning was the clear articulation of goals for the work-force reduction in line with corporate strategy. Thus the company was able to clearly indicate its goals rather than simply fire people.

A task analysis was completed for all functions, and human-resource requirements were established. Then a detailed work-force analysis was completed. People were assessed in terms of their qualifications to perform tasks critical to the business goals, past performance, and seniority. The situations of those employees who were members of protected classes were also reviewed by corporate human resources, the legal adviser, and the divisional vice president. Out of this process came a matrix in which specific reduction targets were established and staffing decisions made on the basis of business need.

The processes employed in both these organizations were by far superior to the approach of mandating a fixed-percentage reduction across all departments. Happily, this almost insane practice is more and more becoming a thing of the past.

Downsizing has become a hallmark of the 1980s. As more organizations have made such large-scale work-force reductions, the process has become more systematic and been more effectively managed. The steps outlined above offer a framework for raising the questions that need to be addressed in tailoring a downsizing strategy to a particular corporation.

Endnotes

[1] Ralph G. Nichols, "Listening Is Good Business," *Management of Personnel Quarterly* 1, no. 2 (1962) 4.

[2] John Child, *Organization: A Guide to Problems and Practice*, 2d. ed. (London: Harper & Row, 1984).

[3] Ezra F. Vogel, "Pax Nipponica?" *Foreign Affairs*, 64 (Spring 1986),754–67.

[4] James Cook, "Bring On the Wild and Crazy People," *Forbes* (April 28, 1986), 54–56.

[5] "The End of Corporate Loyalty?" *Business Week* (August 4, 1986), 42–49.

13

Four Difficult Termination Situations

AS WE HAVE STATED REPEATEDLY, TERMINA-
tion is seldom easy. However, some situations are more
difficult than others. When we asked outplacement consultants to identify the kinds of terminations that are especially
difficult to handle, the following four problems emerged with an
overwhelming degree of frequency. These are also the problems
managers request help with most often.

Problem No. 1: The Long-term Employee

When terminating someone, it seems easier when the person is
young and has only been with the company for a few years. If
people have served the organization for ten, fifteen, or even
twenty-plus years, management feels an obligation to them, and
the manager doing the termination may feel very guilty.

Consider the problems that arise when discharging such employees. First, they have been out of the job market for a considerable length of time. Second, they are likely to suffer from a

parochial viewpoint simply because they have spent so long with one company; they will have set ideas on how things are done and may be so in tune with the company's way that they will be at a distinct disadvantage in selling themselves to other organizations. Third, their co-workers are likely to be especially sensitive to their treatment as a measure of the company's loyalty to its employees.

These employees are especially in need of outplacement counseling after the termination interview. They are most likely to be susceptible to the pitfalls of the job search process, simply because they have been long removed from it. Furthermore, providing OPC helps to demonstrate the company's recognition of their years of service.

Beyond providing OPC support, the company's termination policy should recognize longevity of employment as one of the criteria affecting the specifics of the support package. Generally, long-term employees should receive generous financial and nonfinancial benefits, reflecting the problems of adjustment that confront them, as well as the organization's sense of obligation.

When firing a long-term employee, the company should use the same approach it uses with any other person, however. First, the manager must outline specifically what the employee has done to bring the situation to this point. Second, there should always be three concrete reasons why the situation has come to such a conclusion. It should go without saying that efforts toward improving performance should have been exhausted prior to arriving at the termination decision.

When dealing with long-term employees who are experiencing performance problems, it is imperative that the manager set specific performance criteria or objectives in an effort to turn their work around. Other employees will be sensitive to whether they received a fair shake.

We have often observed new managers, brought in to revive poorly performing departments, firing people almost immediately without making a legitimate effort to allow them to improve performance. Unfortunately, the opportunity for long-term employees to adjust to the new rules of the game is seldom provided. This is almost always a mistake. A manager can, and should, set strict standards for subordinates and require almost immediate evidence of improved performance, but the opportunity to perform should be there.

Nevertheless, when it becomes clear that an employee is not going to improve, a straightforward termination must be made. With long-term employees, one of the cruelest and psychologically most damaging approaches is not to tell them they are fired but to allow them to exist in a kind of never-never land of half-truths. It is equally damaging to give them minor tasks that are of little or no value to the organization. Both the employee and the employee's associates perceive the lack of meaningful contribution, and under such conditions, the empathy of close associates often turns to ridicule. Worse, the employees themselves can lose confidence in their abilities or become bitter. Friends and colleagues may begin avoiding them because of the unpleasantness of the situation.

When dealing with long-term employees, it is best to address the problem directly, giving specific, concrete reasons, and providing them with a substantial support package.

Problem No. 2: The Boss and Employee Are Good Friends

It is easy to say that supervisors and employees should not be good friends because socializing can create long-term problems. In reality, managers frequently become attached to their subordinates, which makes it difficult to discipline them. At managerial levels, this frequently occurs as alliances are forged between executives. Long managerial working hours turn these alliances into a significant part of a manager's social life.

Even when the person being dismissed is a close friend, the manager must be honest and directly state the reasons for the termination. To do less is to compromise the integrity of the organization. The real issue is that the manager has a responsibility to maintain the performance of an organization. When a subordinate is not performing or is violating some other employment criterion, not to apply the same solution that would be applied in other cases is to act irresponsibly. Termination may cost the manager the employee's friendship, but the responsibility for doing so is clear.

To place the matter in perspective, corporate friendships are also interrupted for other reasons. People change jobs or move to other divisions, and gradually relationships fade. Termination is just one aspect of the managerial environment that can affect personal relationships.

There is another side to it. Using a trumped-up rationale for letting a good friend sit and vegetate ultimately costs the manager in dealings with others. Nothing undermines a manager's influence faster than a charge of favoritism; and perceptions of favoritism are difficult to control. Failure to fire a close friend for cause compromises the manager's options in dealing with others.

When managers find themselves facing the prospect of discharging a close friend, often their basic struggle is for some reinforcement of the decision. The support of knowing that they have followed the guidelines of a solid corporate termination policy in which dismissal is the next step helps them over this difficult psychological hurdle. We have found, for example, that simply discussing the points covered above often places an executive's mind at ease. More than one person has said, "Of course I know you're right, but somehow I needed to talk it through anyway."

Problem No. 3: Members of Protected Classes

Minorities, women, and people over 40 constitute a special risk for corporations discharging them. This is true because most performance appraisal systems are inadequate and managers do not coach people properly on how to improve performance or tell them clearly enough what they are doing wrong.

Legislation prohibiting discrimination in employment practices dates back to the Civil Rights Act of 1964. This act established the Equal Employment Opportunity Commission (EEOC), which has the power to take companies to court if they are not in compliance with the act. Essentially, Title VII of the Civil Rights Act makes discrimination illegal in all areas of employment: hirings, promotions, terminations, transfers, and layoffs.

Executive Order 11246, issued in September 1965, established the concept of affirmative action for government contractors. In addition to the requirement that corporations not discriminate, affirmative action mandated that companies doing business with the federal government take steps to eliminate the effects of past discrimination. Subsequent legislation further specified the protections accorded by the EEOC.

Contrary to the opinion of many managers, it is not impossible to dismiss a member of a protected class, although a company should be prepared to defend its decision. Such a decision needs to establish that the termination is being made for "just business cause" and that the person has been warned that his or her work is not acceptable. In short, EEO legislation requires that managers make sound, unbiased, and supportable business decisions, a requirement that nevertheless makes many managers uncomfortable.

Most managers are accustomed to having their biases go unchallenged when evaluating employees. The problem can be complicated by failure to conduct and maintain sound performance reviews. As we have seen, historically courts have held that under common law an employer has the right to discharge an employee at any time regardless of the reason. Thus, with the exception of those protected by union agreements, employees have been more or less at the mercy of their bosses. EEO legislation has altered this condition for certain employees.

These factors have generated an overreaction on the part of

many supervisors and managers—a fear of taking disciplinary action against such employees. This fear is the result of misunderstanding what the law actually requires. If the termination policies and disciplinary process outlined in Chapter Four are followed, there is no problem. Documentation should exist that the employee has been told current performance is unacceptable and given standards for improvement. Specific descriptive reasons for the termination should have been given at the time of the firing. The support package should be consistent with what other employees of similar status within the organization have received. It is always good practice to review the case with the company's affirmative action specialist before taking action.

Of course, it is possible that the employee will appeal the termination to the EEOC. However, if the termination is legitimate, the complaint will cost the company little other than the time of one of its personnel managers—certainly less than maintaining the problem employee. Many complaints never get past the preliminary investigation when it becomes clear that the company acted in a thorough and aboveboard fashion.

In reality, the goal of corporate policy should be to afford all employees the protection the law has provided certain classes: a thorough and documented review of actual performance. As far as federal and state laws are concerned, employers are free to terminate any employee they wish—provided such discipline is not motivated by a discriminatory purpose or handed out in a discriminatory manner. For example, an employer may not fire an employee because the employee has complained of racial bias. Nor may an employer, faced with the need to lay off twenty-five out of one hundred employees, lay off a disproportionate number of minority employees.

Terminations for good cause, imposed in a consistent manner, without regard to race, religion, national origin, sex, or age, are not unlawful. However, objective guidelines and their consistent application are very important elements in preventing claims of discrimination and in protecting the employer when claims are filed. Where an employer has no objective guidelines for imposing discipline, discrimination may be suspected.

For example, terminations should not be based on the subjective decisions of supervisors alone. Clear rules should be established, with corresponding penalties, and both should be explained to employees. Then, any violations should be recorded carefully. Terminating an employee for an unsatisfactory work record is lawful, but ample evidence should be compiled, recorded, and kept available. On the other hand, if a clear policy is instituted, but the penalties are applied inconsistently, with a disparate effect on minorities, the employer will be found to have discriminated.

It is also permissable to terminate a protected class employee for insubordination—refusing to obey reasonable work orders. It is important, however, that a claim of insubordination be supported by ample evidence and that there be no evidence that a young, white, male employee would not be treated in the same manner.

Absenteeism can result in termination as long as the discharge is in accord with reasonable company rules applied to all workers. The same applies to the ability to perform work. Terminating a female employee because she is unable physically to perform her work is not necessarily sex discrimination merely because she is replaced by a male. On the other hand, replacing all female employees with males would amount to sex discrimination in the absence of evidence that the replaced females were all unable to perform the work assigned to them and that all applicants were evaluated by job related criteria.

Employers are prohibited from firing employees for reasons that have a discriminatory effect on minorities. For example, employees may not be fired for having an arrest record or for having their salary garnisheed, unless the employer can prove that such policies do not adversely affect minority employees. Therefore, in applying a personal conduct standard, three questions need to be answered:

1. Will the policy have an adverse effect on minority employees?
2. If an adverse effect exists or will exist, is the standard necessarily related to job performance or warranted by some business necessity?
3. If there is a business necessity, is there an alternative with a lesser impact on minorities that will serve as well?

As the burden of proof on each of these questions will fall on the employer, a personal conduct standard must be carefully thought through before it is instituted, and careful records and statistical information must be gathered and maintained if the standard is instituted. Once again, however, the regulations merely require that employers think through the business reasons on which personnel policies are based.

Problem No. 4: People Who Overrate Themselves

At times, managers are faced with firing people who not only fail to perceive how poor their performance has been, but seem to believe they are doing a superior job. Such employees are generally very resistant to efforts aimed at improving their performance. Attempts to correct their behavior turn into arguments during which the employees maintain that their performance has been strong.

The reasons for such misconceptions can be complex. Most managers have neither the training nor the resources to alter them significantly, and they shouldn't try. Regardless of how frustrating the situation becomes, managers should stick to documenting the situation, clearly describing their expectations to the subordinate, and, when it is clear that the subordinate has repeatedly failed to meet those expectations, proceeding with termination.

During the termination, managers should avoid being

abrupt, despite a show of bravado on the part of the employee. More than likely, the employee is terrified about the future. However, significant behavioral change will require professional counseling. Thus, this employee is a special candidate for outplacement counseling.

If the employee reacts with disbelief, managers should support their position by referring to the performance standard. The theme of the manager's position should be, "Maybe you'll do better elsewhere, but I believe you should examine your performance here carefully." Managers should encourage these employees to discuss what they might do differently in the next job. This can help start the process of self-analysis, laying the groundwork for more effective outplacement counseling.

Managers should not compromise their position by suggesting that another boss might have seen things differently or adopting some similar posture. If these employees' self-perception is ever to come more in line with reality, they will first have to admit their failures. Removing even part of their responsibility for their performance makes it too easy for them to rationalize away all their problems on the job.

14

Outplacement Internationally

THE PAST DECADE HAS SEEN OUTPLACEMENT gain acceptance as a human-resource service throughout the United States. During that same period of time, it has emerged internationally, although its level of acceptance varies greatly. This final chapter draws on the expertise of our international colleagues to survey the current status and future prospects of OPC in Canada, Asia, Europe, and Latin America. Outplacement is clearly not just a North American phenomenon, although the nature of OPC varies throughout the world and remains in its infancy in most other countries.

Canada

Outplacement is well established among larger companies throughout Canada, on virtually the same basis as in the United States. The concept has developed in a parallel manner and the counseling services are almost identical. In 1985, interest in the voluntary window concept began to take off, making the retrenchment strategies of U.S. and Canadian firms yet more similar.

There is not much codified in Canadian law on handling discharges, although precedent is strong. A typical middle-level manager making $50,000 a year and with ten years service will seldom receive less than nine months severance. The trend is toward month-to-month payment with an incentive clause to make it advantageous for the outplaced executive to seek employment as early as possible. Typically this involves a splitting of any unused months once employment is obtained. Thus, if an outplaced manager had a nine-month severance package and found employment in four, the compensation for the remaining five would be split. An increasing number of firms are opting for this approach as a way to reduce the costs associated with executive terminations.

Employment regulations are within the jurisdiction of the province, so regular updating on the provincial situation is called for. Any reduction in excess of fifty people at the same time requires prior approval of the provincial Ministry of Labor.

It is worth noting that Quebec has a reinstatement law under which a company can be forced to rehire with back pay any fired employee with more than five years service, if it is determined that no just cause was involved. It is also the only place in North America with an antiscab law.

Hong Kong

Hong Kong is a unique environment. In February 1984, DBM opened the first locally based outplacement company in Hong Kong for the purpose of serving the strong U.S. corporate presence in the city.

Virtually all the U.S. expatriates who have received outplacement services have held senior positions, with an average salary of $70,000. So far, these clients have had an average of about seven and a half years work experience, with three years in Hong Kong—a background that points to their multinational ori-

entation. Most don't want to leave Hong Kong for a combination
of reasons, which include the excitement of the culture, the domestic lifestyle, and the desire to remain "a big fish in a small
pond." In Hong Kong these executives largely run their own
show. Back home they would have all the constraints of being a
member of a corporate team. Unfortunately, the number of senior jobs available is limited, making this a very competitive market.

These expatriate Americans are very responsive to the offer
of outplacement services, having been exposed to the concept
through the American business press. They readily accept OPC
as a tool that can help them move from one job to another. Their
employers are equally receptive, because if the executive is lucky
enough to find employment in Hong Kong, the company will
save up to $40,000 in relocation expenses. Furthermore, should
relocation prove inevitable, the executive will arrive in the
United States with a job search already underway. Given the typical preferences of clients, this search will be pursued through a
multinational network of contacts.

This points up a major feature of OPC services in Hong
Kong: clients must pursue two searches simultaneously, an over-
seas search and one in the United States. For this reason it would
be difficult for a firm without an international network to serve
this market adequately.

Time pressures significantly compress the job search process.
Seldom is more than one month severance provided. Having
made the decision to change executives, companies don't want to
keep them around. The cost of living is extremely high. Housing
is $2,000 to $3,000 a month, and there are no government-pro-
vided benefits.

While outplacement is readily accepted within the expatriate
community, it is a new concept for the local Asian community.
All indications are that the education process will be slow, built
on a steady increase in the number of appreciative clients who
have experienced the process. The notion of face—manifested as

a sense of shame over job loss and a social need not to embarrass the family—further complicates the process. Clients refuse to do the face-to-face networking basic to the job search process in the United States and most Western countries. Instead they show a marked preference for the impersonal mass mailing approach, which allows them to avoid the personal embarrassment of saying to another individual, "I need help."

Our Chinese clients tell us that, had their counselor been Chinese, they probably would not have accepted the service. This parallels the experience of a leading Hong Kong search firm, whose early search consultants had to be foreigners because of fear on the part of the Chinese that word would get out in the local Chinese community. Experts believe that establishment of OPC will follow the pattern experienced by search firms, noting that ten years ago there was one search firm in Hong Kong consisting of a single person. Today every international search firm is there, and they are used by local residents as well as foreigners.

Japan

It often comes as a surprise to the American personnel executive to learn that outplacement has been introduced into Japan and is gaining gradual acceptance. The often-lauded notion of lifetime employment is a postwar phenomenon and never did apply to all workers—only to regular employees of the largest companies. As the Japanese economy matures, pressures are coming to bear even on those organizations to look for innovative ways of dealing with managerial overhead. Atsuhiko Tateuchi of DBM's Tokyo affiliate says, "When the economy was growing at an explosive pace, the companies could make room. Virtually all college graduates achieved the level of manager. In the good times, so many were hired, now we don't know where to put them. The age of retirement used to be 55; now it is 57 and will probably be 60 in another year."

As one would expect, however, the nature of the outplacement process in Japan is significantly different from that in other countries, reflecting the uniqueness of the Japanese approach to employment. The big companies want to keep their best employees and feel a social obligation to retain the poor performers. Thus, it is the average performer who is the most likely candidate for OPC. Companies are responsive to OPC because, properly structured, it is a viable solution to their staffing problems. Their average employee may very well be better than the best employee in a smaller company. This is because of, first, the dominance these companies have had in hiring the top graduates of the most prestigious universities in Japan's highly structured and competitive educational system; and second, the training and experience they have then been able to offer. Thus, if the average performer can be induced to move, all parties are likely to be winners, an outcome with which management can be comfortable.

The problem is that those who leave a large company must go to a smaller one—they will not find employment in another large corporation—and almost always, this means that their salary will be reduced; for example, from 10 million to 6 million yen. The Japanese solution is for the large company to pay the difference, allowing the manager to move without losing income.

This procedure reflects the reluctance of management in the large corporations to violate its normative commitments even in the face of increasing need to rid its ranks of less productive performers. This cumbersome and expensive approach allows management to claim it has met its social obligations while providing opportunities for younger talent to advance. At the same time, a message is communicated to young people rising in the ranks: superior performance is the only guaranteed method of maintaining one's position in the large corporation.

In this process, outplacement counselors must often function like employment brokers. For example, it is not atypical for DBM to develop a resume from information provided by a sponsoring company's personnel department without the employee's knowledge. The resume will carry no name but will give the age, education, and work history of the individual. DBM will distribute the resume to key contacts and forward any favorable responses to the sponsor's personnel department. The sponsoring company will still not tell the employee he is fired but will say there is a company interested in him, which he should call. Before contacting the new company, the employee is advised to visit DBM, where he will get help in going through the job interview and similar support.

DBM is also called on to do career counseling, which involves a self-analysis process that encourages employees to examine their career options in light of their limited opportunities in their current situation. Interested persons can get interview training, and DBM will write up their resume and cover letter and do the mailings. This too is usually done on a covert basis in which responses are sent to DBM and forwarded to the individual to follow up.

As with the Chinese in Hong Kong, networking does not work well, because termination is still seen as shameful. To save face, no one explicitly admits that it has happened. In this environment, there is little market for counseling per se; it is too intangible a service for companies used to stability in their employee relations. A job offer *is* tangible, however, and thus DBM ties the offer of outplacement service directly to the possibility of a new position.

DBM often seeks to introduce clients to foreign companies with whom the client's salary is likely to stay the same or even increase after the switch. American companies find it hard to recruit in Japan, since they want executives with good credentials but cannot offer the security and prestige of top Japanese firms.

Although the large companies do not fire people directly, they are becoming adept at giving employees subtle encouragement to leave. For example, one large Japanese energy company made a strategic decision that eliminated its need for a group of cargo boat captains—men with degrees in shipbuilding and engineering—and other technical experts. These were all well-educated men, mostly in their 40s. The company told them they were not needed and put them in a big room with no job to do. All the men could do was read the paper all day. As might be imagined, the group was very depressed. After two months the company offered the men a lump sum of money if they would voluntarily leave and accept outplacement help. Some did; others stayed because they did not trust the outplacement consultants. So the company again left them to sit alone all day and a few months later repeated the offer. This continued until all decided to leave.

Another case involved a man sent to the United States by a Japanese textile company as president of its American operations. When he was recalled to Tokyo, the firm had no real place for him because of the bulge in its management ranks, so it sent him to a remote location, without his family, to serve in an advisory capacity. After three years of this treatment, he became frustrated and asked the company's internal outplacement department to find him a new job. Because of his high level, they could not find an attractive position for him and brought in DBM. Within a few months he had found a position with a major corporation.

Cases such as these illustrate the direction outplacement is taking in Japan. Several Japanese corporations have established internal outplacement functions, although these typically lack expertise in resume development, interviewing methods, and self-analysis techniques. Essentially, they operate as matchmakers, even offering to lend employees if a company is not willing to make a formal employment offer. Again the sponsoring corporation will pay a salary differential in such worker loan arrangements. In contrast, DBM provides self-analysis, resume writing and mailing, interview training and job-matching help, serving an increasingly growing niche. In 1982, DBM Japan served 12 client companies, handling 24 cases. In 1985, more than 250 client companies sent more than 324 employees, a trend that promises to intensify.

United Kingdom

In the United Kingdom, the OPC concept is well established, with the larger British firms regularly using it for senior executives. As of 1986 there were fourteen OPC firms in London alone. Beginning in the late 1960s, the demand for outplacement services grew steadily throughout the 1970s.

Terminations in Britain must comply with certain statutory guidelines. Employees can appeal wrongful dismissals, which by law must be preceded by two verbal warnings and one written one. Employees and their boss sign a standardized contract at the time of employment that specifies working hours, holidays, and salary and that forms the basis of the employment relationship. A dismissed employee can petition to have the case heard before an industrial tribunal, which consists of one "local worthy" who knows the law, one employee associate, and one union representative. To defend a discharge as constructive the company must prove that (1) it followed the procedural steps mandated by law, and (2) there is some substance to the complaint being made against the employee.

In work-force reductions of more than ten people, thirty days notice must be given. Cutbacks of one hundred or more must be preceded by ninety days notice. In both instances the company must inform the Ministry of Trade, giving the reasons for the reduction and associated cost data.

Severance payments are set by a schedule based on length of service and age. After two years with the company, employees up to age 40 must receive one week of severance for every year of service; those over age 40 receive two weeks for every year of service. Some companies pay more.

An executive making 25,000 pounds or more will typically get a year's severance. The sum is given after the executive has officially left the employer. Under these conditions, the first 25,000 is tax-free; the rest is taxed at 50 percent of the normal tax rate.

Delivery of outplacement services essentially follows the

same process as in the United States. The principal modification is in the networking approach, which is not as aggresively pursued in Britain. Nevertheless, the networking process appears to be highly effective. As of August 1985, the average time for a senior executive to find a new job through the U.K. DBM outplacement program was three months. The expectation of the staff was that such a person should find employment within four months. Just over 15 percent of the clients find jobs through employment advertisements. The rest locate their new positions through the hidden job market, a testimonial to the job search strategy advocated by the OPC process.

France

In France, OPC is rapidly becoming an acceptable and even important aspect of human-resource management. A new association of outplacement consultants (ASCOREP) was established in 1985, and the topic has received increasing attention in the news media.

A common use of outplacement services is to help people make the decision to leave. An example is a three-day program that is explicitly aimed at helping people decide whether or not they want to stay with the company. The workshop helps prepare employees for a more positive dialogue with their managers.

In the case of plant closings, workshops have been conducted that teach company personnel to train blue-collar workers in job search skills. Outplacement consultants have also organized and run career centers during plant closings.

By law, the National Employment Agency, created in 1946, has a monopoly in job placement activities. No private company can present a candidate for a position. Thus, outplacement firms must be especially careful to avoid any appearance of placing people.

Germany

In Germany (formerly known as West Germany), outplacement was virtually unknown as recently as 1979. Now it is a growing phenomenon. Of the 350 largest companies, about 20 percent have tried the service at least once. Often such work begins as directional counseling and eventually proceeds to outplacement. Current activity has increased dramatically, and the indications are that within the next couple of years a major OPC market will emerge.

By law, the minimum termination notice provided employees is from six weeks to the end of the quarter. Virtually all managers have labor contracts. Once notified, employees have to offer their services to the employer, but it is up to the company whether or not they stay on the job during this period. Managers will often get a redundancy payment of one-half to a full month for each year of service.

Companies cannot discharge a person other than for reasons of personal fault or economic necessity. In the case of the former, there must be two written warnings in the file; in the case of the latter, the company must prove that no other solution exists within the company. People cannot be discharged so that the company can hire less expensive help. With the exception of the most senior executives, a company works council must approve all terminations. In the case of work-force reductions, the works council decides who gets laid off as a matter of social policy.

Holland, Belgium, and Switzerland

OPC has found rapid acceptance in these countries. As OPC firms make the capital investment necessary to provide services, they are experiencing a growing market.

Since the early 1970s, internal outplacement services have been provided by all major Dutch multinationals. Use of external consultants dates from the 1980s. Acceptance of the concept by the multinationals, increasing publicity in the business press, and a decrease in social security and separation indemnities by the labor courts all seem to have contributed to the increased popularity of outplacement services.

Beginning in the early 1970s, the separation indemnities awarded by Belgium's courts were the highest in Europe. These awards could be as high as two to three years' pay for employees with great seniority at middle-management through senior-executive levels. In this environment, there was little motivation for either employers or employees to pursue outplacement. Since 1982, however, changing customs in these awards, combined with a general tightening of the business climate, have contributed to a fast-growing acceptance of professional outplacement services.

In Switzerland, severance pay is typically low—three months—and a recipient cannot live on unemployment compensation. The Swiss can fire at will in an economy that has a level of income second only to Germany. Unemployment is less than 1 percent. In this environment there has been a growing receptivity to OPC.

DBM's experience in all three countries has been that, as facilities and materials in the local language become available, demand for the service has grown. Gaining acceptance of the concept has not proven difficult once these resources have become available.

Italy and Spain

In Italy it is difficult for employers to terminate even two or three people. Hence outplacement will have to evolve in a climate hostile to separation practices. In Spain the OPC concept is practically unknown. Currently an information campaign is being carried out by DBM and one other American-based firm, with expectations of a gradually growing market.

Argentina

In 1983, the opening of DBM's office in Buenos Aires marked the introduction of the OPC concept to the country. Over an eighteen-month period, a DBM representative in Argentina talked with five hundred top executives, three hundred of whom headed South American operations. Only ten had heard of outplacement, and all of them had heard about it in the United States. At present the overwhelming majority of executives find the idea of helping employees to leave their companies new and a bit strange.

All indications are that gaining acceptance of the concept will be a slow process. At present, one out of twenty-five companies that have been exposed to the idea in a systematic way has decided to use the process. Outplacement has been established on a regular basis in approximately forty companies. In 1985, one other outplacement firm entered the marketplace, which will help give the concept further exposure.

Law 2748 regulates everything about working in Argentina, including dismissals. The regulations regarding termination are strict. Severance must include at least one month salary for each year worked, vacation compensation, plus one month notice. Managers frequently get five to twelve months salary on top of what the law requires. The regulations pertain to compensation issues only. Unjust dismissal is not an issue.

During the outplacement process, Argentinean clients resist marketing campaigns with mass mailings, preferring face-to-face networking, which is better suited to the country's culture.

Perhaps indicative of the future was a group outplacement project in a chemical company where three separate work-force reductions occurred without incident, including one plant closing involving eighty people.

During this same period, another company in the same industry cut back forty people, and the workers took over the plant; management could not re-enter for two months. Obviously a number of factors could have influenced these two very different scenarios. The difference in worker reaction has not gone unnoticed, however, and cases like this are part of the gradual institutionalization of outplacement in Argentina. This process is slowed by the reluctance of firms to share experiences because of a sense of guilt over terminations.

In the United States, outplacement has evolved to include several dimensions of the job/career transition process. From a counseling approach that centered primarily on self-analysis and job search skills, a range of related services has grown, including directional counseling, career continuation services, and work-force reduction planning. This evolutionary process reflects the needs of the U.S. employment system and the ways it is changing.

The need to constructively assist people during periods of job transition is spreading throughout the world under the umbrella of outplacement. The exact nature of the services provided is being shaped by the larger cultural context of the society in question, but the idea that both employer and employee need assistance in facilitating transitions between jobs—beyond whatever legal protections society has legislated and whatever monetary severance the company provides—appears to be gaining widespread currency. It is our guess that these services will continue to spread as human-resource professionals continue to grapple with one of the most difficult of all employment situations.

Index